MAKING
CHARACTER
DOLLS' HOUSES
IN $^1/_{12}$ SCALE

MAKING
CHARACTER
DOLLS' HOUSES
IN $^1/_{12}$ SCALE

BRIAN NICKOLLS

David & Charles

For Jenny

A DAVID & CHARLES BOOK

Copyright © Brian Nickolls 1995, 1999
Photography by Jonathon Bosley

First published 1995
First published in paperback 1999

Hardback ISBN 0 7153 0200 0
Paperback ISBN 0 7153 0854 8

Designed and typeset by Les Dominey Design Company, Exeter
and printed in Singapore by C. S. Graphics PTE Ltd
for David & Charles
Brunel House Newton Abbot Devon

CONTENTS

Frontispiece: Georgian House – hallway and landing
Above: Swan Inn – store

INTRODUCTION

Since publication of my first book, *Making Dolls' Houses in 1/12 scale*, interest in making dolls' houses and miniatures has increased yet again. There are now four specialist magazines covering all aspects of the hobby. A large number of modelmakers, who previously may have felt that dolls' houses were not a pastime for males, have found another outlet for their skills in the production of scale model houses and furniture. In planning the projects for this book, I have borne this in mind, and included two designs which I hope will appeal particularly to them. The buildings included here, although more complex than those previously published, do not require a greater level of skill – just time and patience.

At this point a brief word on the subject of copyright is necessary. All the plans and designs in this book are for private use only. It is illegal to use these designs for commercial purposes without obtaining prior written permission from the author. To sell (or permit to be sold) unlicensed copies of these designs is illegal.

For those newcomers to woodworking and modelmaking – a word about timber supplies. For all the projects in this book, timber was bought from a sawmill or timber merchant, sawn 'through and through' from a log in thicknesses from 1 inch to 3 inches and then converted as required. Some mills and merchants sell offcuts, which can often provide a useful source of material. DIY stores are generally unproductive. All measurements in this book are given in imperial units (feet and inches). The only exception to this rule occurs where the standard measurement used by suppliers is metric, for example in the case of plywood thicknesses which are referred to in millimetres.

It is very gratifying to hear of the many models that have been made to the earlier plans; a gentleman from Northern Ireland made all five projects in less than six months, and then telephoned asking for more; and eight ladies from the Midlands worked through the book at evening classes. I hope this book provides an interesting second helping for them, and others like them to get their teeth into.

CIDER

BARN

This is a typical rural building with a thatched roof. In my first book thatch was represented by teak veneer. This time coconut fibre will be used, following as closely as possible the method used in real life. Full instructions are given to enable you to make the press itself and the apple mill, neither of which are available from any other source.

Thatcher at work on the Cider Barn

TIMBER REQUIREMENTS – CIDER BARN & FORGE

WOOD	THICKNESS	AREA sq ft	
Birch plywood	$^3/_8$in (9mm)	9	
	1.5mm	$^1/_2$	
	THICKNESS in	WIDTH in	LENGTH ft / in

WOOD	THICKNESS in	WIDTH in	LENGTH ft	in
Elm	$^1/_{16}$	$^3/_8$	1	6
		$^{15}/_{32}$	6	-
	$^1/_8$	$^1/_8$	5	2
		$^{11}/_{16}$		$3^1/_2$
		$^1/_2$	4	–
		$^7/_8$		3
		$1^1/_4$	1	2
	$^1/_4$	$^1/_4$	4	6
		$^3/_8$	18	6
		1	3	–
	$^3/_8$	$^3/_8$	2	8
		$^3/_4$		$7^1/_2$
	$^7/_{16}$	1	2	2
	$^3/_4$	1	1	3
		$1^1/_4$		6
	$1^1/_4$	$1^1/_4$	1	4

CARCASE

Referring to Figs 1a–1f, cut one base, one end wall, one end truss, one middle truss, and a front and back panel from $^3/_8$in plywood. Rout a rebate $^3/_8$in wide and $^1/_8$in deep on the inside face of the end wall, where shown. Rout the $^3/_8$in x $^1/_8$in housing for the trusses on the inside faces of the front and back panels. Cut out the door and window openings on the front panel and end wall. Using a jigsaw, cut away the internal waste from the trusses to leave vertical posts $^3/_4$in wide and rafters and tie beams $^1/_2$in wide. The middle truss has no housing to locate the front wall, as a slot is provided when the surface veneers are applied. *Do not yet rout the housings in the base.*

DRY ASSEMBLY

Using two $^3/_4$in no 4 woodscrews, fasten the end wall to the back panel 1–$1^1/_2$in from the top and bottom of the joint. Fasten the back of the middle truss into the first housing by the same method. Repeat for the end truss noting that the housing is inset $^7/_{16}$in from the end to allow for a $^1/_{16}$in surface veneer and the removable panel which will fit flush inside the front and back walls. Remove the trusses and, having first marked the front and back edges of each $^1/_8$in from the edge, apply a surface veneer to both faces and inside edges using $^1/_{16}$in elm. On the middle truss, a $^3/_8$in wide gap in the veneer is left where the front wall butts. The outer post on this truss is veneered on all four sides. Note that when veneering, the bottom $^1/_8$in of all uprights should be left clear to fit into the base grooves. Replace the trusses leaving $^1/_8$in margins at the front and back edges. Screw the front panel into position with the butted end screwed from the chimney side of the middle truss.

Mark out the base for the routed grooves, and stand the wall and truss assembly on top. This should coincide with the marks on the base but if not, adjust the marks and rout accordingly, $^1/_8$in deep. Fit the assembly into the grooves on the base and screw from underneath. When satisfied that everything fits together well, cut out the portable panel (Fig 2), from $^3/_8$in plywood, for the open end. The sizes given are for the finished panel. Although not strictly necessary, this

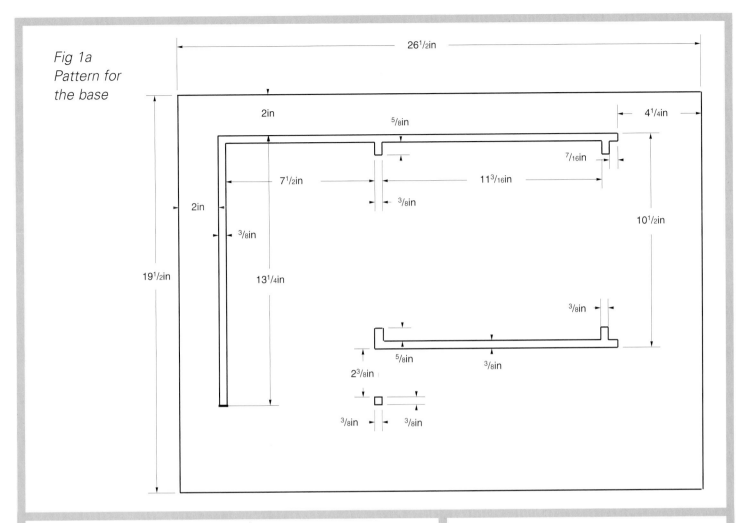

Fig 1a
Pattern for
the base

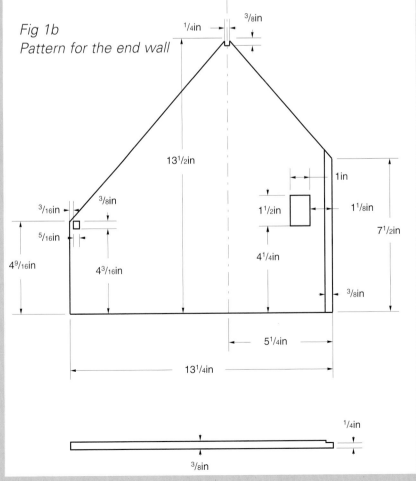

Fig 1b
Pattern for the end wall

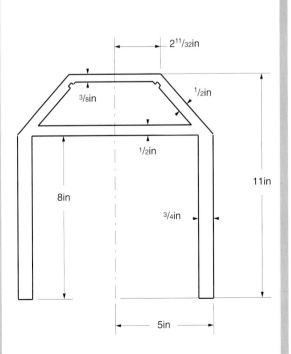

Fig 1c
Measurements for the end truss

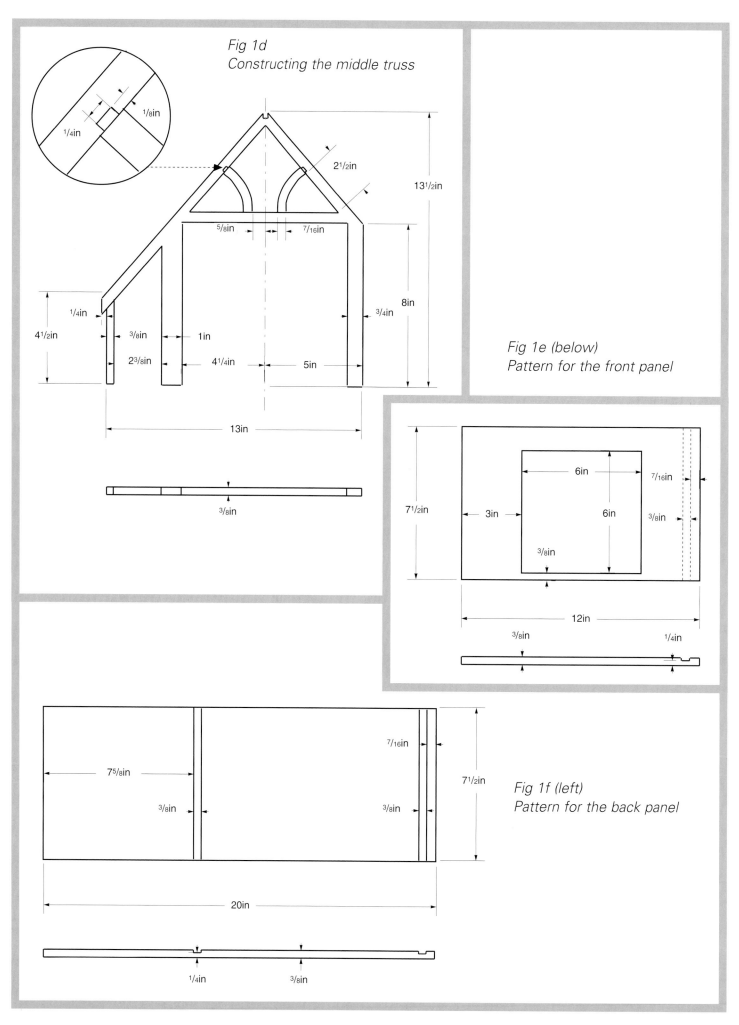

Fig 1d
Constructing the middle truss

¹/₈in

¹/₄in

2¹/₂in

13¹/₂in

⁵/₈in   ⁷/₁₆in

8in

¹/₄in   ³/₄in

4¹/₂in   ³/₈in   1in

2³/₈in   4¹/₄in   5in

13in

³/₈in

Fig 1e (below)
Pattern for the front panel

6in   ⁷/₁₆in

7¹/₂in   3in   6in   ³/₈in

³/₈in

12in

³/₈in   ¹/₄in

⁷/₁₆in

7¹/₂in

7⁵/₈in

³/₈in   ³/₈in

Fig 1f (left)
Pattern for the back panel

20in

¹/₄in   ³/₈in

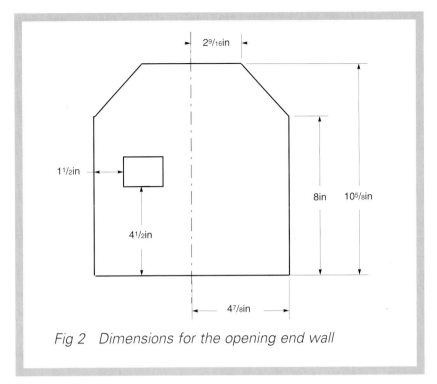

Fig 2   Dimensions for the opening end wall

can be improved by edge veneering at the sides, top and bottom. This necessitates removing $1/16$in from all edges and gluing on $3/8$in wide strips of $1/16$in elm.

Dismantle the whole assembly and continue with more detailed work on trusses, doors and windows.

TRUSSES

Cut slots centrally $1/4$in wide and $3/8$in deep at the apex of both the middle truss and the end wall, for the ridgeboard. Having first cut away the surface veneer, add a piece of elm $3/8$in deep, 6in long, and projecting $1/2$in outwards. This should be glued and dowelled to the outside of the end truss on the open side. Cut off the ends to conform with the roof slope. With the exception of this latter component, texture and wane the edges. Cut the slots $1/8$in deep on the end wall and middle truss for the cross beam which connects the two. This is made from elm $3/8$in deep, $5/16$in thick and $7^3/4$in long. On final assembly, this will be glued in place with pegs from $1/16$in diameter bamboo dowel, drilled and pushed into it through the end wall and truss. Cut two arched struts from $7/16$in elm to fit from under the purlin slot to the tie beam (see Fig 1d). *Do not fix yet.* Mark the midpoint of the rafter sections of the middle truss and cut a slot at each side on the underside $1/4$in wide and $1/4$in deep to house the purlins. From these cutouts, mark the inside face of the end wall and

cut recesses $1/4$in square and $1/8$in deep. Mark the inside of the open end truss in the same way and cut away the surface veneer to form a similar recess. Glue a thickening piece of $3/8$in plywood 1in wide to the inside front edge of the end wall with the top slotted to take the cross beam and the top angled to the roof slope. Note that the bottom edge is $1/8$in above the bottom of the wall to allow the latter to fit into its slot.

DOORS AND FRAMES

Square up the corners of the apertures. Prepare the header and side posts from elm, machined to the profile shown in Fig 3. Place the header in position (no glue yet), and cut the uprights to be a snug fit under it. Mark where the header has to be cut away to allow the uprights to fit right in. Each door is made from 1.5mm plywood, $2^7/8$in wide and $5^7/8$in high. The method of fitting hinges and planking is given on page 186. The planks are $1/16$in thick elm, $15/32$in wide. Braces are fitted to the back (see Fig 3). Chip away at the bottom edges to represent wear and tear. Strap hinges, made from black card $1^1/2$in x $3/16$in are glued to the outside face of the doors in line with the brass hinges already fitted. Complete the door framing and plane flush at front and back. Glue a lintel of elm $7^1/2$in long, $5/16$in deep, and $1/8$in thick above the doorway with its bottom edge level with the top edge of the header. It should overhang equally at each side. Remove the doors and hinges for the more detailed work later on. Note: when slotting the hinges through the frames there may be a small amount of hinge projecting on the face of the frame which butts against the door opening; file this flush.

WINDOW LINING

Referring to Fig 4, line the window openings on the end wall and the opening end panel with elm $3/8$in x $1/16$in. Fit the top and bottom sections first and then the sides. Fit a further framework of $1/8$in x $3/8$in elm inside the lining, inset 2mm from the back, allowing a projection on the outside. Glass or Glodex will be fitted against this from inside, and the outside projection will be trimmed back to the stone cladding. Add the central mullion to the window in the opening wall.

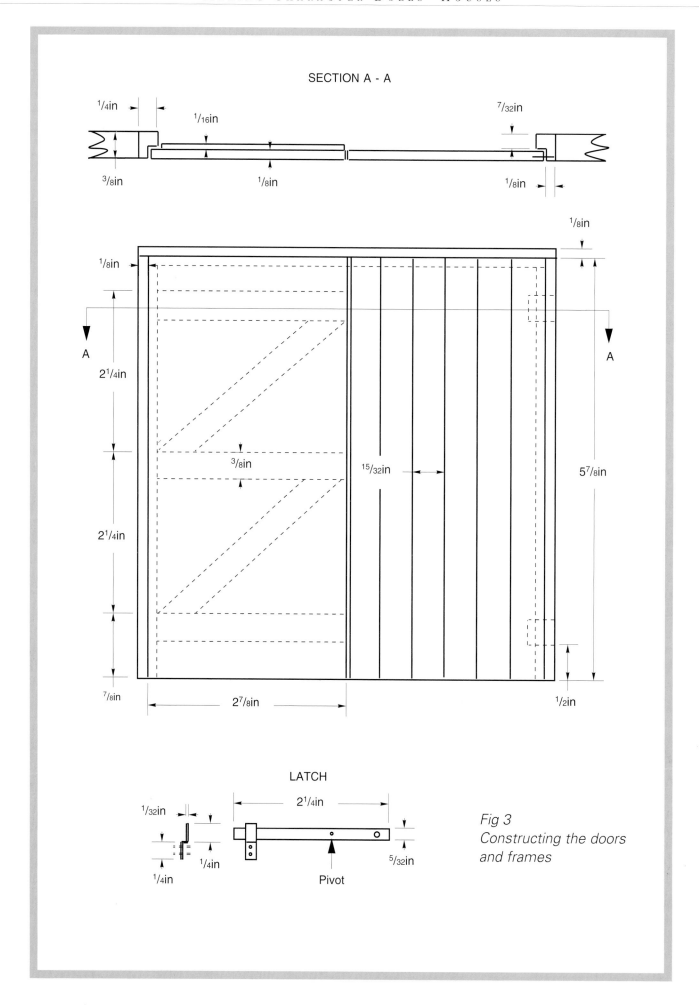

SECTION A - A

¹/₄in
¹/₁₆in
⁷/₃₂in
³/₈in
¹/₈in
¹/₈in

¹/₈in
¹/₈in
2¹/₄in
³/₈in
¹⁵/₃₂in
5⁷/₈in
2¹/₄in
⁷/₈in
2⁷/₈in
¹/₂in

LATCH

¹/₃₂in
2¹/₄in
¹/₄in
¹/₄in
⁵/₃₂in
Pivot

Fig 3
Constructing the doors
and frames

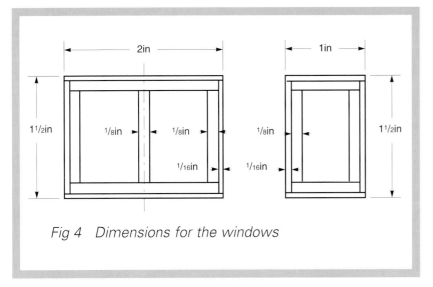

Fig 4   Dimensions for the windows

CHIMNEY

This is optional and if required, details can be found in Chapter 2.

BASE FRAME

Cut two strips of $3/8$in plywood, $1^1/2$in x $26^1/2$in, and two $1^1/2$in x $19^1/2$in. Mitre the corners and glue these strips as a frame round the underside of the base. Cut a further length to fit transversely between the long side members. Impact glue is sufficient, but compress all the edges in a vice to provide a tight joint. The centre strip relies on hand pressure alone. Plane all the edges fair, and veneer them with $3/4$in x $3/32$in elm. Glue the short sections first, trim off the ends flush, and then apply the long sections. Plane the top and bottom edges flush all round.

DECORATING

All the inside wall surfaces should be painted now before the carcase is fastened to the base. To give a rough, plastered effect that is not too even or clean, apply one coat of textured masonry paint, having first masked those areas which must be left clear, such as the $1/8$in margins which are housed into the base and walls. For now the small section outside the truss at the opening end is best left clear as too much paint build up here will impede the opening panel. Stipple the paint to give as rough a surface as possible. The second coat should have a dirtier look. This is achieved by first mixing a small quantity of masonry paint with black poster paint to form grey. Using a sponge or a piece of foam, dab the grey at random and follow this with untextured paint dabbed on liberally and textured with a sponge.

FINAL ASSEMBLY

Reassemble the carcase with PVA glue, adding further screws or panel pins in the joint lines. Screws can be used on the outside walls as they will be hidden by the stonework cladding. When assembling it will be easier to fasten the short front wall to the middle truss first, as the screws are awkward to get at once the end wall is in place.

Make a shelf of elm $3/4$in wide, $1/16$in thick and $7^1/2$in long, with $1/8$in square supports along the underside of the back edge and sides. Glue this to the back wall with its lower edge $4^1/4$in above the floor. It should fit snugly between the end wall and the middle truss.

STONEWORK

Make sure that the opening panel is a good fit. Glue a strip of $1/8$in square elm batten along the top of the roof slopes on the end wall, flush with the outside edges. Mask off any areas not to be coated, such as the $3/8$in deep margins at the tops of the front and back walls where the rafter ends will be glued later. The spaces between the rafters will be touched in later.

The application and scribing of the stonework will take several hours to complete and, once started, it must be finished in one session before the mixture becomes too hard to scribe successfully. The work can be done in two stages by plastering the ends and front in one session and the back in another, but care will be needed to ensure that the colouring of the mixture is consistent. Before starting you should have a trial run on a plywood offcut to familiarize yourself with the various stages. The ideal tool for scribing is a dental scraper with a round cutting edge about $1/16$in in diameter. Alternatively, an old round needle file can be ground to shape.

Powder filler, such as Polyfilla, should be mixed with water to a stiff paste, sufficient to cover the walls to a depth of $1/16$in. As a guide, about half a 585gram standard packet will be needed. It is better to have too much than to have to stop and make another mix. Add a tablespoon of PVA glue, and tone the mixture to a light greyish brown with poster paint – remember that the colour will be lighter when the filler has dried.

Prime the walls with diluted PVA glue (plus

Internal view of bare shell of the Cider Barn

10% water), and then spread on the paste keeping the thickness as even as possible. With a damp paintbrush, smooth the surface to remove any ridges, avoiding excessive build-up against the sides of the door frames and window linings. Work from side to side so that any brush marks are horizontal.

When the filler has dried sufficiently to be reasonably firm (usually half- to three-quarters of an hour), lightly scribe the stone courses $1/2$in–$5/8$in apart, using a graduated batten with a pin driven through the end. Take care not to cut right through the coating, and if it shows any sign of lifting off or clinging to the panel pin let it dry a little longer. Do not scribe the lines too precisely.

Following the pattern in Fig 5, lightly pencil the outline of the stones on to the surface and cut the joints with the scraper. The cuts should not mark the plywood underneath. Leave to

harden overnight, and then remove any high spots with a chisel and sandpaper. Use a coarse paper very lightly to retain the same surface texture as the remainder. With a Skarsten scraper, clean off all the faces of window sills, linings, door frames, and lintels.

COLOURWASH

Mix a little green, brown and yellow poster paint in about one pint of water to give the basic stone colour required, and brush this liberally over all the stonework. While the surface is still moist, mix a more concentrated combination of these colours in a saucer and with a $3/8$in chisel-edged brush, vary the tones of random stones – some with more yellow, others with more green, and so on until the desired overall effect is achieved. Allow to dry thoroughly before sealing with two coats of matt varnish. If the stonework is not completely dry, the varnish will bloom.

FLOOR

This should be painted next, before starting on the roof. Mix textured masonry paint with a little black and brown poster paint, to make a medium grey. Carefully cut in round the edges and then stipple on the paint. While the paint is still wet, use a foam scrap to sponge more black, brown, yellow, and green on top to give the appearance of beaten earth. The floor inside the fixed end wall, where the hearth will be fitted, should have a sooty appearance.

ROOF

Cut a ridgeboard from elm $^1/4$in thick, 1in deep, and $18^1/4$in long. Referring to Fig 6, cut notches $^1/4$in deep on the underside to fit into the slots on the end wall and middle truss. Angle the outer end downwards at 50° to take the central hip rafter. Cut two purlins from $^1/4$in square elm, each $19^1/2$in long, and fit them into the slots already cut in the end wall and the undersides of the middle and end trusses. Cut off the purlins at the open end, so that they fit inside the portable end wall.

Prepare four long rafters (for the catslide section at the front) and sixteen short rafters (Fig 7). They should be $^3/8$in deep, $^1/4$in thick, and nominally $12^1/2$in, and 9in long respectively. To make these, first prepare one piece of elm $^3/8$in thick, $12^1/2$in long, and 2in wide, and three pieces $^3/8$in thick, 9in long, and 4in wide. Start by routing a V-slot on one face of each piece, $^7/32$in deep, with its centre $^3/4$in from one end.

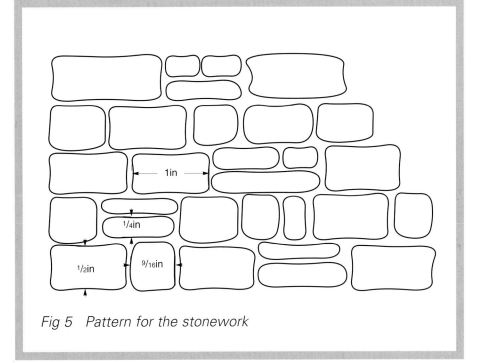

Fig 5   Pattern for the stonework

With the ridgeboard resting in its slots, cut one strip $^1/4$in wide from a short piece, and another $^1/4$in wide from a long piece, to use as patterns. Rest the inverted V-slot of the long pattern on the cross beam between the end wall and the middle truss, and angle its top edge to fit against the ridgeboard with its sloping top edge lying fair with the roof slopes of the end wall and trusses. Similarly, use the short pattern, with its V-slot resting on the top edge of the front wall, to establish the length of these rafters. Use the same pattern between the ridgeboard and the back wall to find the length of the back rafters.

Still referring to Fig 7, rout or saw slots, $^1/8$in wide and $^1/8$in deep, across the top faces of the elm blocks, starting from the angled top edge, at $^3/4$in centres. Using a circular saw, cut four long rafters and sixteen short rafters from the blocks, and individually angle the upper end of each to fit against the ridgeboard. The remaining sections of the short blocks will be used later for the hip rafters. Reduce the depth of the top edge by $^1/8$in for $^1/2$in from the bottom of each rafter. This forms a rebate for the $^1/2$in x $^1/8$in plywood tilt boards. Cut the bottom of each rafter as shown in Fig 7, so that when fitted the bottom edge is horizontal. Check that the rafters fit against the ridge and locate nicely at the

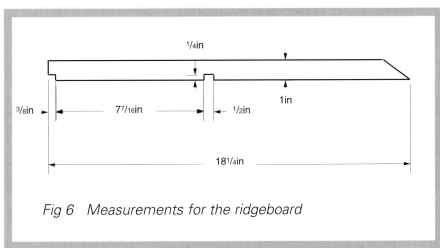

Fig 6   Measurements for the ridgeboard

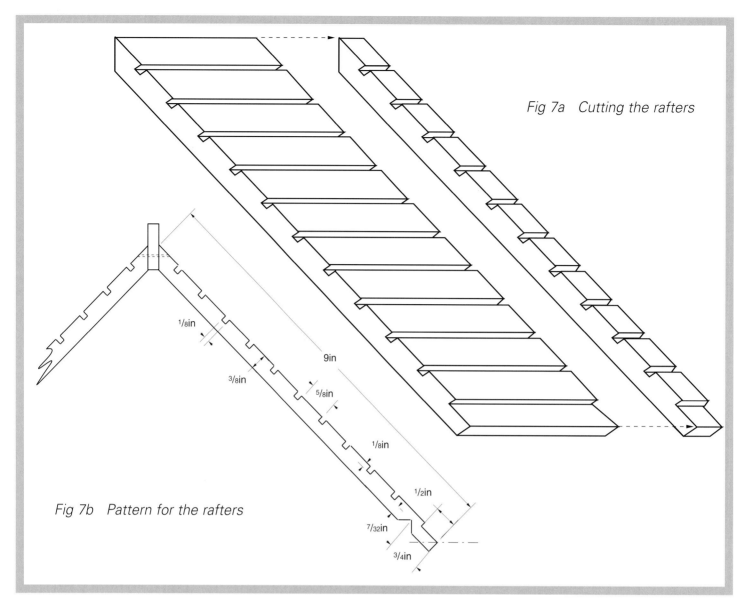

Fig 7a   Cutting the rafters

Fig 7b   Pattern for the rafters

bottom, and also that they bear evenly on the purlins. When satisfied, remove the ridgeboard, rafters, and purlins and weather them.

WEATHERING

To $1/4$ pint of vinegar add a handful of rusty nails and leave to stand overnight, or longer if possible. Stir well. Using a scrap of elm as a test piece, paint on the mix. When dry, the surface of the wood should be silvery grey. If too dark, the mixture should be diluted with water.

Prepare sufficient 20in lengths of $1/8$in square elm for the battens, and weather them. Drill a $1/16$in diameter hole vertically through the centre of the tie beam on the middle truss, and then gouge a $1/16$in wide groove, $1/16$in deep, along the top edge of the tie beam from the hole to the inner face of the sloping section of the truss at the back wall. (This will be needed later for wiring.)

WIRING

Drill a $1/16$in diameter hole through the floor on the end wall side of the middle truss, tight in the corner between the truss and the back wall. Thread the wire tail of the centre light (Wood 'n' Wool) up through the tie beam on the truss, along the groove on the top, round the back edge of the truss, and down through the hole in the floor. Drill a $1/8$in diameter hole horizontally through the base edge at the back to coincide. Drill a further $1/16$in diameter hole through the floor close against the end wall in the centre, and a third close against the back wall 2in from the middle truss, towards the open end of the building. About $1/2$in above these last two holes drill a pair of holes at $1/4$in centres into both the end wall and the back wall to accept Cir-Kit 1023-2 hollow eyelets. Take care in both cases not to drill deeper than the length of the eyelets to avoid breaking through to the outside. Cut two lengths of Cir-Kit twin wire to reach from each pair of eyelet holes, down through the floor holes beneath them, to the hole drilled through the base edge at the back. One small connector block is required and a recess should be cut in the underside of the base, about $^1/2$in inside the frame, to receive it. This prevents the connector from projecting below the base frame. Screw the connector in place in line with the hole in the base edge. Thread sufficient heavier twin wire for the transformer feed through the base edge and fasten it to the connector.

Each of the wires from the eyelet positions should now be soldered at one end round the collar of an eyelet. Thread one pair of wires through each of the holes in the floor and then push and gently hammer the eyelets into the holes in the respective walls. Take care not to damage the wire which should lead downwards from the eyelets to the floor. Connect all the wire tails from the three positions under the base in parallel, and secure them to the other side of the connector block.

ROOF ASSEMBLY

Glue and pin the ridgeboard in place, and then glue in the purlins. Glue the arched struts in place, and pin at the top through the sloping part of the truss.

Start with a pair of rafters (front and back), and using a $1^1/4$in wide spacer, hold these in position on either side of the ridgeboard $1^1/4$in from the middle truss towards the open side of the building. Make sure that the V-slots locate, and then drill a $^1/16$in diameter hole horizontally through both rafter tops and ridgeboard (see Fig 7b). Glue this pair of rafters in place using $^1/16$in diameter bamboo dowel at the top, and $^3/4$in veneer pins at the bottom, driven downwards into the top edges of the walls.

Continue by fixing four more pairs of rafters, at the same spacing, towards the open end of the building, then work from the middle truss to the end wall in the same manner, using the four long rafters over the extended catslide section.

HIP

Take one of the spare rafters and glue and pin it centrally on the elm block at the outside of the end truss. Fix the top of this rafter, with glue and a pair of $^1/16$in dowels, into the angled end of the ridgeboard (see Fig 8). Cut the rafter off flush at the top of the ridgeboard. Next take the tenth pair of rafters and fasten these as before to the walls and ridgeboard, ensuring that their tops are inside the slope of the hip rafter.

CORNER RAFTERS

Cut two $^1/4$in square strips of elm, each 6in long. Lay one in position with its top resting between rafter no 10 on the front wall, and the central hip rafter. Angle the top end vertically to fit against the ridgeboard, and then angle the sides so that it fits snugly between rafter no 10 and the central hip rafter. The bottom end is positioned to lie with its outer edge at the corner of the projecting elm cross beam on the truss. With a knife, mark this cross beam on either side of the corner rafter, and then saw and chisel a notch in the cross beam to receive it. Drill through the rafter into the ridgeboard at the top and into the cross beam at the bottom, and fasten with glue and $^1/16$in diameter bamboo dowels. Note, take care when drilling the bottom of this rafter that the hole is angled to avoid coming through the bottom of the cross beam. Repeat this and fasten the corner rafter between the ridgeboard and the back wall. Using a razor saw and a file, notch each face of each corner rafter to line up with the notches on both side rafters and the central hip rafter.

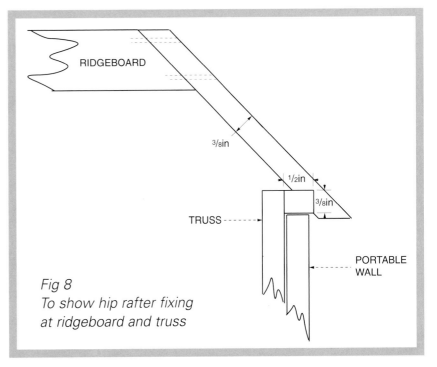

Fig 8
To show hip rafter fixing
at ridgeboard and truss

Where the edges of the trusses are housed into the front and back walls, cut back both sides of the end truss, and the back of the middle truss, by $^1/8$in above the tops of the front and back walls, and in each place glue and pin a triangular fillet of $^3/8$in plywood to continue the slope of the truss to the outside of each wall.

BATTENS

Glue a strip of elm, $^1/8$in square, along both roof slopes of the end wall, flush with its outside face. Glue a similar strip on the catslide section of the middle truss slope, flush with the face nearest the opening end. Glue the upper four battens into the slots on the back roof and pin through each batten where it crosses the end wall and middle truss. Similarly fasten the upper four battens on the front roof. Cut two strips of $^1/8$in plywood, each $^7/8$in wide, with their top edges angled and bevelled to fit against the underside of the fourth batten and against the face of the corner rafter at the front and back. Cut these to length so that their bottom edges correspond with the projecting rafter ends, and bevel accordingly. These will provide a smooth underface to the thatch where it overhangs the slopes of the removable wall. Glue and pin one of these to each sloping face of the end truss, leaving a $^1/8$in gap on the inside face to act as a ledge for the remaining battens. This leaves a $^1/2$in overhang outside the face of the truss.

Fasten the remaining battens at the back and front, continuing down over the catslide. Glue and pin the top three battens across the hip.

Paint the exposed top surfaces of the front and back walls between the rafters with matt medium-brown paint. Cut two 21in lengths of $^1/8$in plywood, each $^1/2$in wide, for the tiltboards (Fig 9). Starting on the back roof, cut one of these to fit in the reduced lower section of the rafters, between the $^1/8$in square strip on the end wall slope and the $^1/8$in thick plywood facings on

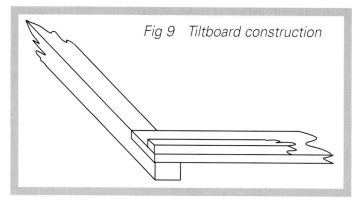

Fig 9   Tiltboard construction

the end truss. Remove the $^1/8$in plywood strip and, using impact adhesive, fix a length of $^1/8$in square elm along the lower edge of its upper face (see Fig 9), overhanging the tiltboard at the open end of the building so that it reaches from the back wall across the $^1/8$in plywood facing on the end truss.

Using the other length of $^1/8$in plywood, make the tiltboard for the front roof in two sections, and add further lengths of $^1/8$in square elm to these. The bottom edge of all three sections should now be bevelled so that when fitted in place they are horizontal. Glue and pin these boards across the recesses at the bottoms of the rafters, with the $^1/8$in strips uppermost. Model railway track pins are best used here, with holes pre-drilled for them. Make up a further tiltboard for the hip, this time using 1.5mm plywood, $^3/4$in x 6in, as it will need to be curved slightly. Cut off the hip and corner rafters flush with the outside of the elm cross beam. Using a small plane, trim the plywood facings on the end truss roof slopes so that they are just proud of the portable panel (about $^1/16$in).

Now, reduce the depth of the three hip rafters by 1.5mm from the upper edges, and glue and pin the tiltboard to these three members so that the upper edge of the $^1/8$in square section is in line with the outer edges of the plywood facings on the end truss roof slopes. Saw and plane the ends to conform with the roof slope on each side. Cut two strips of 1.5mm plywood, each $^3/16$in wide, and glue and pin these across the rafters at the front and back, close against the ridgeboard.

THATCHING

Before attempting to thatch the roof it is recommended that you read *Thatch and Thatching* by Jacqueline Fearn (Shire Publications), or any similar books on the subject. If possible, look closely at thatching demonstrations at your local agricultural show and ask about points you do not understand. Thatchers are usually more than willing to help. You will then understand that the bundles (*yealms*) of straw or reed are laid nearer to the horizontal than the vertical. This gives the bristling end grain appearance of reed thatch, and I have tried to recreate this in miniature. However, wheat reed (or water reed) is, by nature, thinner at its head than at its base whereas the coconut fibre used here is more or less even throughout its length. For this reason the

Close up of thatch on the Cider Barn, showing rafters and battens

tapered yealms in real life cannot be reproduced in miniature. Reed or straw can be butted upwards with a leggat, but coconut fibre cannot and therefore all the shaping has to be done by cutting. It is recommended that you practise on a trial section about four rafters wide and five battens deep.

Six bundles of fibre will be needed, together with a large pair of scissors (preferably of the size used by paperhangers), a pair of anvil secateurs and a craft knife. Hot-melt glue from a gun will be used for fastening. Before proceeding further, cut a piece of card to cover the floor of the building to protect it from glue drips.

First, cut the ties on a bundle and lay it out flat on a large board. Separate smaller bundles or yealms with finger and thumb. These should be about $5/16$in in diameter (little more than a pencil thickness). Cut one end of a yealm square with the secateurs, dab the end grain with hot-melt glue, and clip the end in a bulldog paper fastener. Continue making yealms until you have

used up the whole bundle; further bundles can be processed as you need them. Cut some yealms with angled tops (up to 45°), for the roof edges. The angle should start to splay outwards about three rafters from the edge (Fig 10). Starting at the lower right-hand corner of the back roof, glue a row of yealms to the tiltboard. Trim the yealms back with the secateurs so that they project $3/4$in outside the wall at the eaves and $1/2$in outside the wall at the gable end. Use a plywood spacer as a guide. When trimming, re-glue the cut off yealms as you go to avoid too much wastage. Take the lower course right across the roof, and then start again at the right-hand side with the second row, this time gluing at both the tiltboard and the first roof batten (see Fig 10). Again, trim off $3/4$in and $1/2$in at the eaves and gable ends respectively. From now on the cut off sections of yealm will be too short to use again, so cut all the remaining yealms in half (approximately 4in), and re-glue the cut ends. Lightly brush the roof to remove loose

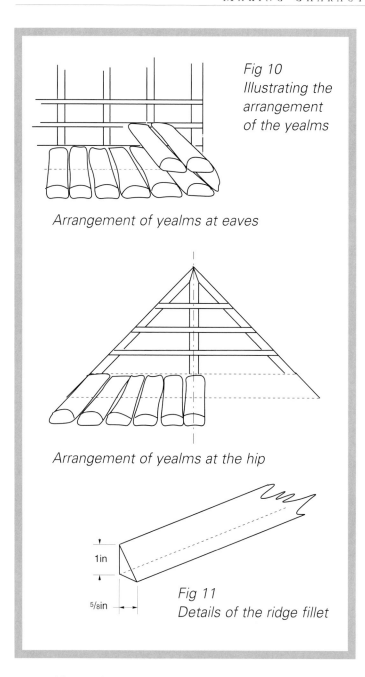

Fig 10
Illustrating the arrangement of the yealms

Arrangement of yealms at eaves

Arrangement of yealms at the hip

1in

5/8in

Fig 11
Details of the ridge fillet

fibres after laying each course. After four courses, give the roof a light trim using secateurs or scissors held parallel to the roof slope and approximately $^7/_8$in above it. This will help with subsequent courses which are glued in three places (the upper three battens that they cover), and will ensure that glue is not placed too far down where it will show when the roof is finally trimmed to between $^5/_8$in and $^3/_4$in thick. When you reach the hip (see Fig 10), continue at 45° over the corners, gradually straightening each yealm until you reach the centreline. Next, trim under the eaves so that the bottom edge of the thatch is horizontal. Continue thatching the back roof until you reach the top course which is glued at its upper edge to the plywood batten that is fitted against the ridgeboard. The front

roof can now be thatched in the same way, but this time start at the lower right-hand side of the catslide and continue to the level of the tiltboard on the remaining roof. Continue as before up to the ridge. Note partly for demonstration purposes, and partly to allow more light inside, a section has been omitted on the front roof. If you wish to fill this in, continue thatching the whole roof to the ridge. Otherwise, stop thatching on the catslide seven battens from the bottom and two rafters in from the left-hand edge, and then continue upwards, with the course laid on the eighth batten stopping two rafters in, and each successive course leaving the last two yealms of the previous course uncovered (see colour illustration page 21).

TRIMMING

Once all the yealms have been glued in place, the final trim can be done. The following tools are required here:

Paperhanger's scissors (which will need frequent sharpening with a file), tin snips, and disposable razors with the blade guards removed. Four of these razors will be required as they blunt very quickly.

The aim is to reduce the thickness of the thatch to between $^5/_8$in and $^3/_4$in. The work has to proceed gradually or the scissors will not cut. Make sure you hold the scissors parallel to the roof slope. Using a stiff churn brush in an upward direction lift the fibres, and then trim any high spots by about $^1/_8$in at a time. Further trimming can be done with the razors but *do not press down too hard*. The best results are achieved with a diagonal downward stroke.

RIDGE

Cut a piece of medium-thick card, 5in x 26in. Starting 1in in from one end, lay loose bundles of fibre across the card closely butted, and about $^1/_8$in thick. Apply two lengths of masking tape over the top, from end to end, $2^1/_2$in apart. Press well down on to the fibre, and at the uncovered ends. With a sewing machine and black or brown thread, run a line of stitches down the length of the card and fibre, just clear of the inside edge of the tape on each side. Run a further line of stitches $^1/_2$in inside each of the first rows. Mark a line lengthways on the masking tape at each side, $^3/_4$in outside the first row of stitches, and with secateurs cut along these lines to leave a card/fibre strip 4in wide. Leave the tape in place for now. Turn the card upside down and score the centreline. Holding a straight edge on the centreline, carefully fold the card into a 'V' which should be compressed in a vice, making sure that both edges coincide. The tapes can now be removed, taking care to pull towards the edge to avoid damage to the fibre. Do not worry if the card has crinkled a little inside the 'V'. The ridge, in real life, is built up with up to three layers of yealms, interspersed with lengthways rolls of reed or straw, fastened to each other with hazel spars. This is where we cheat. Add a further $3/4$in in height to the top of the ridgeboard (a piece of $1/4$in plywood $3/4$in deep will suffice). It should be $18^3/4$in long with one end angled to the slope of the thatch on the hip. (Note that it is about 1in longer than the first ridgeboard, and extends over some of the thatch already placed.) Pre-drill this additional ridgeboard and glue and pin it in place. Now add a further course of yealms about 2in long on top of the last course at the front and back, and trim these to match the rest of the thatch. Next cut a piece of elm $1^1/8$in x $3/4$in, 19in long. Cut this in two diagonally to produce two triangular sections (see Fig 11). Glue and pin one of these on either side of the ridgeboard, flush at the top. Trim off and lightly round over the top edge. Trim the ends flush at the hip slope. Take the card/fibre ridge covering and, using scissors, cut back the card to $1/8$in inside the fibre edge. Using impact adhesive, fold 1in of plain card, without fibre, underneath at the end over the fixed end wall, rest it in place on the wooden ridge and cut to length. Note, spot-glue the stitches before cutting to prevent them from undoing. Again using impact adhesive, glue the ridge cover over the wooden ridge taking extreme care to line it up correctly before pressing down firmly. Cover the exposed hip end with selected yealms with the ends trimmed close and square, leaving very little glue showing. Using PVA adhesive, glue a few strands across the ridge, over the seam between the ridge card and the end yealms. Trim the yealms on the hip end to match the card ridge.

SWAYS

These are made from very small diameter cane stained dark brown, or from fishing line or floral wire, and follow the two rows of stitches on the ridge card and round the hip. They are held in place with hooks bent from track pins and

inserted at $1/2$in intervals. Mask all the walls of the building with plastic sheet, and spray the thatch with two coats of Windsor and Newton fixative.

OPENING END PANEL

Make a lintel of elm, weathered and textured, $2^7/8$in long and $3/32$in thick, with an average depth of $3/16$in. Lay this on the stonework with its bottom edge flush with the top of the window opening, and with an equal overlap each side. Mark with a knife, and then cut away the stonework back to plywood level. Glue the lintel in place.

Next, make the window sill from elm $2^1/4$in long and $3/16$in square. Plane one face to reduce one edge to a thickness of $3/32$in. Position this below the window, mark and cut back the stonework as for the lintel and glue in place. Both this window and its sill, and the window at the other end of the building should now be painted matt green. Two $1/4$in ball catches are required for this panel. Skim the collars from the catches, using a lathe, to leave a clear $1/4$in barrel. Drill $1/4$in diameter holes centrally in the left- and right-hand edges of the panel, 6in from the bottom. The holes should be approximately $1/32$in deeper than the barrel. Press the catches firmly in place until the brass barrels are flush, and only the balls project. Push the panel in place on the building, and mark the indents where the balls press on the front and back walls. Drill a $1/4$in diameter hole, $1/8$in deep at each of these points, and file a shallow rounded groove from the outer edge of the wall to the hole.

FINISHING

Paint the top of the base outside the building a mixture of green for grass areas, and grey and mud for the paths, using tinted textured paint. Leave the veneered base edge clear and give this two coats of matt varnish. Shortened track pins are inserted as required in the internal walls to represent nails for hanging various items. Pilot holes should be drilled first about $1/32$in diameter, and $1/4$in deep, and the cut off pins glued in to leave a projection of $1/8$in.

EQUIPMENT

Cider Press Referring to Figs 12a and 12b, cut from $1^1/4$in square elm, one base beam A $8^1/2$in long, and one press beam B $7^1/4$in long. Drill

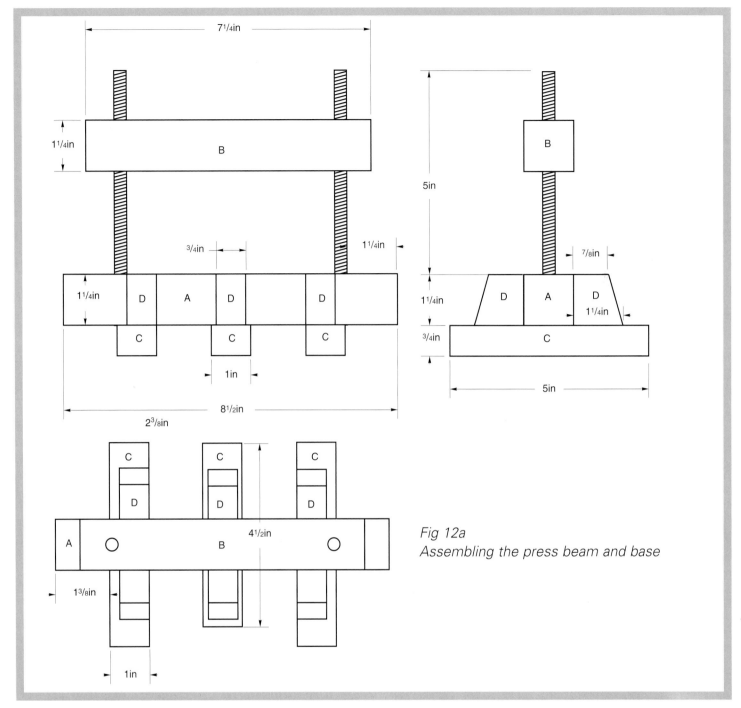

Fig 12a
Assembling the press beam and base

two $^9/_{32}$in diameter holes into the base beam, on the centreline, $1^1/_4$in from each end. Screw a $6^1/_4$in length of 8mm studding into each hole. Drill a corresponding pair of holes through the press beam B, this time $^{11}/_{32}$in diameter, ensuring that the press beam is inset from the base beam equally at each end. From elm, cut the lifting beam E $^3/_4$in wide, $^3/_8$in thick, and $7^1/_4$in long. Drill $^{11}/_{32}$in diameter holes through this to coincide with those in the press beam B. The two lifting screws are formed from 8mm nuts, drilled $^1/_8$in diameter on three faces with $^1/_2$in lengths of $^1/_8$in outside diameter brass tube soldered into them (see enlarged detail). The three

base supports C are now cut from elm $^3/_4$in x 1in. The outside supports are each 5in long, and the centre support is $4^1/_2$in long. Glue and pin these under the base beam A as shown, with an equal projection front and back, except for the centre support which is inset by $^1/_2$in at the front.

Steadying blocks D, cut from $^3/_4$in thick elm, are now fastened on top of the base supports C at the front and back of base beam A. The outer steadying blocks are flush with the inside edges of the outer supports, and the centre pair of steadying blocks is centred over the middle support C. Four press boards again from elm, 1in

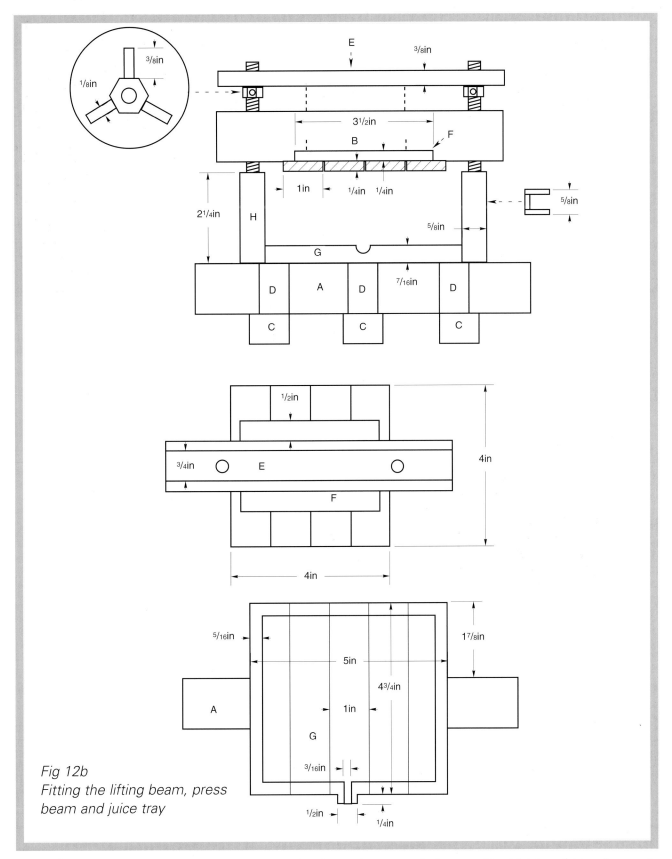

Fig 12b
Fitting the lifting beam, press beam and juice tray

wide, 1/4in thick, and 4in long, are now glued together to form a square 4in x 4in. Before proceeding further, texture the assembly so far completed, and apply the weathering mixture (see page 18).

The press board assembly should now have the two side battens F, of 1/2in x 1/4in elm, each 3 1/2in long, glued and pinned on top of it, 1 1/4in apart. This structure should now be positioned under the press beam B, and secured to it with a pair of short chains 1/2in from the ends of F on either side. The press beam B should also be

The cider press

suspended by chains under the lifting beam E, so that there is a space between them of about ^{5}/8in. This is done as follows:

Cut two pieces of 10 links-per-inch chain, each eight links long, fit a very small screw-eye at one end of each, and fasten these eyes centrally on top of the press beam 1^1/8in from the threaded rod at each end. Drill ^{1}/8in diameter holes through the lifting beam E to correspond with the chain positions on B. Gouge a ^{1}/16in wide slot across each of these holes on the top face of E, each extending ^{3}/16in on either side of the hole. Pull the chain through from underneath and insert ^{3}/8in lengths of brass wire to stop the chain unthreading. These components can now be put aside.

The juice tray G should now be made from elm 5in square and ^{7}/16in thick. The front edge should be cut back to leave a ^{1}/2in wide spout projecting ^{1}/4in. Mark a margin, ^{5}/16in wide, around the edge, cut away the area inside this to a depth of ^{3}/16in, and file a ^{3}/16in wide slot in the spout to the same depth. With glue and pins, assemble the tray G on top of the main beam A and the steadying blocks D. Texture and weather all parts not previously treated, and chemically blacken the threaded rods (see page 187).

The thread guards H are now made as open-sided boxes from ^{1}/8in thick elm, and positioned round the lower part of the rods at each side. They are secured in place by drilling ^{1}/32in diameter holes through the open ends of the

The apple mill

sides outside the rods and inserting veneer pins which are cut off flush. Reassemble the press and lifting beams to the rods, remembering to insert the lifting screws with washers above and below each. The tommy bars for operating the press are each 4^1/2in long, and approximately ^{5}/32in in diameter. These should be formed by planing lengths of ^{3}/16in square elm or other hardwood, so that they are nearly round, and fitting a ferrule of ^{1}/8in tube, ^{1}/8in long, on to one end of each. These ends are then drilled and have a length of ^{3}/32in diameter rod glued into each to project ^{3}/8in.

The cheeses are made next. These represent layers of sacking with apple pulp folded inside. Cut eight pieces of ^{1}/8in plywood, 3^1/2in x 3in

and cover each with hessian. The outer edges of each can now be spotted with yellow and green poster paint, and the cheeses stacked on the juice tray beneath the press boards.

Apple Mill This model is based on an original from Somerset, dated 1825. Referring to Figs 13a–13d, cut from ^{1}/4in square elm, two base rails D, four long uprights B, and two short uprights A. Using a router, cut a ^{1}/4in x ^{1}/8in deep notch at the top of one face of each short upright A, and a similar sized slot on one face of each upright B, ^{1}/4in from the top. Three similar sized slots should be cut in the tops of both base rails D. Two panels of 1.5 mm plywood, H, each 2^1/2in wide and 1^5/16in deep, are now cut

Fully equipped interior of the Cider Barn

out and drilled for the roller and axle holes. Each panel has a $^1/_8$in diameter hole $^3/_8$in either side of its vertical centreline, and $^3/_4$in below its top edge, and a further $^1/_8$in diameter hole on the centreline above these two, equidistant by $^3/_4$in from each. Stain both panels medium oak.

Cut the two cross rails G, and glue each one between a pair of long uprights B, noting that there is $^1/_8$in of slot at the outside of each upright B, which is exposed. Clear surplus glue from these slots, as they will later house the side tie rails. Now glue the 1.5mm panels between the uprights, close under the cross rails, and allow the glue to set. Next, machine the front cross rail C to the pattern shown, and glue this across the front uprights A. When dry, these assemblies are glued into the base rails D, with the exception of the front frame AC which must wait until the flywheel is made and fitted. Ensure that the slots on B face each other. At the same time, the side rails F should be glued in place.

The diagonal braces E between the front uprights A should be made next. Cross-halve two pieces of $^1/_4$in square elm, glue the joint, and angle the ends so that at the top they fit under the cross beam C, and at the bottom they fit between the uprights A. Do not yet glue the diagonal braces to the frame AC.

Now the flywheel can be made. This has a core of $^1/_8$in plywood with the rim thickness increased by the addition of 1.5mm plywood on either side. Cut three $4^1/_2$in squares, one of $^1/_8$in plywood, and two of 1.5mm plywood. Drill a 3mm diameter hole through the centre of each square. With either a router or a jigsaw cut the $^1/_8$in square to a disc 4in in diameter. Mark a $^3/_8$in margin round the edge, together with the four spokes as shown in Fig 13a. Cut out the waste area between the spokes and glue a square of 1.5mm plywood to the rim on one side only, using a short length of 3mm diameter rod, to centre the holes. Impact adhesive should be used, and pressure applied in a vice. Cut the 1.5mm plywood rim back to the profile of the core with a craft knife. Repeat this on the other side of the core. Cut a $^1/_8$in thick slice of $^1/_2$in dowel, drill the centre 3mm diameter, and glue this to one side of the wheel, centred at the hub. This will now be the outer face of the wheel. Stain the whole assembly with medium or dark oak.

Four plastic gearwheels, 20mm diameter, from Hobby's Gearwheel Set Z7 are required,

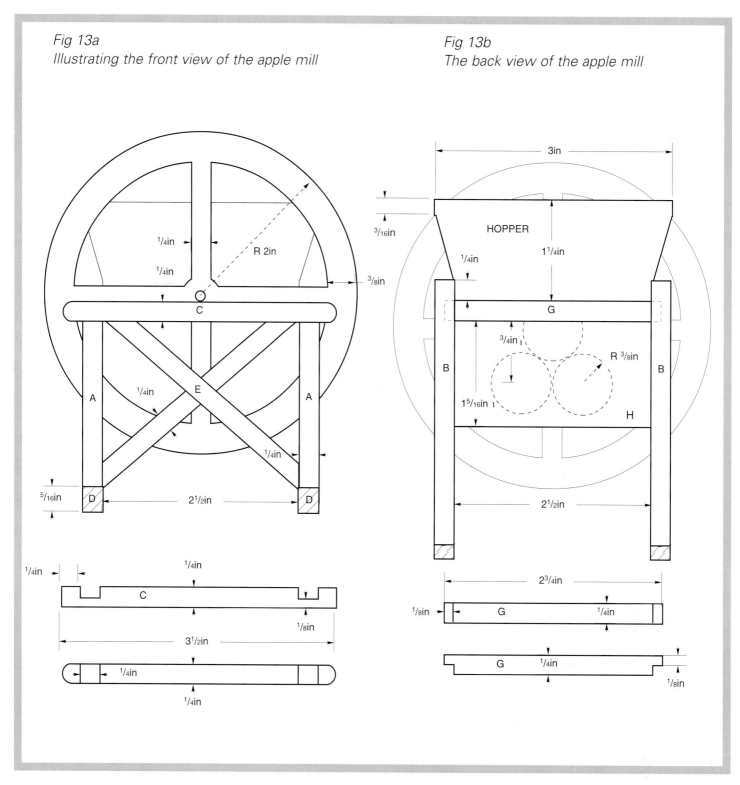

Fig 13a
Illustrating the front view of the apple mill

Fig 13b
The back view of the apple mill

together with one 120mm axle and two 50mm axles, for the rollers and crank. Take the 120mm length of 3mm axle and bend it at right angles, 3in from one end. Now bend back again $^1/_2$in down the short section already bent. This forms the crank and axle with the handle displaced by $^1/_2$in from the axle centreline. Two rollers should now be made from hardwood, each $^3/_4$in diameter, with a 3mm diameter hole through the centre. Their length is determined by the dis-

tance between the 1.5mm panels, less $^1/_4$in, which is the thickness of the gearwheels used. Allow a further $^1/_{16}$in clearance. A gearwheel should now be glued with epoxy resin to one end of each roller, ensuring that the holes are concentric. Set the rollers in place between the panels, with the gears towards the front (fly-wheel side), and push a 50mm axle through each. When viewed from the flywheel side, the right-hand roller axle has an additional gear-

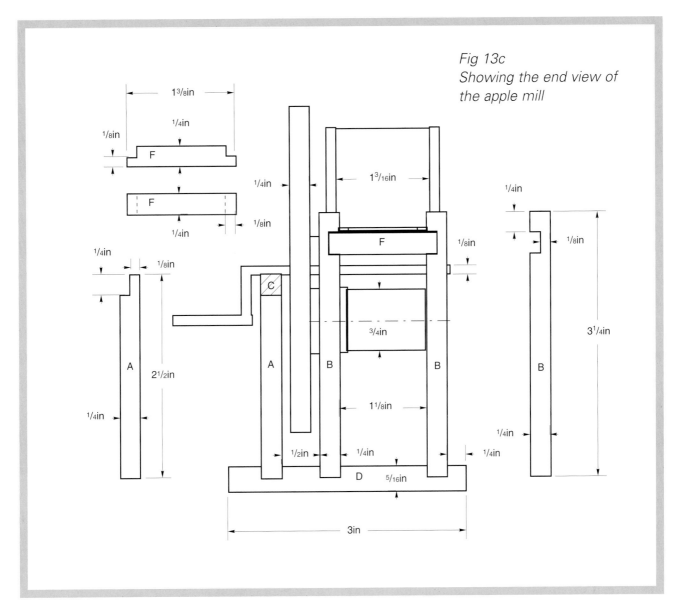

Fig 13c
Showing the end view of
the apple mill

wheel on the outside of the front panel. Now push the crankshaft through the flywheel, and set the fourth gearwheel on this shaft behind it. Push the crankshaft through the upper holes in the front and back panels and test for free rotation. When satisfied, trim off any surplus crankshaft at the back.

Dismantle the moving parts, and give everything one coat of matt varnish. The crank handle outside the flywheel should be painted black, and a length of black card should be glued around the rim of the flywheel. When dry reassemble, and then glue the front frame AC in place on the base rails D, and add the diagonal braces. A short strip of brass can now be bent to sit over the crankshaft and rest on the cross beam C, where it can be glued in place, as a dummy bearing.

The hopper is made from $1/8$in thick elm , with the sides cut first to the profile shown in Fig 13b and 13d, and the ends butt jointed and glued between them, parallel with, and inset $1/8$in from, the sloping ends. When the glue has set, trim the bottom square and check that the assembly will fit on top of the cross rails G, inside the upper projections of the uprights B. Give the hopper a weathered finish.

Now make the shutters and shutter guides from 1.5mm plywood (Fig 13d). The shutters are each $11/16$in wide and $13/4$in long, and butt over the crankshaft at the centre. The guides are nominally $1/2$in wide, and are glued on top of the cross rails G, $11/16$in apart, with their ends notched to fit round the uprights B. The shutters are now free to slide between them. Glue the hopper in place, taking care not to glue the shutters.

The pulp tray is made in the same way to the dimensions shown, with the ends inset by $1/8$in. Sand the bottom edge true, and add a base of

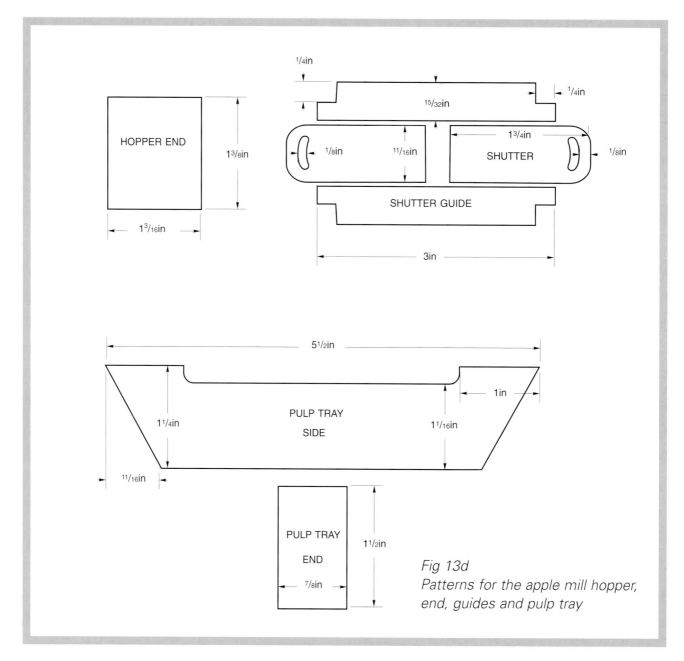

Fig 13d
Patterns for the apple mill hopper, end, guides and pulp tray

1/16in thick elm, trimmed back flush with the sides. This tray should now slide on top of the base rails D, between the long uprights B.

Barrel Rack Referring to Fig 14, make ten legs from 3/8in square elm, each 1 1/4in long, and slotted as shown. The easiest method is to use the router in the manner described for making window bars on page 184–5. Four legs should also be slotted on an adjacent face, in handed pairs, for the corners. Cut four 8 1/2in lengths of 1/4in x 3/16in elm for the front and back rails, and four 1 3/4in lengths for the end rails. Glue one long rail into the lower slot of a corner post at each end. The rail end should extend halfway across the front face of each corner post, flush with the inside of the slots on the end faces.

Now glue three more posts to the rail, evenly spaced, 1 3/4in apart, and then glue in the top rail. Repeat this for the other side. Allow the glue to set, and add the 1 3/4in lengths of rail across each end.

Five elm boards 3/8in wide, 1/16in thick, and 1 3/4in long are now glued across the top of this assembly, from front to back, in line with the pairs of posts. The completed structure can now be textured and weathered. Provision is made for four barrels, whose size may vary from one maker to another. Four wedges will be needed to support each barrel. These should be cut from 1/4in square elm strip in 3/4in lengths, with the top edges shaped to the barrel radius using a Dremel drum sander in a Minicraft drill. The wedges are then glued in place on the top rails.

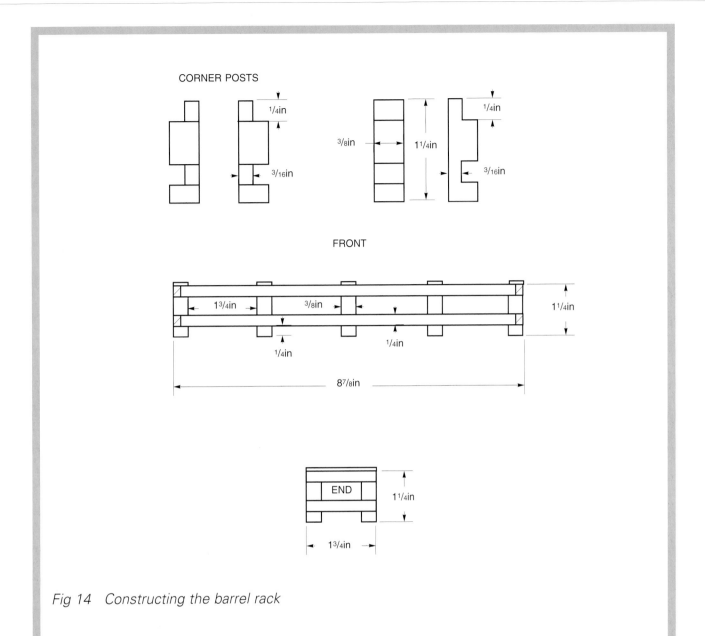

Fig 14   *Constructing the barrel rack*

CIDER BARN – LIST OF SUPPLIERS

Irene Campbell: Pottery.
C. & D. Crafts: Baskets.
Dijon: Cir-Kit wire and eyelets, and Tortoise stove.
Dolphin Miniatures: Barrels, buckets, beer crates, hay rake, sack trolley, and ladder.
Mainly Men Minis: Doll.
Nursery of Miniatures: Coconut fibre for thatching.

Lights, made by Peter Kennedy, and the dog are from the author's own collection.

FORGE

This has the same basic building as the Cider Barn with the addition of a chimney. The contents include the forge hearth and smoke-hood, water tank, bellows, and anvil, for which full instructions are included.

Tea break at the Forge

Following the instructions for the Cider Barn in Chapter 1, construct the building, up to the point of carcase assembly. The chimney, which was optional on the Cider Barn, should now be made and fitted on the Forge.

CHIMNEY

Referring to Fig 15, cut two $3/4$in wide strips of $3/8$in plywood A each 16in long, and two strips B and C $1^1/2$in wide. B is 16in long, and C is $10^1/2$in long. Glue and pin these with the $3/4$in widths A sandwiched between the $1^1/2$in widths B and C, to form a box section $1^1/2$in square. All four sections should be flush at the top. Lay the box down with the shorter side C uppermost, and glue a piece of lime or pine D, $1^1/8$in square, with the top angled as shown, to either side of the box, flush at the bottom edge. Cut a piece of $3/8$in plywood E, $5^1/2$in long and $3^3/4$in wide, with the top edge cut to conform with the angles of the side pieces D. Glue this to the box with its top edge close butted under section C. Use PVA glue and $3/4$in panel pins for assembly,

except for the side pieces D which are better fixed with impact adhesive. The chimney can now be planed fair all round, and glued and screwed to the outside of the end wall. It should be positioned centrally at the ridge, and screwed from the inside of the end wall. Now carry on and complete the building as shown in Chapter 1.

EQUIPMENT

Hearth and Smoke-hood Cut a backboard of $1/4$in plywood, $3^3/4$in wide, and $8^3/4$in long. Shape this to the profile in Fig 16, with the lower part cut back by $5/32$in on each side for a height of $2^{11}/16$in. Cut a block of pine $3^7/16$in wide, $2^7/16$in high, and 2in thick and, using impact adhesive, glue this to the bottom of the backboard, flush at the sides and bottom edge. Next, cut the smoke-hood to the profile shown, from a block of pine, $3^1/2$in long, $3^3/4$in wide, and 2in thick. Mark a $1/4$in margin round the underside of the smoke-hood and cut away the area inside this to a depth of $1/4$in. Drill a line of

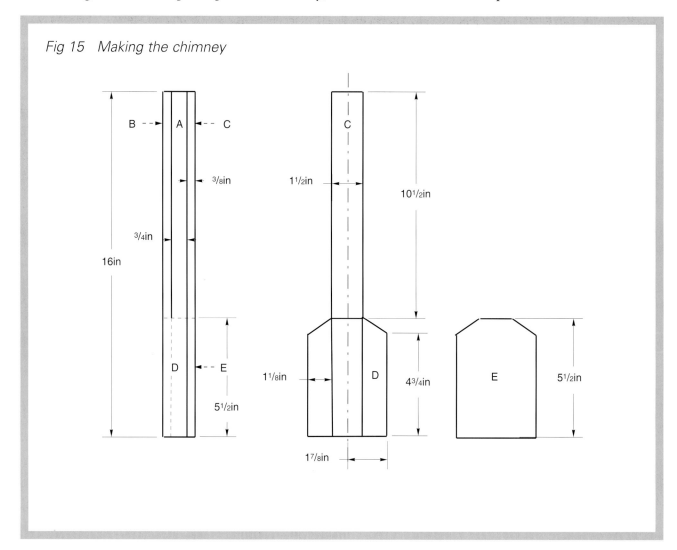

Fig 15   Making the chimney

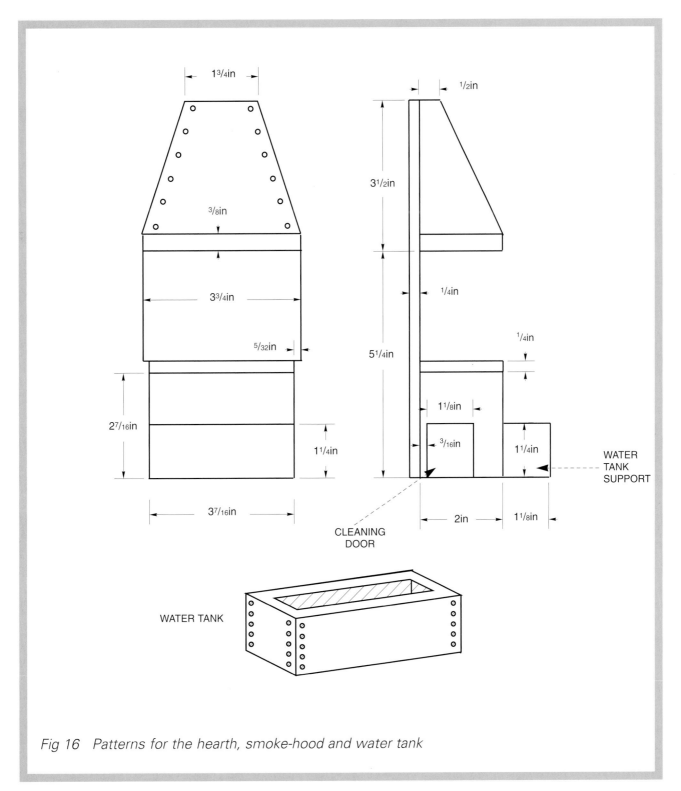

Fig 16   *Patterns for the hearth, smoke-hood and water tank*

holes parallel to, and inset $^3/16$in from, the edges of the front face. These holes should be $^1/16$in diameter, evenly spaced, and each should have a $^1/16$in copper snaphead rivet glued into it.

Now glue the smoke-hood centrally at the top of the backboard, with both top edges flush, and trim the backboard to the profile of the smoke-hood sides. Sand smooth, and then paint the smoke-hood dull black. Drill a $^1/8$in diameter hole from the centre of the top face of the

lower block diagonally downwards to emerge behind the backboard. This will be used later when fitting a grain-of-wheat bulb under the fire.

The water tank support should be added next. This is a block of pine or lime, $3^7/16$in long, $1^1/4$in high, and $1^1/8$in deep, glued against the lower front edge of the hearth. Houseworks mesh-mounted bricks from Blackwells are used to face the front and sides of the hearth, and the

Fig 17
Illustrating the
construction of the
bellows

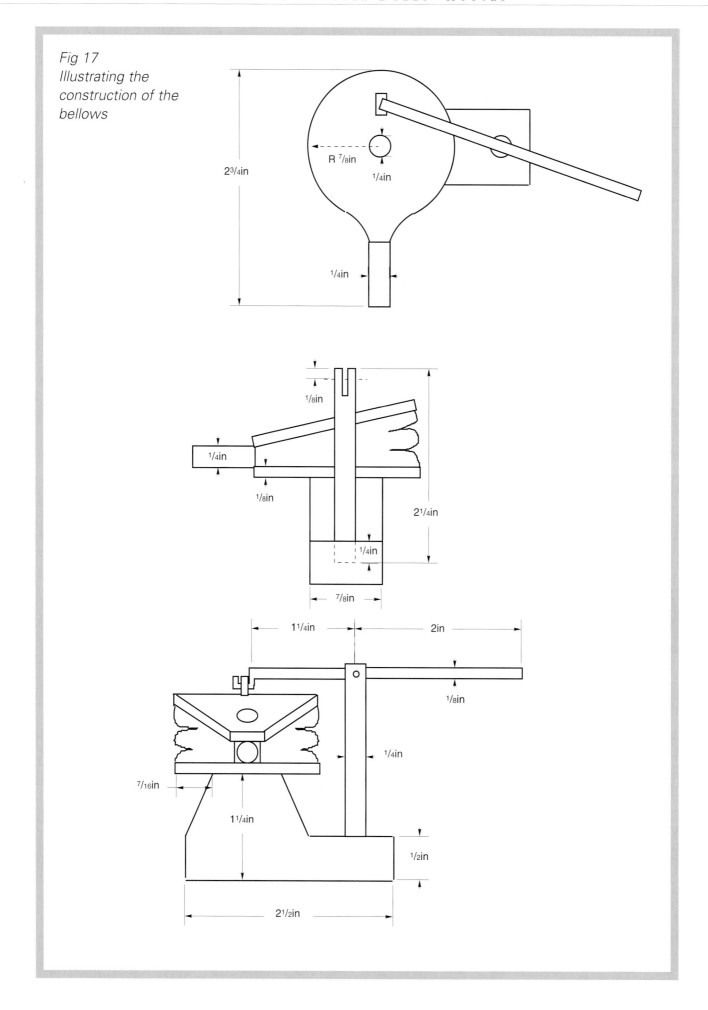

front face of the backboard, up to the level of the smoke-hood. The top of the water tank support can be left uncovered. These bricks can be cut with a small cold chisel, and glued with PVA adhesive. When the glue has set, grout them with Polyfilla. The top of the hearth should now be raised by one course of bricks at its perimeter. Individual bricks are available, but you will have sufficient facing bricks left to be able to glue three strips to a timber backing to increase their depth, before cutting to length and gluing to the hearth. Now paint the inside of the hearth top matt black.

The cleaning door is cut from black card, $1^1/4$in high and $1^1/8$in wide, and glued to the left-hand side of the hearth where shown in Fig 16. Two dummy strap hinges, each $^1/8$in x $^3/4$in are cut from black card and glued to the door $^3/16$in from its top and bottom edges. These strips should overlap the door at the left-hand side by $^1/8$in. This overlap is then folded back on itself to represent the pivoted section. To achieve the soot-blackened effect, all the brickwork is brushed with medium oak spirit stain. Follow this with a wash of matt black, well thinned, and wipe downwards with fine wire wool, leaving the darkest areas on the back wall round the top of the hearth and by the cleaning door. Cut a piece of black card to fit the hearth and cut approximately $^3/4$in square from its centre. Glue a reddish-coloured translucent toffee wrapper, or something similar, over the hole, to form a slightly raised hump. Cover the remainder with simulated coal and wood ash. A grain-of-wheat bulb is now threaded through the hearth, in the hole previously drilled, with a two-pin plug added at the back for connection to the eyelets at the back wall of the building. Replace the prepared card over the bulb, but do not glue as the bulb may need to be replaced at some time.

Water Tank Cut a block of pine $1^1/4$in square and $3^7/8$in long. Mark a $^3/16$in margin round one long face and cut away the area inside this to a depth of $^1/4$in. Now reduce the block on a circular saw by $^1/16$in on each long face, to give a wall thickness of $^1/8$in at the top. The additional thickness was left on the block to help prevent splitting of the margin at the edges. First drill pilot holes, and then hammer a line of track pins cut to about half their length, and evenly spaced about $^1/4$in apart, into the block at each side of

the tank front, and the tank ends, inset $^1/8$in from the edges. These represent the rivets. Paint the tank silver, and fill the space at the top with polyester resin to represent the water. The completed water tank is now glued on top of the support at the front of the hearth.

As an alternative to polyester resin, a product called E-Z Water, produced in the form of meltable plastic granules, is also available. This can be used in the same way as resin but must be melted first and then poured into the tank. The product is non-toxic, has little or no smell, and sets in a very short time. The only slight disadvantage is that its surface is rather less resistant to scratching than resin. It is intended for use on model railways and is therefore available from good model shops.

Bellows Cut two pieces of $^1/8$in thick elm to the profile in Fig 17, and drill a $^1/4$in diameter hole centrally through one of them. Cut two pieces of $^1/8$in plywood, to the same profile, but $^1/16$in smaller all round. Again drill a $^1/4$in hole through one piece only. Cut a strip of thin leather long enough to reach round the perimeter of the smaller patterns. It should be 1in wide at its centre, tapering to $^3/8$in at each end. Using impact adhesive, glue this round the edges of the plywood patterns. Trim the leather flush at the spout end, and on the top and bottom faces. Now glue the $^1/8$in elm profiles on to the top and bottom faces, noting that the holes should be uppermost and should coincide. Drill into the spout end $^1/4$in diameter, and $^3/8$in deep. Into this, glue a 1in length of $^1/4$in diameter tube, so that $^3/4$in projects. Cut a small brass plate, $^1/2$in x $^1/4$in, from .016in brass strip. Drill a $^1/16$in diameter hole in the centre and into this glue or solder a small eye bent from $^1/32$in diameter wire. The eye should have an inside diameter of $^1/8$in. Glue this plate to the top of the bellows where shown, midway between the hole and the back edge.

From a piece of $2^1/2$in x $1^1/4$in elm, $^7/8$in thick, cut the base block to the pattern shown, and drill a $^1/4$in diameter hole for the fulcrum pillar. Cut a $2^1/2$in length of $^1/4$in diameter mild steel rod, and slot the top $^1/16$in wide to a depth of $^5/16$in. Drill a $^1/16$in diameter hole through the rod, midway up the slot. A $3^1/2$in length of $^1/8$in brass rod is needed for the lever. This should be bent at right angles for $^1/2$in at one end and heated and hammered flat both here

Fully equipped interior of the Forge

and at the pivot point. At both these positions the thickness should be ¹/16in after flattening. File a hook on the bent section to engage with the eye on the bellows.

Glue the bellows and the fulcrum pillar to the base block (see plan view, Fig 17), and then set the lever in place. A ¹/16in diameter hole is now drilled through the lever at the pivot point, and a ¹/4in length of ¹/16in brass rod inserted.

Place the completed bellows beside the hearth at the right-hand side, and mark where the spout touches, midway along the hearth side. Drill a ¹/4in diameter hole at this point, ³/8in deep. All the woodwork on the bellows should now have two coats of matt varnish, and the metal parts one coat of dull black paint. The bellows are attached to the hearth by pushing the spout into the previously drilled hole.

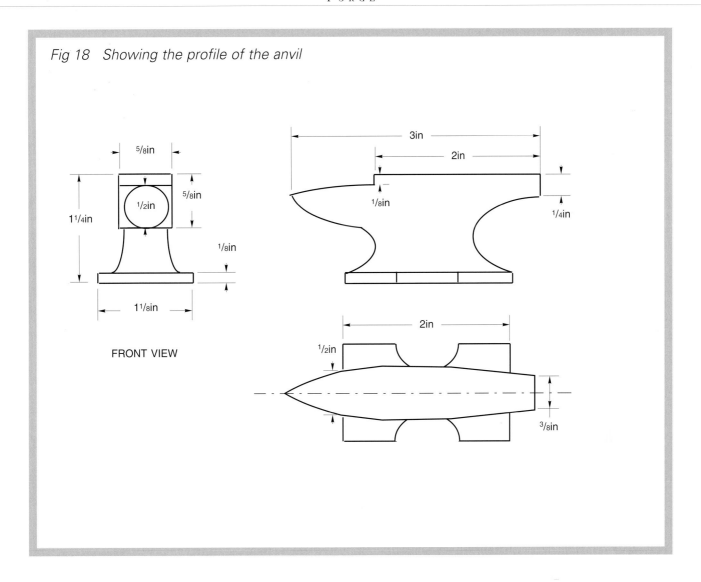

Fig 18 Showing the profile of the anvil

FRONT VIEW

Anvil This is carved from a solid block of beech, to the profile and dimensions given in Fig 18. After roughly cutting with a jigsaw, the final shaping is done with a small sanding drum and disc used in a Minicraft drill. On completion, paint the anvil dull black, and glue it on to a slice cut from a small branch about 2in in diameter and 1^{1}/$_{4}$in thick.

Workbench This is made in the same manner as the barrel rack for the Cider Barn (Fig 14), except that the legs are now 2^{1}/$_{2}$in long, and only six are required – at the ends, and centrally at the front and back. The finished dimensions of the framework should be 8in x 2^{1}/$_{4}$in. The bench top is cut from ^{1}/$_{8}$in plywood 8^{1}/$_{4}$in x 2^{1}/$_{2}$in, and glued on top of the frame, with a ^{1}/$_{8}$in overlap all round. A further covering of rusty tin plate, with the sides and ends turned down, is glued over the plywood.

FORGE – LIST OF SUPPLIERS

Dolphin Miniatures:
Tools, paint pots, and farrier's box.
Marie Theresa Endean:
Doll.
Sussex Crafts:
Bucket and fireback.
John Watkins:
Weather vane and wrought iron panels.

SWAN INN

This model is a representation of a small country pub. The bar area, which extends the whole width of the ground floor, includes the bar itself, bottle shelf, and rack for barrels, all of which are removable for access. A landing, small sitting-room, and one bedroom are provided on the first floor. A store has been added to the left-hand end of the building, in the form of a disused stable.

The Swan Inn, fully furnished

TIMBER REQUIREMENTS – SWAN INN

WOOD	THICKNESS	AREA sq ft	
Birch plywood	0.8mm	$1/2$	
	1.5mm	1	
	$1/8$in (3mm)	5	
	$1/4$in (6mm)	$4 1/2$	
	$3/8$in (9mm)	21	

	THICKNESS in	WIDTH in	LENGTH ft	in
Pine	$3/8$	$1/2$	2	4
	$1/2$	$1/2$	2	6
	$3/4$	$1 3/4$	2	4
	$1 1/8$	$3 1/2$	3	7
Elm	$1/16$	$3/8$	8	-
		$7/16$	9	-
		$15/32$	8	-
		1	2	1
	$3/32$	$1 5/8$	1	6
	$1/8$	$1/4$	1	3
	$5/32$	$3/8$		7
	$3/16$	$1/2$	10	-
	$1/4$	$1/4$	2	4
		$5/16$	8	-
		$3/8$	5	2
	$5/16$	$5/16$	1	8
		$3/4$	1	4
	$3/8$	$3/8$		7
		$1/2$	1	1
	$5/8$	$5/8$	1	4
		$7/8$	2	1
	$11/16$	$13/16$		7
	$3/4$	1		4
		$2 11/16$	4	-
	$7/8$	$1 3/16$	2	-
Lime	$3/32$	$3/8$	11	-
	$1/8$	$1/8$	11	-
		$3/8$	5	-
	$3/16$	$3/16$		4
	$1/4$	$1/4$	1	4
	$7/16$	$7/16$	3	-

Referring to Figs 19a–19d, cut from $3/8$in plywood, one base, two end walls, two partition walls, and one back panel. Rout the grooves in the back and base where shown. Each is $3/8$in wide and $1/8$in deep. Trim $1/16$in from the front edges of the end walls and partitions and replace this with a $1/16$in thick edge veneer of elm. Cut out the two window openings on the back wall.

The two end walls each have a $1/4$in wide and $3/32$in deep groove cut across their inside faces with their top edges $2 3/4$in below the apex, to house the bedroom ceilings. The partitions should have this groove routed on both faces. Cut out the fireplace opening on the left-hand end wall, and glue a frame of 1in x $3/4$in pine or lime to the outside face with the inner edges

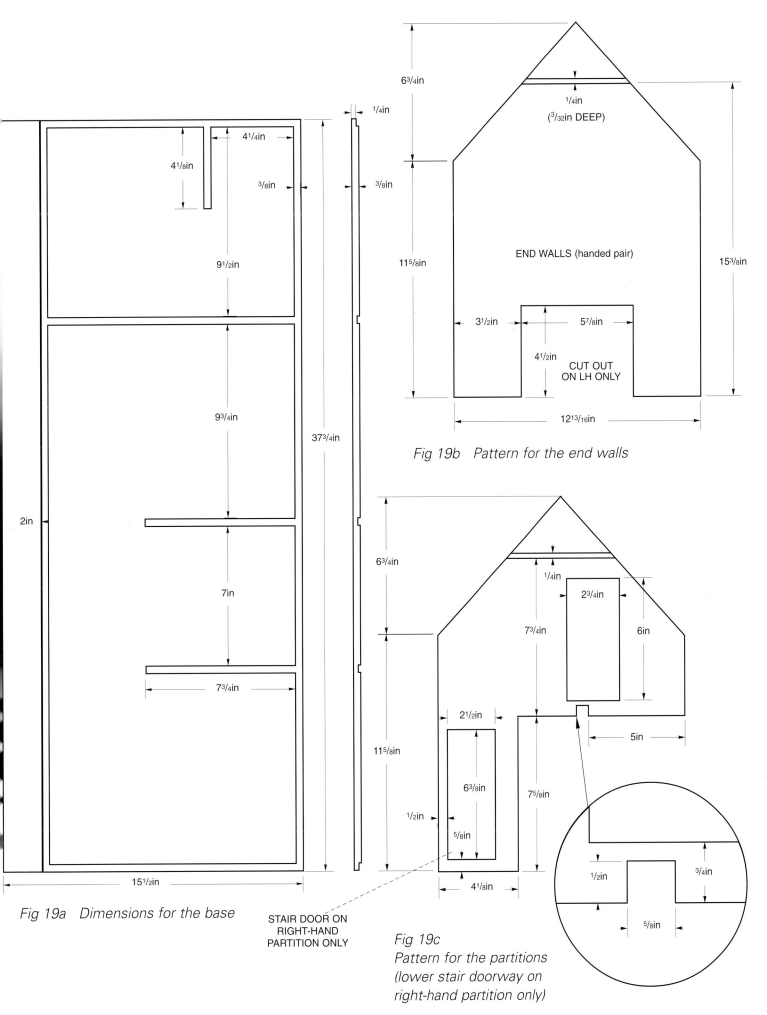

Fig 19a   Dimensions for the base

STAIR DOOR ON
RIGHT-HAND
PARTITION ONLY

Fig 19b   Pattern for the end walls

END WALLS (handed pair)

CUT OUT
ON LH ONLY

Fig 19c
Pattern for the partitions
(lower stair doorway on
right-hand partition only)

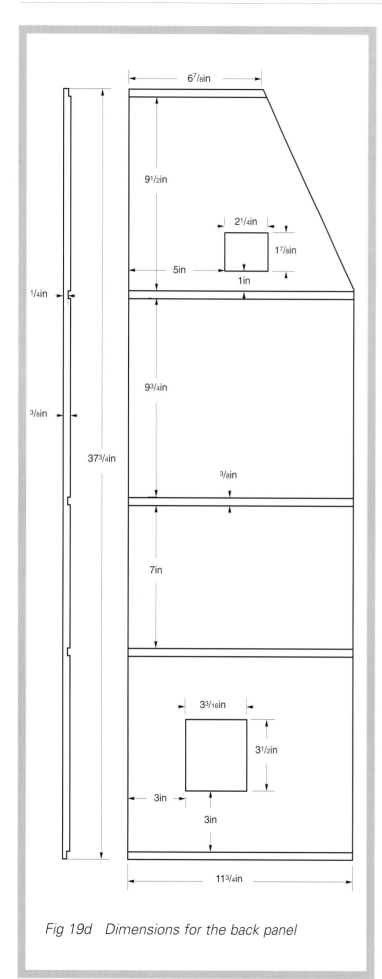

Fig 19d   Dimensions for the back panel

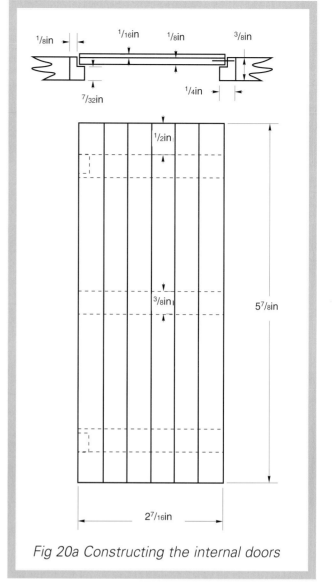

Fig 20a Constructing the internal doors

flush with the opening. The frame is not applied across the bottom of the opening. Cut a piece of $^1/4$in plywood, $7^7/8$in x $5^1/2$in, and glue and pin this over the outside of the frame. Bevel the outer edges at 45°. This will form the back of the fireplace which is deeper than that on the right-hand end wall.

DOORS

Cut the door openings on the partition walls. Note that the lower stair door is only on the right-hand partition. Frame these openings with lime (see Figs 20a–20c), machined to the profile shown, and then make the three doors from 1.5mm plywood, planked on both faces with $^1/32$in thick lime. Instructions for making and hanging doors will be found on pages 185-6. The doors from the landing open into the bedroom and sitting-room, and are hung at the back. Make the dummy door for the back of the

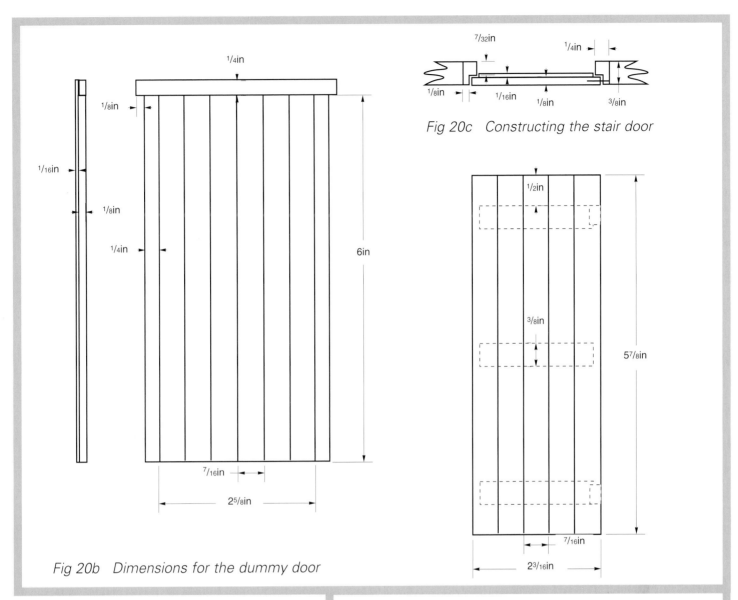

Fig 20c   Constructing the stair door

Fig 20b   Dimensions for the dummy door

bar area, and plank this with elm. This door with its framing, is mounted on a backing of 1.5mm plywood, to be fitted in the bar after decoration. The stair door should also be made now. Do not fix any of the doors yet, put them aside for painting.

FLOOR BEARERS
Referring to Fig 21, cut sufficient $^1/2$in x $^3/16$in elm for the floor bearers, and glue two sections to the back wall where shown, inset $^3/16$in at each end from the vertical grooves. No bearer is needed in the central stairwell section. Notch the two partition walls $^5/8$in wide and $^1/2$in deep to receive the pillars (see fig 19c). Veneer the underside of the notched section on each partition with $^1/16$in elm and plane this flush on both faces.

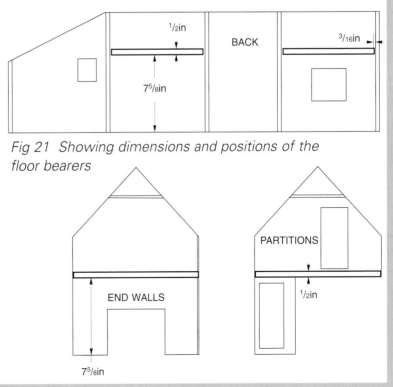

Fig 21   Showing dimensions and positions of the floor bearers

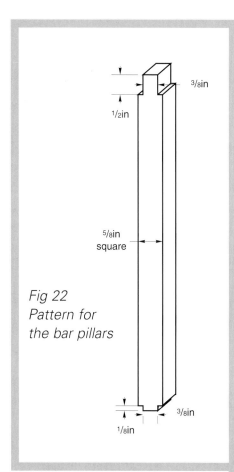

*Fig 22
Pattern for
the bar pillars*

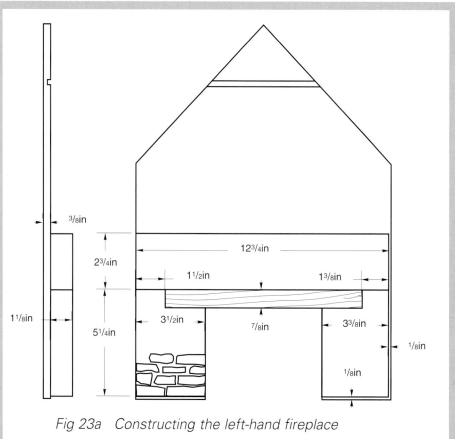

Fig 23a   Constructing the left-hand fireplace

Again following Fig 21, apply floor bearers to both sides of each partition. This will leave a mortise for the upper end of the pillars. *Note that the bearers stop ¹/₈in from the back edges to allow these to enter the grooves in the back wall.* Glue and pin a length of ³/₈in square elm to the front edge of the ground floor section of each partition Cut the two pillars from ⁵/₈in square elm, each 8¹/₄in long (see Fig 22). Use the router to reduce two opposing faces at each end of both pillars by ¹/₈in to leave a tenon at the top ¹/₂in deep and a tenon at the bottom ¹/₈in deep, both ⁵/₈in x ³/₈in. Rout a ¹/₁₆in wide x ¹/₈in deep groove down the back of each pillar for wiring. Using a small disc sander and a length of hacksaw blade, texture the surface of the pillars to produce a rough-hewn effect. Do not glue in position yet.

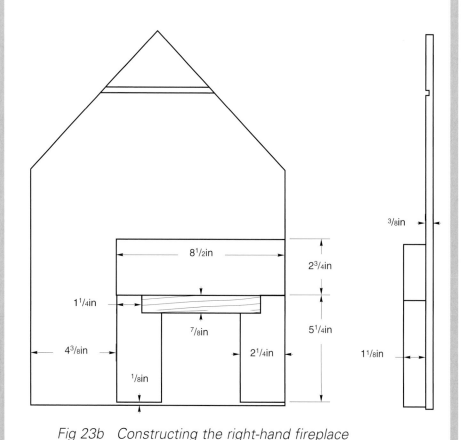

Fig 23b   Constructing the right-hand fireplace

Unfurnished interior of the Swan Inn showing bar sections and landing floor

FIREPLACES

Fire surrounds are now fitted to both end walls. Starting with the left-hand wall, cut two blocks of pine, each $1^1/8$in thick, $3^1/2$in wide, and $5^1/4$in long. Reduce one block to a width of $3^3/8$in. Both blocks should be stepped down on their top edges by $7/8$in for the lintel (Figs 23a and 23b). The narrower piece is glued to the back section of the wall, inset $1/8$in from the edge and bottom, to allow this wall to fit the grooves in the base and back wall. The inner edge of the block should be flush with the inside of the fireplace opening. Apply the wider block to the front section of this wall, again flush with the fire opening and inset $1/8$in from the bottom, but flush with the front edge. Cut a lintel from elm, $1^3/16$in x $7/8$in, to fit the gap between the stepped blocks. Now add a further block of pine $1^1/8$in thick, $2^3/4$in deep, and $12^3/4$in long. Glue this to the wall above the lintel with its front edge flush with the outer edge of the wall. Texture the lintel as for the pillars.

Next repeat this procedure for the fireplace on the right-hand wall, noting that the fire surround is only on the front section of the wall. This leaves a clear space of $4^3/8$in at the back. Glue in a short length of floor bearer here in line with the top of the fireplace blocks and also inset $1/8$in at the back.

Following Fig 23a, carve the stonework on the wood blocks at either side of each fireplace opening up to the level of the top of the lintel. The joints between the stones should be about $1/16$in deep. Cut them with a small gouge, or a burr in a Minicraft drill. Apply one coat of textured masonry paint to the stones, followed by two coats of magnolia emulsion applied to both stones and wall. Varnish the lintel, which can now be fixed in position. All interior walls can now be painted with two coats of magnolia emulsion taking care that the back edges of the end walls and partitions, where they are housed in the back wall, are kept clear of paint for subsequent gluing.

Fig 24a   Detailed plans for constructing the upper windows

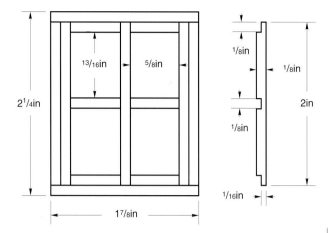

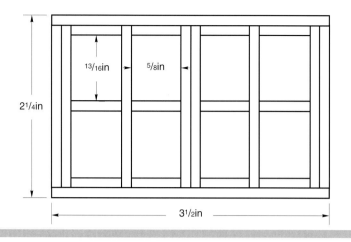

Fig 24b   Lower windows

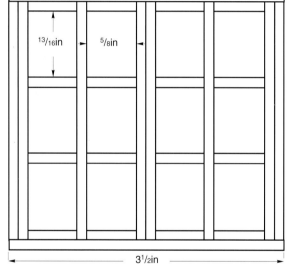

TRIAL ASSEMBLY

Assemble the carcase with screws only (two $^3/4$in no 4 countersunk screws in each joint line), and check that everything fits satisfactorily. Glue fillets of lime $^3/8$in x $^1/8$in in the spaces in the floor grooves behind the pillars and in the left-hand fireplace opening.

ELECTRIFICATION

This will be done partly with Cir-Kit twin tape, and partly with wire which will be more convenient in the hidden areas, particularly the roof void. Starting from a position on the floor in the centre bay $3^1/2$in from the back wall and close beside the right-hand partition, apply a length of

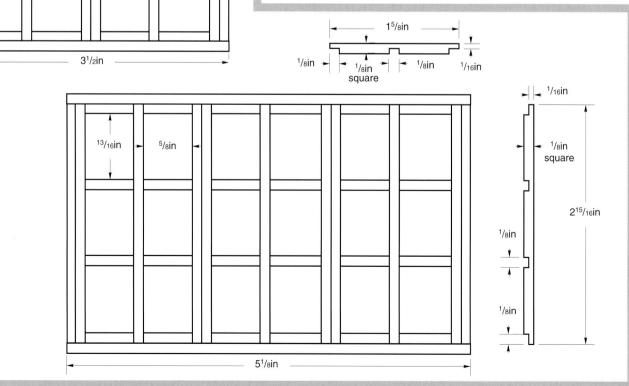

tape across the floor between the partitions. Mark the right-hand partition at this point. Remove the partition and cut a shallow notch in its bottom edge $^5/32$in deep, and just wider than the tape. Glue a corresponding fillet of $^3/8$in x $^1/8$in lime into the floor groove to give a flat run for the tape. Extend this tape across the floor to a point just behind the right-hand fire surround, and brad the tape joint. Replace the right-hand partition and its pillar, apply a further length of tape from a position close behind the left-hand pillar to the cross-floor tape between the partitions, and brad the joint. Repeat this behind the right-hand pillar, but continue over the cross tape for a further 1in and brad again at this point. These last two brads form the connection point for soldering the transformer feed wires. The tapes behind the pillars should each have a pair of socket eyelets fitted. A further pair of eyelets should be fitted to the tape just behind the right-hand fire surround.

Gouge a groove $^1/8$in wide and $^1/8$in deep down the left-hand edge of the right-hand fire surround and across its top edge from this point to meet the end wall. Prepare a length of twin wire long enough to reach from the floor to 2in above the top of the fire surround when following the line of the groove. Connect the top end to a small connector block which should be screwed to the end wall centrally over the fireplace and $1^1/2$in above upper floor level. The lower end of this wire should be bared, and soldered into the floor eyelets after final assembly of the carcase. When fitted, the light (Dijon) for the dartboard will also be connected here, with its wire tail extended if necessary. Add a further connector block in a similar position on the left-hand end wall.

WINDOWS
Referring to Fig 24a and 24b, make the windows. Constructional details for these are given on page 184–5. Line the openings in the back wall.

PAINTING
Paint all the door frames with two coats of Humbrol matt white and all downstairs walls and upstairs walls in the centre section (stairwell and landing) with two coats of magnolia emulsion. The windows and internal doors should now be painted with two coats of Humbrol satin white, excluding the dummy door which is varnished. Apply two coats of matt varnish to all beams, bearers and pillars made so far.

FINAL ASSEMBLY
Glue the windows in place in the back wall, inset 2mm from the back face, to allow for 2mm thick glazing. Now assemble the carcase with glue and screws, adding panel pins at 3in centres. Remember to insert the pillars under the partitions before assembly.

FIRST FLOOR AND CEILINGS
Referring to Fig 25, cut the three ceiling sections from $^1/4$in plywood, and glue them in place between the end walls and partitions. Bevel the front and back edges of each fair with the roof slopes. From the patterns in Figs 26a–26c, cut the three first-floor sections. Rout the $^3/8$in wide x $^1/16$in deep grooves on the underside for wiring. Rout a further groove, this time $^1/8$in wide and $^3/16$in deep centrally in the first groove, and glue in a $^3/8$in x $^1/16$in strip of lime to fill the surface. This leaves a channel $^1/8$in square through the floor for the wire. Notch the outer edges of the left- and right-hand floors,

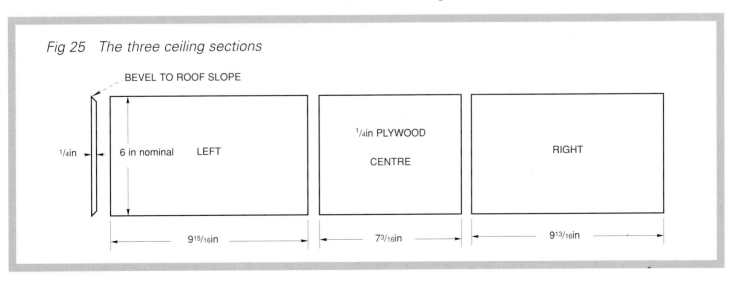

Fig 25 The three ceiling sections

BEVEL TO ROOF SLOPE

$^1/4$in

6 in nominal   LEFT

$^1/4$in PLYWOOD

CENTRE

RIGHT

$9^{15}/16$in

$7^3/16$in

$9^{13}/16$in

$^3/8$in wide x $^1/2$in deep in line with the channels. Drill a $^1/8$in diameter hole into this channel from the underside of each floor at the light position.

Scribe all the floors with $^1/2$in wide planking on both the top and bottom faces. This planking should run from front to back. Veneer the front edge of each floor section with $^1/16$in lime. Cut two beams from elm, $^1/2$in square and $12^1/2$in long. Glue one of these under each side floor section $1^1/8$in from the notched edge and inset $^3/16$in from the back edge.

When the floors are fitted, these beams will lie against the outside faces of the upper fire surrounds. Glue a further beam of $^1/2$in square elm across the middle floor just in front of the light position. This beam is inset $^3/16$in at each end to fit between the floor bearers already in place on the inside faces of the partitions. All three beams should be textured to a rough-hewn finish. A Fluorette lamp holder (Dijon) is glued and pinned to the underside of the floor on the middle section behind the cross beam with its wire tail leading through the channel in the floor, and ending in a two-pin plug at the back. Paint the

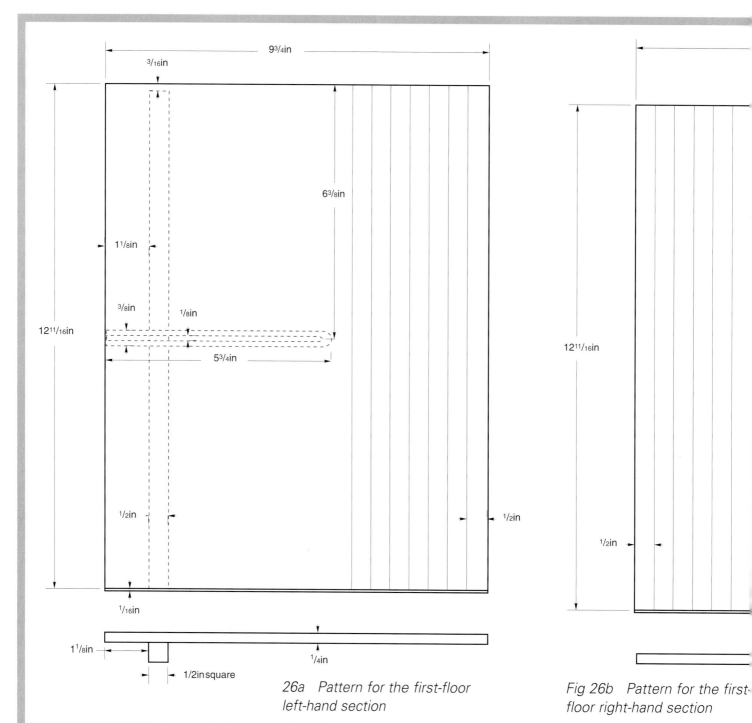

26a   Pattern for the first-floor
left-hand section

Fig 26b   Pattern for the first-floor right-hand section

underside of each floor with two coats of magnolia emulsion and give the top face and front edge of each floor two coats of matt varnish.

STAIRS

The stairs can now be made following Fig 27a and 27b. These are made from stacked blocks of elm (or other hardwood) $2^{11}/16$in wide with each successive step $3/4$in shorter than the previous one. A $1/8$in square nosing is formed on steps 2, 3, and 4 by routing away part of the front edge. The nosing on step 2 is cut away at the sides to fit into the door opening. Step 1 fits flush against the right-hand partition and has a rebate $1/4$in wide and $1/4$in deep cut on its underside, where it butts this partition, to allow for the transformer feed wire. A separate bullnosed step (Fig 27b) is fitted against the outside of the partition, as a continuation of step 1. Steps 9 and 10 are angled at 30° to form a right-angled turn at the top of the stairs. Nosings are not necessary on steps 5 to 10 as they cannot be seen. Glue and pin the blocks to each other as shown in Fig 27a. Once dry, this assembly can be glued and

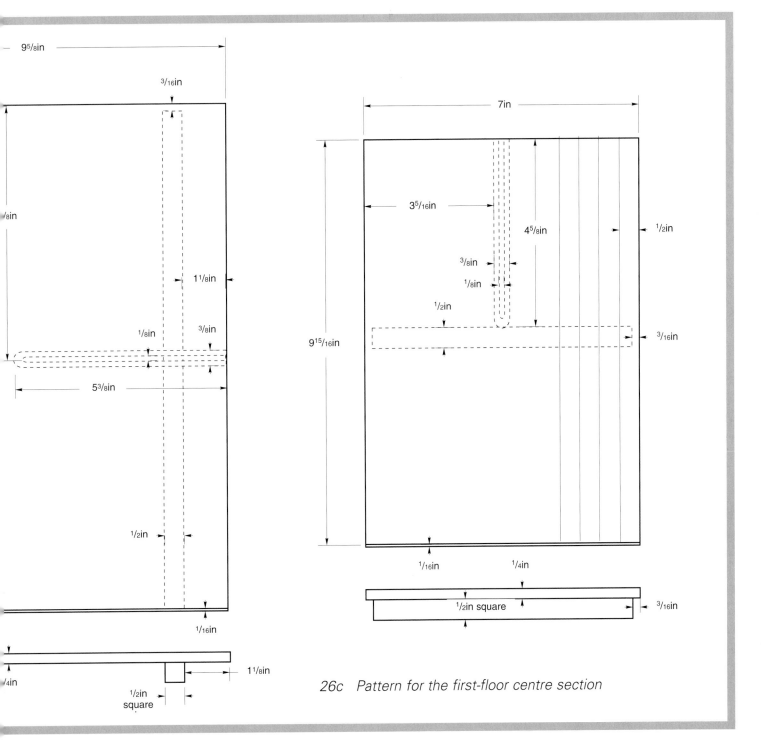

26c   Pattern for the first-floor centre section

Fig 27a
Assembling the staircase

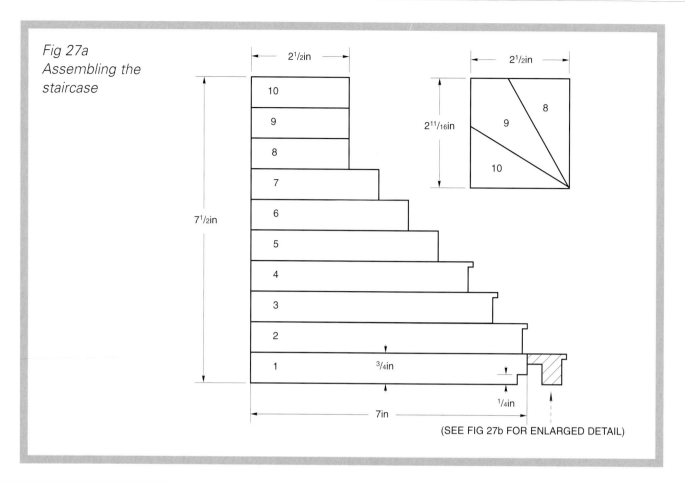

2½in

10
9
8
7
6
5
4
3
2
1

7½in

2½in

2¹¹⁄₁₆in

8
9
10

³⁄₄in

¼in

7in

(SEE FIG 27b FOR ENLARGED DETAIL)

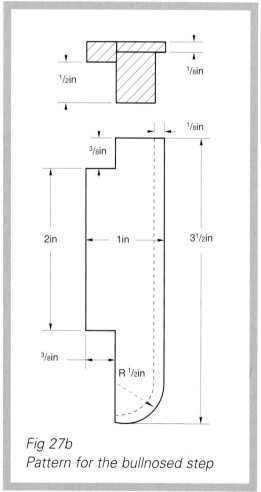

½in

⅛in

½in

⅛in

³⁄₈in

2in

1in

3½in

³⁄₈in

R ½in

Fig 27b
Pattern for the bullnosed step

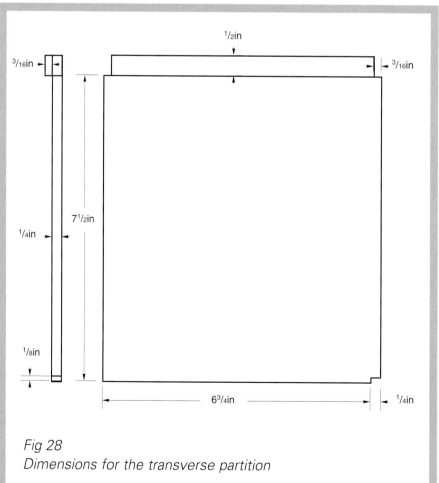

³⁄₁₆in

½in

³⁄₁₆in

¼in

7½in

⅛in

6¾in

¼in

Fig 28
Dimensions for the transverse partition

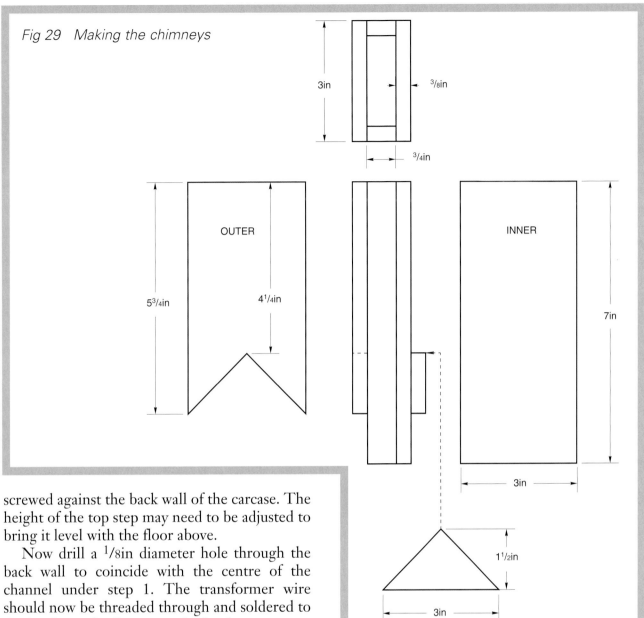

Fig 29   *Making the chimneys*

screwed against the back wall of the carcase. The height of the top step may need to be adjusted to bring it level with the floor above.

Now drill a $1/8$in diameter hole through the back wall to coincide with the centre of the channel under step 1. The transformer wire should now be threaded through and soldered to the brads on the floor tape. Make the transverse partition (Fig 28), and glue a section of elm floor bearer across the top. Note that the top is notched at each side to fit round the floor bearers on the partition walls, and that a $1/4$in x $1/8$in notch is cut at the lower right-hand corner to fit over the feed wire. Apply a length of Cir-Kit twin tape across the back from the notch at the bottom to the centre of the top edge, and fit a pair of eyelets at this point (for the Fluorette plug). Insert a pair of brads at the bottom close to the notch. Solder two short wires, each about 2in long, to these brads. Bend the wires forward under the notch to the front face.

Glue and pin the partition to the outside face of the stair assembly, and apply two coats of magnolia emulsion. The two short wires should now be soldered to the extended tape running back from the right-hand pillar.

CHIMNEYS

Referring to Fig 29, make the two chimneys from $3/8$in plywood, glued and pinned to form a box section 3in x $1 1/2$in. The outer face of each is cut to fit over the apex of the end wall. Note that the inner face and the narrow front and back faces are longer, and extend downwards to the top of the ceiling. A triangular pad is glued to the inside face of each chimney at the level of the gable apex, to provide a landing for the roof. Drill a $1/8$in diameter hole through the inside face of each chimney below the triangular pad to allow for wiring. Drill further $1/8$in diameter holes through the ceilings $1/2$in out from the end walls for the wire, and centrally through each section for the lights. Drill another $1/8$in diameter hole through each partition centrally

Bedroom at the Swan Inn, showing the pivoting roof support

1/2in above floor level. Thread approximately 4ft 6in of twin wire through the chimneys and partition walls with the ends running down through the ceilings to the connector blocks on the end walls below. The chimneys can now be fastened from the outside of the end walls with glue and 3/4in no 4 screws. A banding of 1/4in x 1/8in lime is glued round each chimney 1/4in below the top.

ROOF
Referring to Fig 30, cut out the front and back roof panels from 1/8in (3mm) plywwod. Put the front panel aside. Plane the top edge of the back carcase wall to the bevel of the roof slope, and then glue and pin the back roof panel in place. Trim the ends to leave an overhang of 3/16in at each end. Glue three pads of 3/8in plywood, each 1/2in wide, to the underside of the roof panel flush at the top edge and fitting snugly between the chimneys and partition walls. These provide a thicker top edge for the fixing of the upper front roof section. Plane and chisel this

top edge fair with the front slopes of the chimney pads and the partition walls. The undersides of the ceilings and the inside sloping roof faces should now have two coats of white emulsion.

LIGHTS
The three lights for the upper rooms are now glued to the underside of the ceiling. These lights are from Dijon and have replaceable bulbs. These are necessary here, as the wiring becomes inaccessible when the front roof is fixed. The sticky pads on the lights should be removed and the lights fixed with quick-setting epoxy resin. Screw a connector block to the top of each ceiling section close to the light position, cut the twin wire that passes across between the chimneys in three places, and reconnect via the connector blocks on the ceiling. The lower ends of this wire should be connected to the blocks on the respective end walls. Now connect the wire tails from each light to its connector block. Test the whole circuit for continuity. Drill a

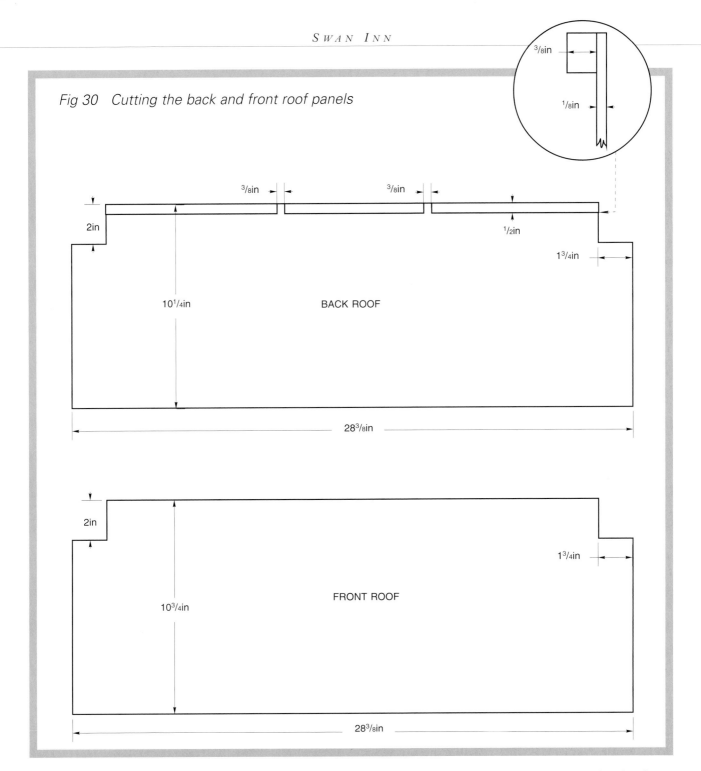

Fig 30 Cutting the back and front roof panels

$^3/_8$in

$^1/_8$in

$^3/_8$in $^3/_8$in

2in $^1/_2$in

$1^3/_4$in

$10^1/_4$in   BACK ROOF

$28^3/_8$in

2in

$1^3/_4$in

FRONT ROOF

$10^3/_4$in

$28^3/_8$in

$^1/_8$in diameter hole centrally through the left-hand end wall, $^1/_4$in above floor level. The light in the store (Peter Kennedy or Wood 'n' Wool) has sufficient wire tail to reach through this hole to the connector block when required.

BAR

With the upper floors not yet in place, this is best made now while there is still easy access. It also needs to be in place so that the ground-floor flagstones can be fitted round it. The bar is made in three sections, each slotting together so that although fitted round the pillars, it can always be removed for access.

Referring to Figs 31a and 31b, make the front from three pieces of $^3/_8$in plywood glued in a sandwich; the inside piece fitting snugly between the bar pillars, and the outer two glued into elm corner posts at each end. Note that these blocks project $^1/_{16}$in in front of the outer piece of plywood, to allow for subsequent $^1/_{16}$in thick planking, and are slotted at the back to accept the tenons on the front of the bar side sections. Round over the elm blocks to $^1/_2$in radius and glue them in place. Next, fill in the front face of the plywood between these posts with $^3/_8$in wide x $^1/_{16}$in thick elm planks. These are fixed with impact adhesive.

Fig 31a
Details of the bar front

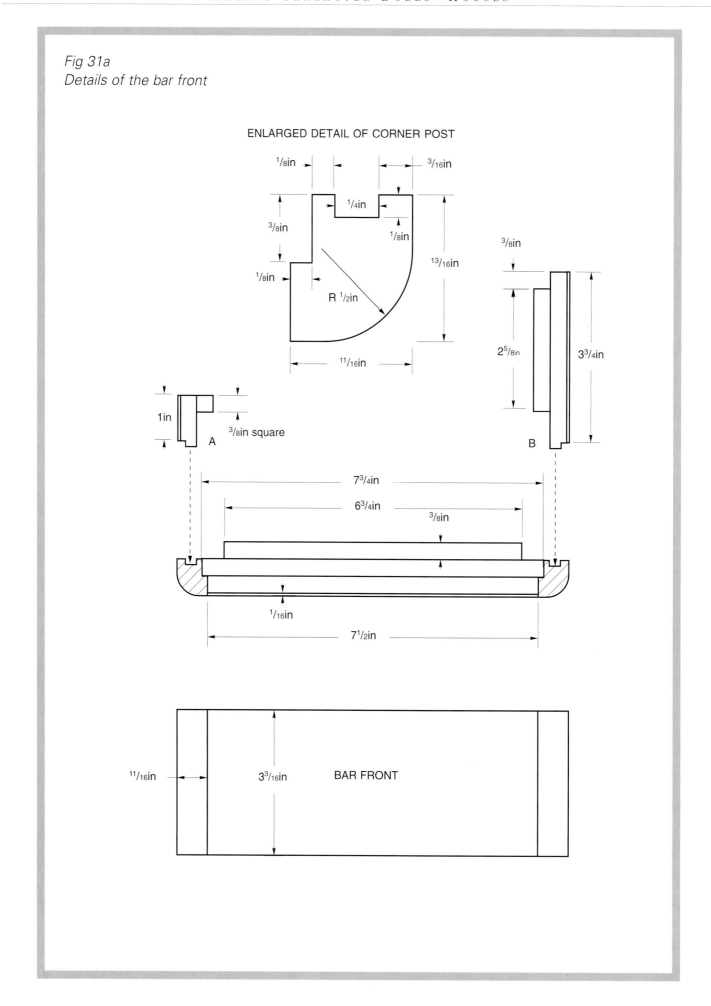

ENLARGED DETAIL OF CORNER POST

Fig 31b
Assembling the bar

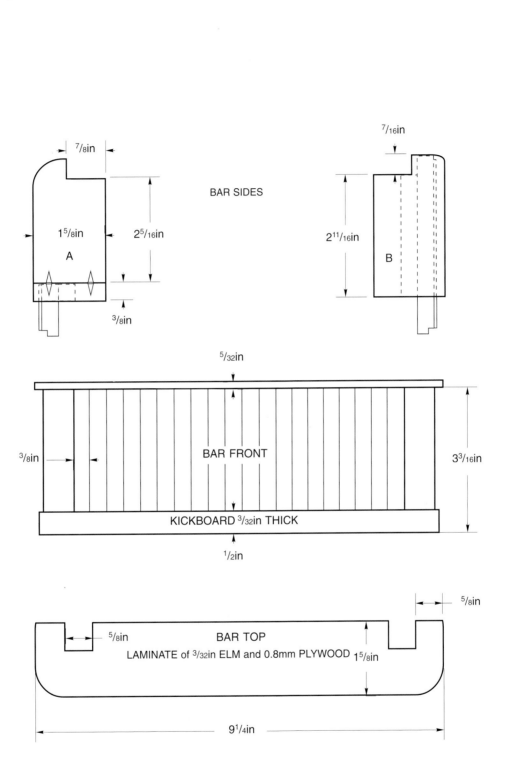

BAR SIDES

Swan Inn bar, left-hand end

The $1/2$in x $3/32$in elm kickboard is now glued along the bottom edge and continued round the curved ends. This requires steaming which can be done easily by placing the kickboard in the spout of a boiling kettle for a few minutes, and then moulding it to shape with the fingers. Use a cloth as the wood will be very hot. Hold the kickboard in place with clamps and rubber bands until dry and set in shape, then remove the clamps and fix with impact adhesive.

The top is made from a laminate of $3/32$in elm and 0.8mm plywood. The plywood stiffens the weak sections at the ends outside the notches for the bar pillars. It is glued on top of the plywood sandwich with a $3/16$in overlap at the front and sides. Again following Fig 31b, make each side from two sections of $3/8$in plywood, with the inner section on the right-hand side fitting snugly between the back of the bar pillars and

the $3/8$in square elm facing on the front of the partition walls. The outer end of each section at A and B is routed to form a $1/4$in x $1/8$in tenon which engages in the back of the bar front. The outside faces of both side bar sections are planked and kickboard fitted.

Make a laminated top for the right-hand section B, and glue this on top of the plywood, noting that the outside of the back extends $3/8$in outside the partition wall, and that the front of the top edge of the plywood is left exposed for $3/4$in to fit under the top of the bar front. The left-hand section A is shorter, and extends only $3/8$in beyond the pillar. Again the front $3/4$in is left exposed, and the top is in two pieces with the inner $3/8$in section glued to the plywood and the remainder hinged on to it to form a lifting flap. The hinges are Hobby's part no D2. A small block of elm $3/8$in wide and $3/8$in deep is

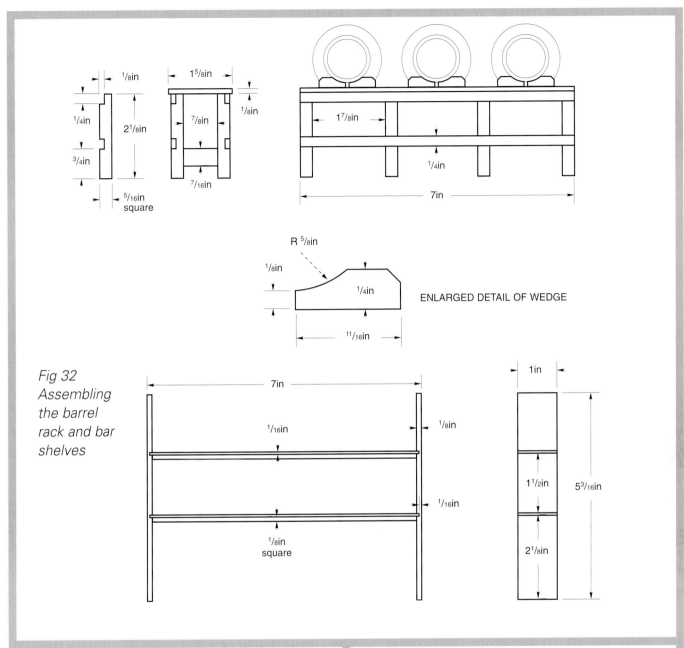

Fig 32
Assembling
the barrel
rack and bar
shelves

ENLARGED DETAIL OF WEDGE

glued to the front of the elm facing on the left-hand partition, to provide a rest for this flap. Give all parts two coats of matt varnish.

BARREL RACK AND SHELVES

The rack, and the shelves above it, should now be made from elm following Fig 32. Both are free-standing. The shelves should be a tight push fit between the partition walls, resting on top of the rack and fitting snugly under the floor bearers on each side at the top. Each shelf has a 1/8in square stiffener glued under the back edge. Note that the right-hand back leg of the rack is cut away below the lower rail, to clear the feed wire connection on the floor. Both components should now have two coats of matt varnish.

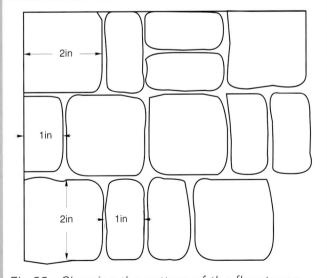

Fig 33 Showing the pattern of the flagstones

Swan Inn bar, right-hand end

FLAGSTONES

These are now cut in pieces 2in square and 2in x 1in from Formica with the edges sanded irregularly. They are fixed upside down with impact adhesive leaving a gap of approximately ^{1}/16in between adjacent stones (see Fig 33, and page 186 for further details). The gap between the stones is grouted with Polyfilla, and tinted with poster paint. Remove excess filler from the surface and sand smooth before applying two coats of satin varnish. Before fixing the flagstones, rest the bar in place so that they can be fitted round the outside. The area behind the bar is left uncovered for access to the wiring and tapes, but will have a loose mat, cut from thin rubber, laid over it.

HEARTHS

Fill in the base of each fireplace with Houseworks mesh-mounted facing bricks from Blackwells, and grout with Polyfilla. Use diluted black poster paint to dirty the inside of the fireplace.

BACK DOOR

This is now glued in place on the back wall with its frame ^{3}/8in out from the left-hand partition wall.

GROUND-FLOOR LIGHTS

The chandeliers from Peter Kennedy have replaceable bi-pin bulbs, and can therefore be permanently wired in place. Thread the wire tails of each up through the rose and through the floor channel to emerge in the notch at the side of each floor section. Glue and pin the roses to the underside of each floor section. Ensure that the wiring from the ground floor to the chimney is well located in the groove at the top of the right-hand fireplace, and then glue and pin the right-hand floor section in place. Avoid pinning near the concealed wire in the grooves. Connect the wires from the light to the connector block on the wall. Repeat this operation for the left-hand floor section, and connect that light to its connector block. The middle floor is not fixed. It will remain portable for access to the bar area.

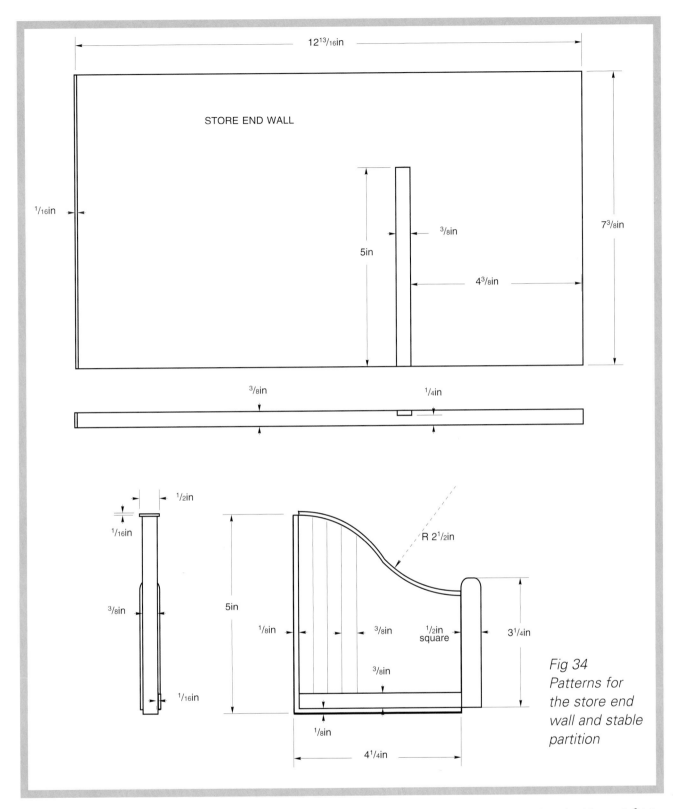

Fig 34
Patterns for
the store end
wall and stable
partition

STORE

Referring to Fig 34, cut out the end wall for the store from $^3/_8$in plywood, and rout the groove for the stable partition. Still following Fig 34, make the partition from $^3/_8$in plywood cut to the profile shown, noting that planking is scribed on the front face only and that it has a $^1/_2$in x $^1/_{16}$in capping which may need to be steamed to shape. A post of $^1/_2$in square lime or elm, $3^1/_4$in long, is glued to the open end, and a kickboard $^3/_8$in deep and $^1/_{16}$in thick is glued along the bottom edge. Note that a $^1/_8$in margin must be left at the bottom and at the edge which butts the store wall, for the partition to enter the grooves. The top of the post should be lightly chamfered. Paint this partition matt dark green, and then glue and screw both this and the end wall in place on the base of the building.

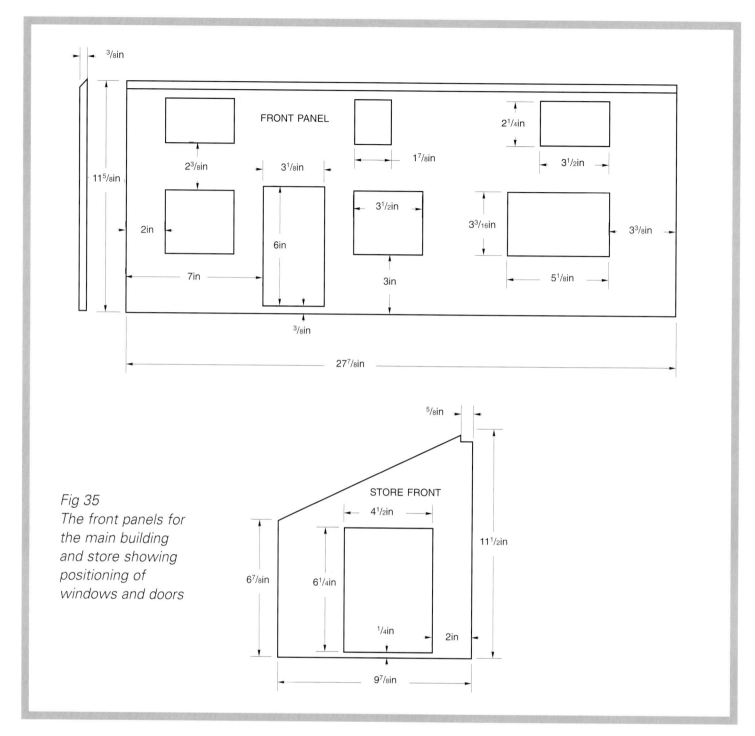

Fig 35
The front panels for the main building and store showing positioning of windows and doors

FRONT PANEL

Following Fig 35, cut out the front panel, and rout the window and door openings. Referring to Fig 36, frame the front door opening and make the door. *Do not fix yet.* Line the window openings (Fig 24). Bevel the top edge of the panel to conform with the front roof slope. The windows should now be dry fitted but not fixed yet.

FRONT ROOF

From the panel already cut, separate the top and bottom sections where indicated in Fig 37, and rout a rebate 1/2in wide and 1/16in deep on the top surfaces where shown. (The 1/16in depth is to accommodate the leather hinge, and may need to be adjusted depending on the thickness of the leather used.) Cut a 1in wide strip of leather 28 1/2in long. Apply impact adhesive to half the width of this leather, and to the rebate in the upper roof section. Assemble these two, and then glue the other half of the leather to the rebate in the lower section, taking care to maintain the alignment of the panel edges and a close butt at the join. With a sharp craft knife, trim the ends of the hinge flush with the panel edges.

With the front panel resting in the base groove at the front of the building, and temporarily fastened to the end walls with masking tape, temporarily pin the upper section of the roof at the ridge. Mark the underside of the lower section where it overhangs the front panel, and glue a triangular section batten to the underside (see Fig 37). This batten should rest evenly against the outside of the front panel at the top. Trim off the lower edge of the roof, bevelled flush with the underside of the batten. The bottoms of the batten and panel may need to be planed further so that they do not project downwards over the upper linings of the upper windows. The roof slopes on the walls and partitions should now be veneered with elm about 1/64in thick (they could be painted instead of veneered, but the veneer enables you to give them a varnish finish).

Paint the undersides of the front roof panels with two coats white emulsion, leaving bare those areas at the top and sides of the upper section which will be glued. When satisfied that everything fits properly, glue and pin only the upper section to the ridge, triangular pads, and roof slopes of the end walls and partitions. Plane the ridge flush with the back roof edge.

PORCH

From the pattern in Fig 38, cut out the front panel from 3/8in plywood, to the profile shown. Cut two side walls, each from 1 5/8in x 3/4in pine with their tops angled as shown, and glue these behind the front panel, flush at the bottom and outside edges. Glue a small block of the same material, with its top edges planed to the roof slope, behind the apex of the front panel. Trim the outside edges fair, and then add a roof of 1.5mm plywood projecting 1/8in at the front, and overhanging 1/16in at the eaves.

Set the porch against the front panel, centred on the doorway, and mark round it with a pencil. The porch can then be fastened with impact adhesive, taking care that its bottom is level with the top of the base, and that the front panel is resting fully in the base groove. Remove the front panel and add four 3/4in no 4 screws from the back of the panel into the porch.

STORE

Referring to Fig 39, make two roof support battens from 7/8in x 5/8in elm, one 12 3/4in long and the other 12 1/8in long. Bevel the top edges of

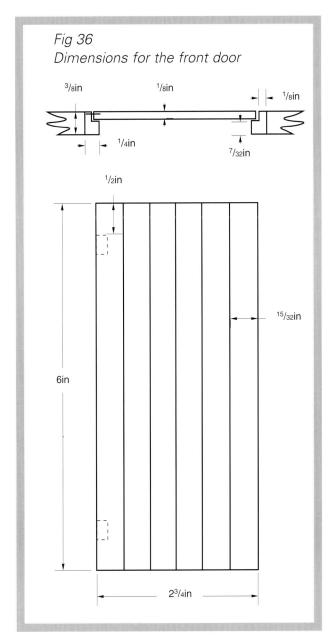

Fig 36
Dimensions for the front door

each to the roof slope. The long length fits along the outside of the house wall from inside the back wall of the store to finish flush with the house wall at the front. Glue and pin this in place, ensuring that the bevelled top edge is fair with the slope on the store back wall. The second length is glued and pinned inside the end wall of the store starting inside the back wall and finishing 5/8in inset from the end wall at the front.

Now cut out the front wall for the store from 3/8in plywood (Fig 35), and cut out the door opening. Frame this with elm or lime as shown in Fig 40, and then make the planked door. The strap hinges are strips of black card glued to the door in line with the small brass hinges used to hang the door. Notch the upper right-hand corner of the front wall to fit under the roof support batten.

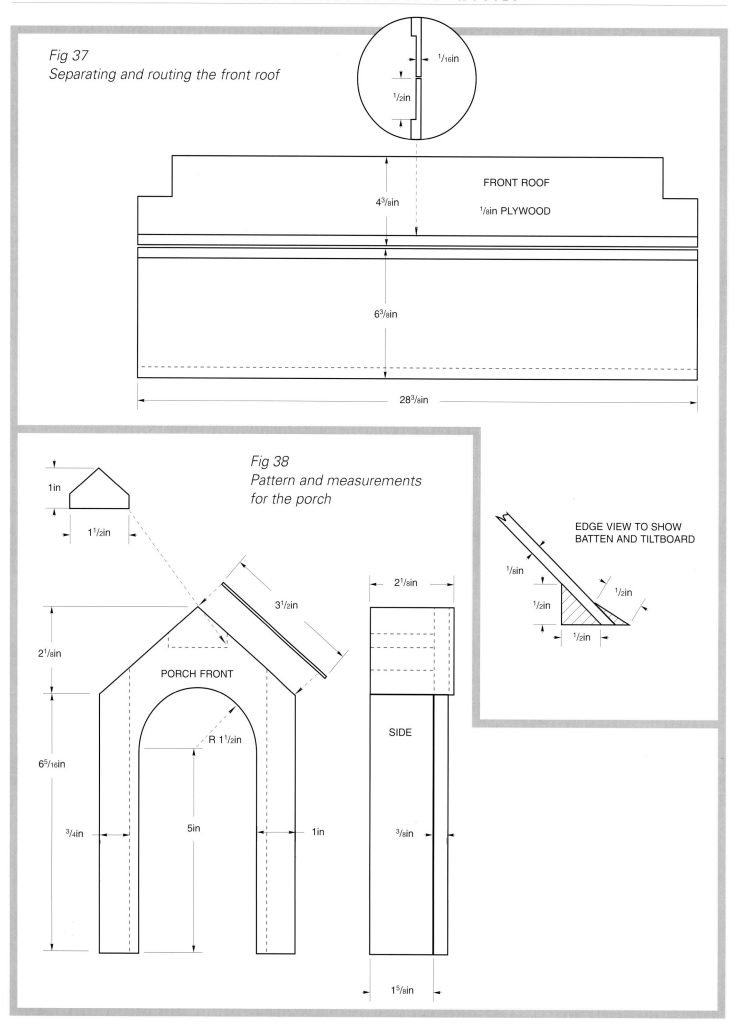

Fig 37
Separating and routing the front roof

¹/₁₆in
¹/₂in

FRONT ROOF
¹/₈in PLYWOOD

4³/₈in

6³/₈in

28³/₈in

Fig 38
Pattern and measurements
for the porch

1in
1¹/₂in

3¹/₂in

EDGE VIEW TO SHOW
BATTEN AND TILTBOARD

¹/₈in
¹/₂in
¹/₂in
¹/₂in

2¹/₈in

PORCH FRONT

2¹/₈in

R 1¹/₂in

SIDE

6⁵/₁₆in

³/₄in
5in
1in

³/₈in

1⁵/₈in

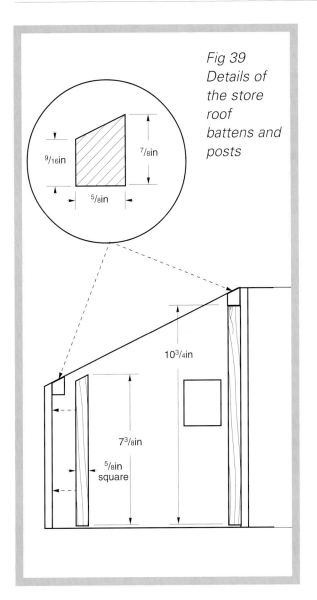

Fig 39 Details of the store roof battens and posts

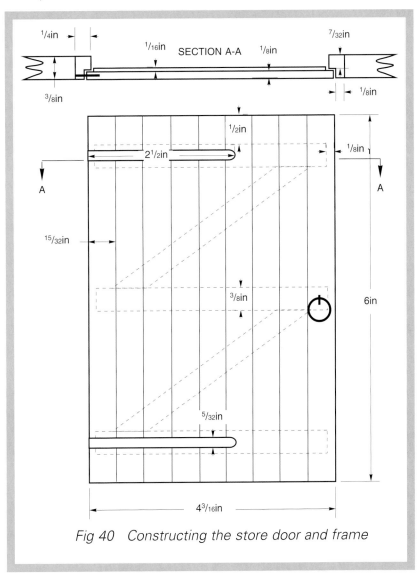

Fig 40   Constructing the store door and frame

Bevel the end wall of the store to the roof slope and then, referring to Fig 41, cut the store roof from $^1/8$in plywood. The edge that butts the house wall should be bevelled to give an even fit and there should be $^3/16$in overhangs at the front, back, and over the end wall.

Before fixing the roof, make the two front posts from $^5/8$in square elm (Fig 39). After texturing and weathering, they should be glued in place. One is fixed to the house wall and the other inside the end wall of the store. Both should be flush with their respective walls on the outside. The top of the left-hand post is angled to the roof slope. The right-hand post butts under the support batten. A transverse beam of $^1/2$in square elm is cut to fit across the underside of the roof between these two posts and is glued in place. A longitudinal beam of $^1/2$in x $^3/8$in elm is glued to the underside of the roof, running back from this cross beam, to the inside face of the back wall, and $^1/4$in x $^5/16$in joists are fitted

and glued across the roof on either side at $1^1/2$in centres. The upper and lower ends of each pair of joists are angled to fit against the support battens. Texture and weather the beams and joists, but do not varnish over.

Make a length of scribed panelling $3^1/2$in high to fit along the inside of the store back wall. Use 1.5mm plywood with $^3/8$in wide planks scored on it. Add a top rail to the outside face $^5/32$in deep and $^1/16$in thick, and a kickboard at the bottom, $^3/8$in deep and $^1/8$in thick. Paint this dark green to match the stable partition and glue in place on the back wall. Make a lintel of elm $^1/16$in thick, $^1/4$in deep, and $5^1/4$in long. Texture and weather this, and glue it in place with its bottom edge in line with the top of the door frame and overlapping $^3/8$in on either side of the opening.

Paint all the inside walls of the store with one coat of textured masonry paint, followed by one coat of magnolia emulsion. Paint the floor with

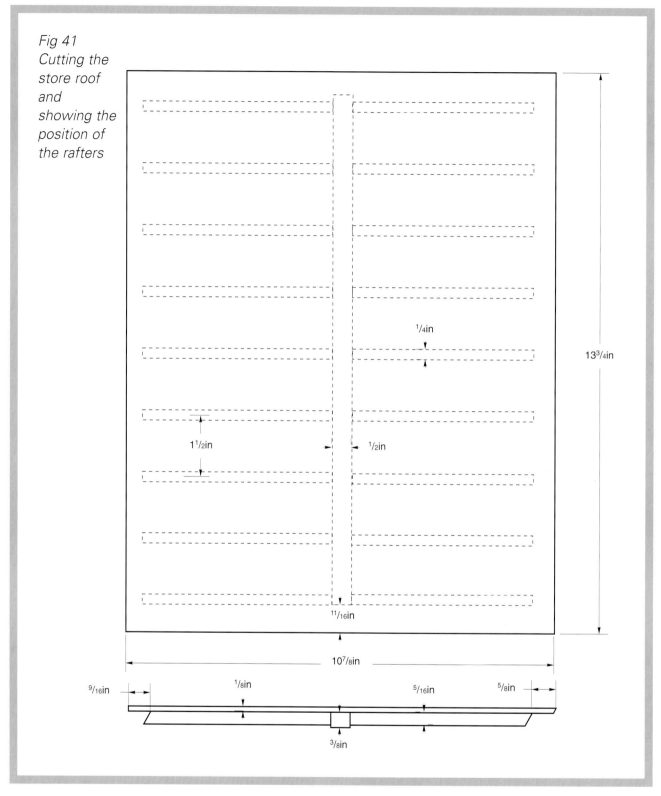

*Fig 41
Cutting the
store roof
and
showing the
position of
the rafters*

one coat of textured paint followed by one coat of Humbrol dark grey. Drill obliquely through the longitudinal centre beam, and thread through the wire tails from the light (Peter Kennedy). Thread the wire tails onwards through the house wall to the connector block on the inside. The roof can now be glued and pinned in place and the light connected and tested.

INTERNAL FIXTURES

Referring to Fig 42, make the two chimney breasts for the first-floor rooms. The cutouts for the fireplaces also provide access to the connector blocks. The one on the left-hand wall is covered by a fireplace, while the one on the right-hand end wall has a removable cover of 1.5mm plywood which is papered over. Although not shown, a further fireplace could be

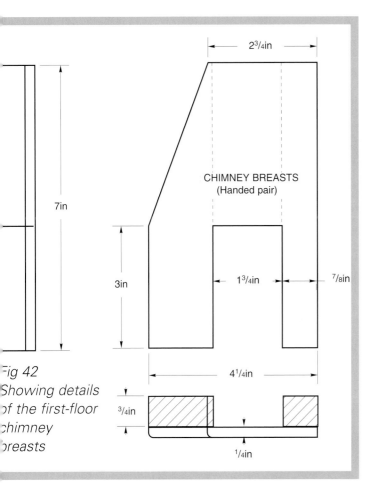

2³/₄in

CHIMNEY BREASTS
(Handed pair)

7in

3in

1³/₄in

7/8in

4¹/₄in

3/4in

1/4in

Fig 42
Showing details
of the first-floor
chimney
breasts

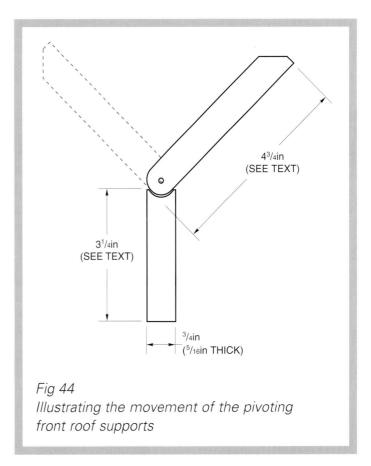

4³/₄in
(SEE TEXT)

3¹/₄in
(SEE TEXT)

3/4in
(5/16in THICK)

Fig 44
Illustrating the movement of the pivoting
front roof supports

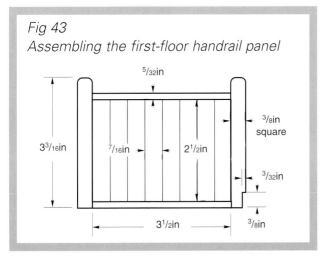

Fig 43
Assembling the first-floor handrail panel

5/32in

3/8in
square

3³/₁₆in

7/16in

2¹/₂in

3/32in

3¹/₂in

3/8in

ture is now glued and pinned at the right-hand back edge of the floor. Note that a ³/₈in x ³/₃₂in notch is cut at the bottom right-hand corner so that it can slide past the skirting.

PIVOTING FRONT ROOF SUPPORTS

Cut two of these from elm following the pattern in Fig 44, noting that the lengths of the two components on each are approximate only, and should be adjusted as follows:

The top of the upright fixed section should be level with the vertical front edge of the house end wall when resting on top of the floor. The movable section should support the roof flap in a horizontal position when swung forward (with its top edge butting the underside of the roof just inside the triangular eaves batten). A ³/₄in no 6 screw is used for the pivot. When closed, the upper movable section should lie with its upper edge flush with the roof slope of the house wall. It is supported in this position by a ¹/₈in diameter dowel glued into the wall and projecting ¹/₈in.

ROOF COVERINGS

The main building has a slate roof made from thin card and the store has a corrugated iron roof made from recycled tin cans.

fitted here. If fitting a portable cover, two strips of ¹/₈in square lime should be glued inside the opening to provide a landing. These strips are inset 1.5mm from the outside face.

The portable middle floor should now have the handrail panel fitted. This is made from ¹/₄in plywood, 3¹/₂in long and 2¹/₂in high and, following the pattern in Fig 43, faced on the outside only with ⁷/₁₆in x ¹/₁₆in elm planks. A ³/₈in square elm post is glued at each end and the handrail and base rail added. Both of these are ³/₈in wide and ⁵/₃₂in deep. The whole struc-

MAIN ROOF

Cut sufficient dark grey card into $3/4$in wide strips, each $28^1/_2$in long, to reach from the eaves to the ridge when overlapped by $1/8$in ($5/8$in exposed). These strips are cut through to a depth of $5/8$in from the lower edge at $7/8$in intervals, to leave an uncut upper edge $1/8$in wide. Make a pair of tiltboards (front and back) from $1/2$in x $1/8$in lime, planed to a feather-edge at one side. They should each be $28^3/_8$in long and glued across the front and back roof panels, flush at the bottom with the feather-edge uppermost. Using PVA glue and starting at the eaves, glue the first strip of card slates to the tiltboard, flush at the bottom edge. Position this strip so that the row begins with a complete slate at the left-hand edge. Each successive course is staggered by half a slate ($7/16$in), and overlaps the course below it by $1/8$in. The upper course of slates on the lifting section of roof must not extend upwards over the centreline of the leather hinge. Check this before starting to fix the slates, and adjust the overlap accordingly. This upper course is laid with individual slates (with the $1/8$in strip removed from the top edge). This $1/8$in wide strip is now applied across the bottom edge of the upper roof section, and the next course applied over it with the bottom edge about $1/32$in above the centreline of the leather hinge. When this course is glued in place, check that there is free movement of the lower section to the horizontal plane. Continue to the ridge where the $1/8$in top border of the last course should be flush.

Repeat this on the back roof, and then, using card, make ridge tiles each $3/4$in wide and $1^1/_2$in long and folded to give two equal faces $3/8$in deep. Glue these in place along the ridge. The end ridge tiles will need to be cut shorter to fit between the chimneys. Avoid getting glue on the upper faces of the slates as this will act as a barrier to the colourwash which is applied next.

The whole roof should now have a wash of poster paint (not too wet, or the glue will dissolve). The colours are black, dark brown, and green which, when wiped downwards with a sponge, give a realistic effect with varied tones and streaks. When dry, seal the roof with one coat of matt varnish.

STORE ROOF

You will need twelve empty food cans with ribbed centre sections. As size of the ribs can

Exterior of the Swan Inn and local drunk

vary between products, you should ensure that all twelve match. With a can-opener, remove the bottom of each can and, using tin snips, carefully cut each can down the seam if there is one; otherwise, cut vertically from top to bottom. Cut around the circumference about $1/2$in outside the ribbed area. Using a blowtorch heat these sections to red heat and flatten them against the face of a house brick by pressing down with a large block of wood. Do not hammer them as this will also flatten the corrugation. When cool, cut them into sections, each about $2^5/_8$in x

5¹/₂in. Use a file to smooth the edges, taking care not to cut your fingers.

Starting at the back lower corner of the roof, fix the first sheet with hot-melt glue. This is best applied to the roof and then, with the sheet placed over it, reheated with a domestic iron to form a strong bond. Press down with a block of wood or, better still, a piece of heavy steel plate until the glue has cooled and set (around 30 seconds). Next, add the upper sheet at the back of the roof, flush at the back edge, butting the house wall at the top, and overlapping the sheet below it. Continue to the front with each suc-

cessive pair of sheets overlapping those previously applied. No colouring is needed, as the heat treatment will have done this for you.

FRONT PANEL

Paint the window linings black and, when dry, glue the windows in place inset 2mm from the back face. Make window sills from elm or lime ⁵/₁₆in wide and tapering from ³/₁₆in deep at the back to ¹/₈in deep at the front. They should each overlap the bottom window lining by ¹/₄in at each end. Glue them in place with their top edges flush with the upper edge of the lower

Store, showing the stable partition and chimney breast

lining and, when dry, paint them black. The outside of the front panel, the store front, and the remaining exterior house walls should now be painted with one coat of textured paint followed by one coat of white emulsion. Add a 1in high band of matt black to the bottom edge of each wall. The inside faces of the removable front walls can be either painted or varnished. The latter is recommended as it will not show finger-marks.

GLAZING

The two back windows are glazed with Glodex which is lightly glued in place, but the front has windows of 2mm glass. These are held in place by narrow strips of masking tape about ¹/₄in wide which cover ¹/₈in each of the back panel and the glass. Ensure that where it is applied to

the glass it does not extend over the window to show from the front.

BASE

Referring to Figs 45 and 46, make the base frame from 2in wide strips of ³/₈in plywood, halved where they cross each other. Assemble this structure with glue and pins and, when the glue has set, lay the house on top inset 1in at the back and sides. Fasten further strips of ³/₈in plywood, this time 1in wide, to fit round the house on top of the frame but ending flush with the 2in house-base extension at the front. A further section of ³/₈in plywood is now fixed across the front, its width being sufficient to reach the front edge of the frame.

Remove the house and clean off any surplus glue from the rebate formed on the inside.

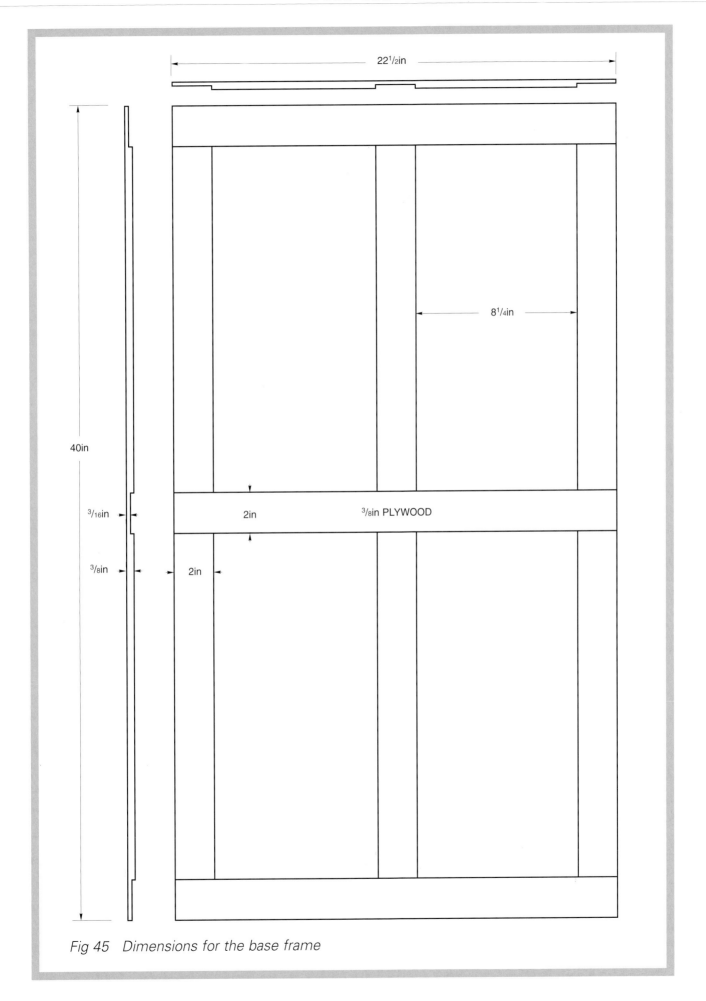

Fig 45   *Dimensions for the base frame*

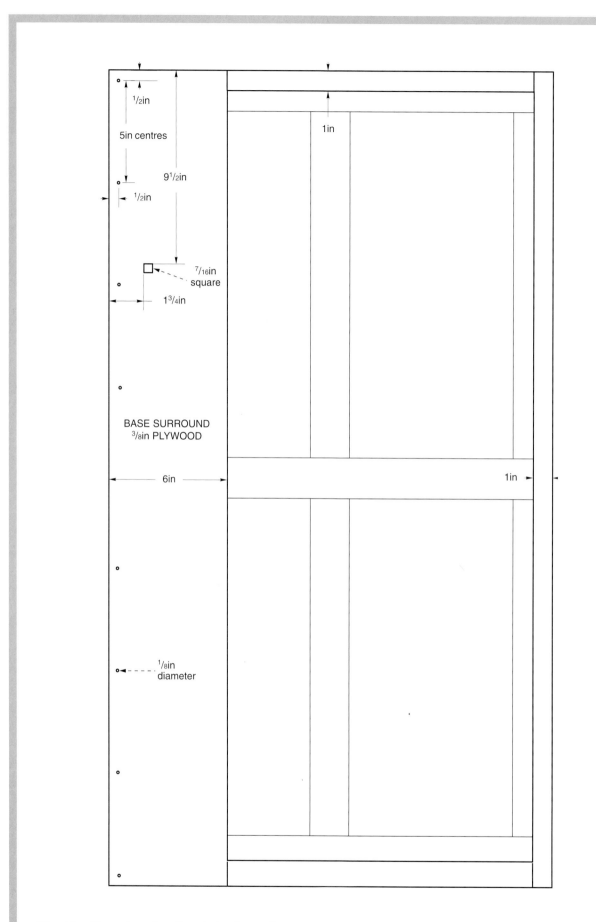

Fig 46   Showing details of the base frame surround

Sitting-room and landing at the Swan Inn

When dry, the outer edges of this base are planed fair and veneered with $^1/_{16}$in lime before varnishing or painting green. Replace the house on the base and mark the base at the opening to the porch. Remove the house.

Now paint the path area from the porch, and the house-base extension to the front edge of the base frame with textured paint and then, with poster paint, tint this to gravel colour and seal with one coat of matt varnish. The house-base extension is scribed in 2in squares to represent flagstones before colouring.

Referring again to Fig 46, drill $^1/_8$in diameter holes along the front of the base where shown. These will locate the fence posts. Cut the $^7/_{16}$in square hole for the signpost. The front of the base should now be grassed over, using model railway powders, but leaving the path area clear. When dry, clean out surplus glue and powder from the holes. Referring to Fig 47, cut eight posts from $^7/_{16}$in square elm or lime, round over the tops in one plane only, and drill four of them with $^1/_8$in diameter holes for chain. The remaining four posts each have a small hook glued into one face. This hook is made from brass wire. All

the posts have $^1/_8$in diameter holes drilled $^3/_8$in deep into their bases, into which $^3/_4$in lengths of $^1/_8$in dowel are glued. These dowels will locate the posts in the holes on the base. Paint all the posts white with a $^3/_4$in wide black band round the bottom of each. Cut two lengths of chain (Hobby's) so that, when set up, they hang loosely between the posts. The chain can be either painted or chemically blackened with Haematite (Liberon).

SIGN

Referring again to Fig 47, cut a length of lime $^7/_{16}$in square and $8^1/_8$in long. Cut the slot in the top and glue and pin the wedge-shaped supports round the base of the post leaving a $^3/_8$in projection below them. Now construct the outer frame, from $^1/_4$in square lime, with bridle joints as shown. Glue and pin the bottom rail of this frame into the slot at the top of the signpost, and add the $^3/_{16}$in square supports underneath. Paint this structure white with the exception of the base supports which should be black. The sign itself is made from 1.5mm plywood with a border framing of $^1/_8$in x $^1/_{16}$in lime applied to it.

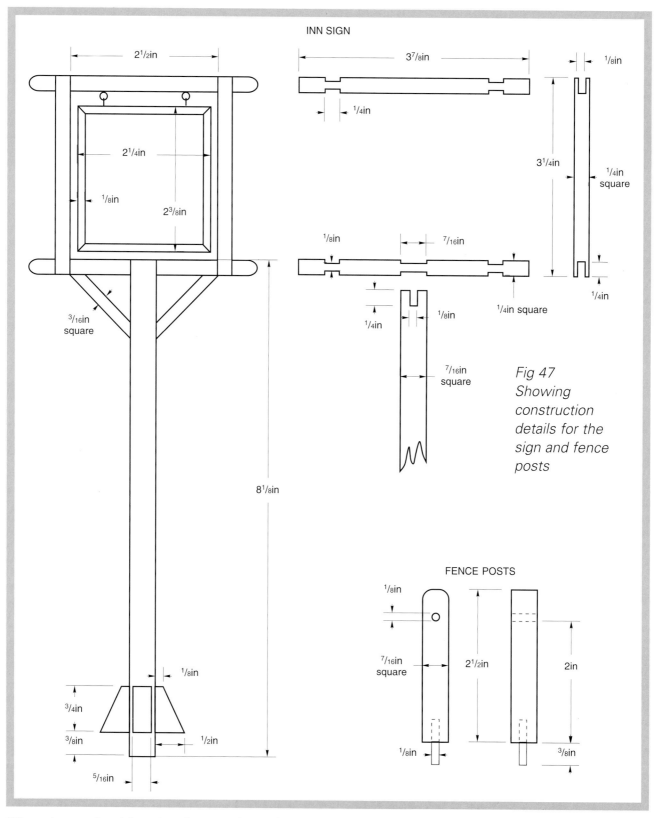

INN SIGN

2¹/₂in

3⁷/₈in

¹/₈in

2¹/₄in

¹/₄in

3¹/₄in

¹/₄in
square

¹/₈in

2³/₈in

¹/₈in

¹/₈in

⁷/₁₆in

¹/₄in square

¹/₄in

³/₁₆in
square

¹/₄in

¹/₈in

¹/₄in

⁷/₁₆in
square

⁷/₁₆in
square

*Fig 47
Showing
construction
details for the
sign and fence
posts*

8¹/₈in

FENCE POSTS

¹/₈in

¹/₈in
square

⁷/₁₆in
square

2¹/₂in

2in

³/₄in

³/₈in

¹/₂in

¹/₈in

³/₈in

⁵/₁₆in

The picture is either hand-painted as shown here, or cut from a magazine illustration. The sign is hung from the frame with small screw-eyes.

FINISHING

The upper rooms are papered. The left-hand one has paper by Mini Graphics, from Dijon, and the other two rooms have papers from The Singing Tree.

When the papers are dry, make up skirting from lime ³/₈in wide and ³/₃₂in thick, with the top edge rounded over (Fig 48). Pre-paint this with Humbrol satin white and cut it, with mitred joints at the corners, to fit each room. The skirting round the bases of the chimney breasts are best made from painted card which will bend easily over the rounded edges. The landing area has no skirting on the back wall. A short length of elm $1/4$in deep and $3/16$in wide is glued on top of the left-hand floor bearer at the back of the landing to provide a stop for the portable floor and to fill the space above the bearer up to skirting level.

The doors, with the exception of the dummy and the front door, which are varnished, should be painted now if you have not already done so. The door handles are Houseworks no 1123 from Blackwells, pinned in place with track pins filed off at the back. The latches on the opposite faces of the doors are thin strips of black paper. The doors can now be fixed in the house by gluing the hinges into the slots in the door frames. The name board is made from 1.5mm plywood with a

$1/8$in wide frame of the same material applied to one face. This is painted with white emulsion, and the lettering is applied over it. In this case, pre-cut self-adhesive vinyl letters are used. No board measurements are given as you may wish to use a different name with more or less letters. Glue the board in place on the front wall.

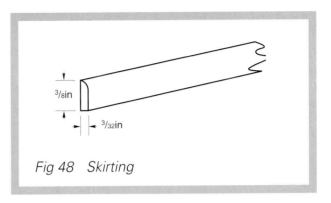

Fig 48   Skirting

SWAN INN – LIST OF SUPPLIERS

And Other Bits: Barrel furniture.
Sue Austen: Ducks.
Gordon Blacklock: Pipe and silver ashtray.
Bryntor Miniatures: China casks, jugs, Torbay pottery, and flagons.
Irene Campbell: Flagons.
Cassel's: Vase.
Veronique Cornish: Flower fairy.
Terry Curran: Flagons and rum bottle.
Dijon: Upstairs lighting, bar and dartboard lights, Mini Graphics wallpaper for sitting-room; bed and wardrobe, glowing fire embers, dartboard, coffee table, fireguard, tin bath, garden bench (kit), and Cir-Kit tape and eyelets.
Dolphin Miniatures: Chest of drawers, mirror, washstand, fire dogs, settle, beer crates, barrels, sack trolley, yoke, wheelback chair, flower tubs, and long case clock (Bodo Hennig).
Dorking Dolls' House Gallery: Slippers.
Hobby's: Glass beer mugs.
Victoria Fasken: Dressing table set.
Just in Case: Beer bottles

Lilliput Miniatures: Tea chest.
Carol Lodder: Mug, spongeware, wash basin, and jug.
Mainly Men Minis: Dolls.
John & Pauline Meredith: Toby jug and swan figurine.
Phoenix Model Developments: Kit for cash register.
Leo Pilley: Yard of ale.
Quaintways Miniatures: Stuffed pike in case and shelf.
Quality Dolls' House Miniatures: Wine bottles and garden tools.
The Singing Tree: Wallpapers for landing and bedroom.
Sussex Crafts: Fireback and bucket.
Thames Valley Crafts: Pasties and tray, cigarettes, matches, and beer bottles.
Pat Venning: Ashtrays.
The bell, ships lights, bedspread, and mower, and the sofa, armchair and radio in the sitting-room are from the author's own collection, as is the knitted twinset kindly made by June Stowe. The bar chandeliers and the light in the store, made by Peter Kennedy, are also from the author's collection.

GEORGIAN
HOUSE

This is still the most popular style, for which a wide range of furniture and accessories is available. A grander house than that in my first book, it has nine rooms. On the ground floor a large central hall opens on to the kitchen and dining-room. A double staircase leads to the library above, which connects with the main bedroom, drawing-room, and the balcony at the front. The central room on the second floor is equipped as a schoolroom, with a small bedroom at each side. A drawer with a drop down front is incorporated in the base to provide a pull-out garden with iron railings at the front and steps leading up to the house.

The Georgian House fully furnished

TIMBER REQUIREMENTS – GEORGIAN HOUSE

WOOD	THICKNESS	AREA sq ft		
Birch plywood	0.8mm	$1/2$		
	1.5mm	$3^1/2$		
	$1/8$in (3mm)	2		
	$1/4$in (6mm)	25		
	$3/8$in (9mm)	42		
	THICKNESS in	WIDTH in	LENGTH ft	in
Lime	$1/32$	$3/8$	2	-
		$9/16$	5	6
		$5/8$	150	-
	$3/32$	$1/4$	14	-
	$1/8$	$1/8$	21	-
		$1/4$	23	-
		$5/8$	28	-
	$5/32$	$5/16$	20	-
	$3/16$	$3/8$	14	-
		$1^1/4$	1	4
	$7/16$	$7/16$	28	-
		$5/8$	8	-
	$5/8$	$3/4$	1	8
	$7/8$	$7/8$	3	-
	$1^1/2$	$1^1/2$	6	-
Pine	$3/4$	1	3	4
		$3^1/2$	5	-
		$3^3/4$	13	-
		$3^7/8$	4	-
		6	1	6
Mahogany	$1/16$	$1/16$	15	-
		$1/8$	2	-
		$1^1/16$	8	-
	$3/32$	$3/16$	5	-
	$1/4$	$1/4$	2	-
	$11/32$	$7/16$	1	6
	$1/2$	$7/8$	8	-

CARCASE

Referring to Figs 49a–49e cut, from $3/8$in plywood one base, one back, two sides, and two partitions. From $1/4$in plywood cut one upper floor and one upper floor extension. Rout the grooves and rebates where shown to the appropriate widths. All are $3/16$in deep, except for the grooves in the upper floor which are only $1/16$in deep. Cut out the door and window openings and notch the top of the back panel in the centre, $3/4$in wide and $5/8$in deep. Next, following Fig 50, construct the base frame from $3^3/4$in x $3/4$in pine. Note that the underside of the side members and the adjacent transverse member are routed where shown, $3/8$in wide and $1/4$in deep to accept the $1/4$in plywood drawer carrier. When satisfied that it fits together properly assemble with PVA glue and 40mm panel pins.

Cut the drawer carrier from $1/4$in plywood $8^1/8$in wide and $44^1/4$in long. Glue and pin this in place on the frame. Now fasten the base on top of the frame with glue and panel pins, ensuring that a $3/16$in wide space is left along the back edge and the sides to receive the back and side

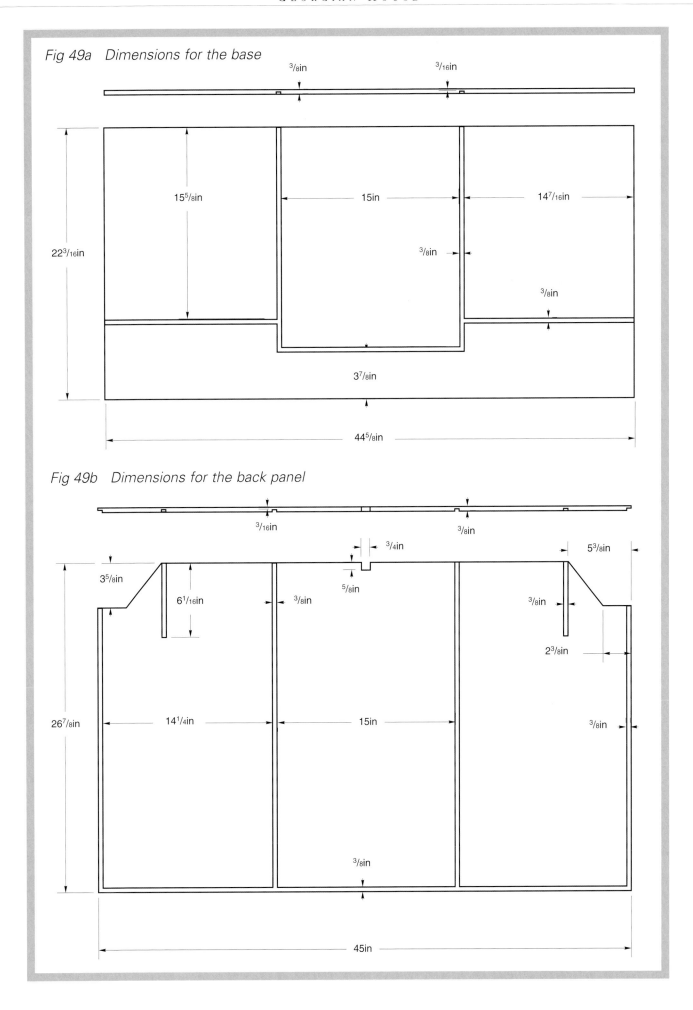

Fig 49a   Dimensions for the base

Fig 49b   Dimensions for the back panel

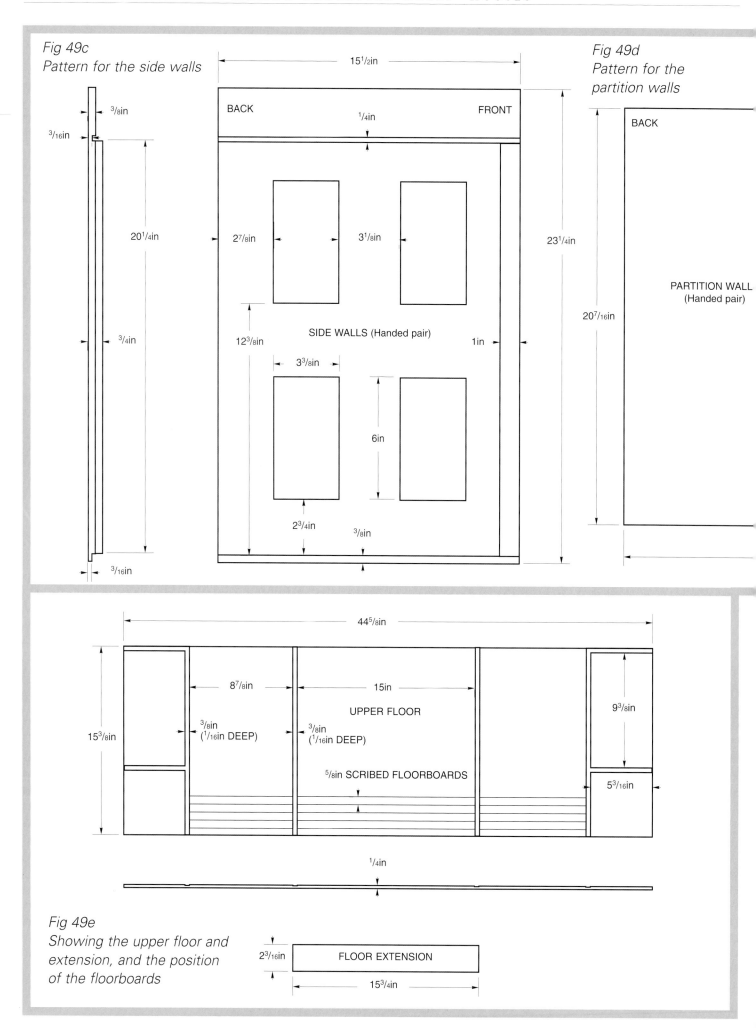

Fig 49c
Pattern for the side walls

15¹/₂in

BACK
¹/₄in
FRONT

³/₈in

³/₁₆in

20¹/₄in

23¹/₄in

2⁷/₈in

3¹/₈in

20⁷/₁₆in

³/₄in

12³/₈in

SIDE WALLS (Handed pair)

1in

3³/₈in

6in

2³/₄in
³/₈in

³/₁₆in

Fig 49d
Pattern for the
partition walls

BACK

PARTITION WALL
(Handed pair)

44⁵/₈in

8⁷/₈in

15in

UPPER FLOOR

9³/₈in

³/₈in
(¹/₁₆in DEEP)

³/₈in
(¹/₁₆in DEEP)

15³/₈in

⁵/₈in SCRIBED FLOORBOARDS

5³/₁₆in

¹/₄in

Fig 49e
Showing the upper floor and
extension, and the position
of the floorboards

2³/₁₆in

FLOOR EXTENSION

15³/₄in

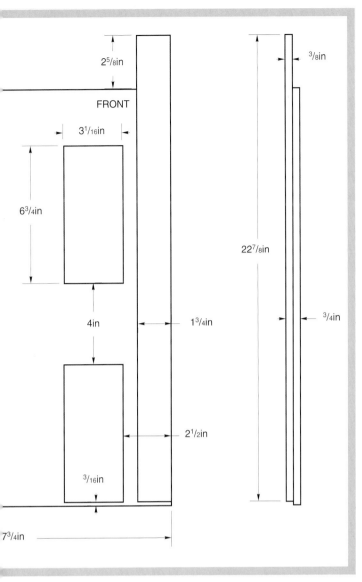

panels which overlap it. Glue wood fillets at either side of the base to fill the $^3/_{16}$in space from the transverse grooves to the front edge. Plane flush at the top and sides.

TRIAL ASSEMBLY

Assemble all the carcase components and temporarily fix in position with three $^3/_4$in no 4 screws in each joint at the top, bottom, and centre. When thus assembled, there should be a space of $^1/_8$in between the front edges of the sides and partitions, and the grooves for the front panels. This will be taken up by an edge veneer of $^1/_8$in thick lime. Dismantle the carcase and, following Figs 49c and 49d, glue thickening strips of $^3/_8$in plywood, 1in wide and $20^1/_4$in long, to the inside face of each side wall, flush at the front and inset $^3/_8$in from the bottom, and strips $1^3/_4$in wide and $22^7/_8$in long to the outside face of each partition, flush at the front and inset $^3/_{16}$in from the bottom.

Plane the thickening strips flush with the front edges of the sides and partitions and then veneer across the total thickness of the front edges (now $^3/_4$in), with $^1/_8$in thick lime. Note that the veneer at the front of the partition walls should remain at the full width of $^3/_4$in, right to the top of the thickening piece. Following Fig 51, and the method described on page 185–6, make the internal door frames and the doors, not forgetting the two dummy doors for the library. These follow the same pattern but are panelled on the outside face only. The doors and architraves are mounted on 0.8mm plywood, and glued in place when the decorating is completed. Fix the frames in place in their respective openings, and remove the doors for later painting, taking care to mark where each door belongs.

ELECTRICS

Cir-Kit twin tape is used throughout this house. Dismantle the carcase and start by applying a length of tape centrally up the back panel from the upper edge of the rebate to the top. Brad both conductors $^1/_2$in up from the bottom of the tape. Mark the back wall panel at the level of the top of both the first and second floors. Horizontal tapes will be applied across the back wall in both places, with their bottom edges $^1/_{16}$in above the floors. Before applying these tapes, small fillets of wood must be glued into the vertical grooves that house the partition walls so that the tape has an even surface under it. The partitions must be notched at their back edges to fit over these fillets. Brad through the horizontal tapes to make contact with the vertical tapes. To avoid a short circuit, the upper conductor of each horizontal tape is connected to the left-hand conductor of the vertical tape, and the lower conductor of each horizontal tape is connected to the right-hand conductor of the vertical tape. Mark the light positions centrally on the underside of the upper floor, midway from front to back in the side rooms, and 1in further out in the centre room. Draw parallel lines $^5/_8$in apart from each of these positions to the back edge of the floor, to indicate the width of the tape.

Next, notch the back edge of the floor $^1/_{16}$in deep in each position, and run tapes from the light positions to the back edge allowing an extra 2in in length which is folded back on itself to form a tab 1in long for later connection to the

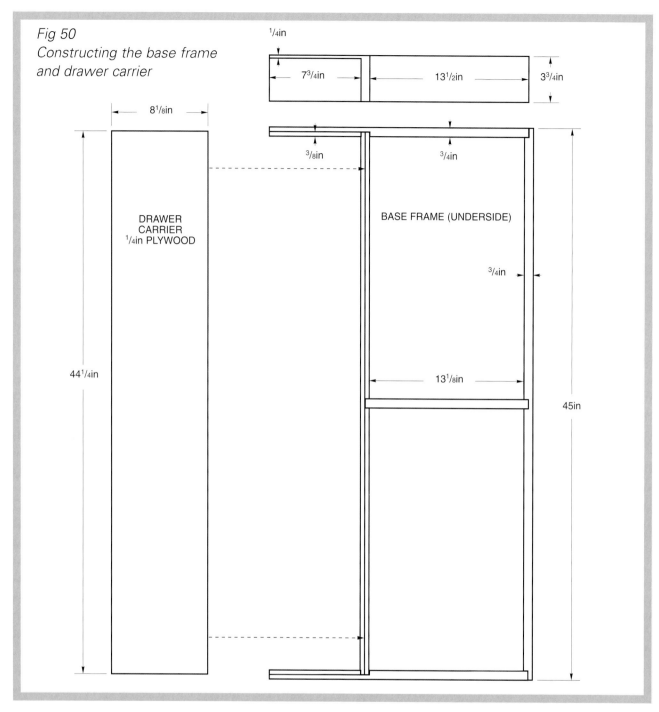

*Fig 50
Constructing the base frame
and drawer carrier*

DRAWER
CARRIER
1/4in PLYWOOD

8 1/8in

44 1/4in

1/4in

7 3/4in   13 1/2in   3 3/4in

3/8in   3/4in

BASE FRAME (UNDERSIDE)

3/4in

13 1/8in

45in

upper horizontal tape. Drill a 1/8in diameter hole through the back carcase wall in the hall, just above floor level, and solder a 3ft length of twin wire to the bottom of the Cir-Kit tape. This is threaded through the hole to the outside for connection to a transformer. Test this tape run on the back wall with a transformer and test bulb to ensure continuous conductivity. Do not yet join the floor tape tabs to the tapes on the back wall.

CORNICE AND FLOOR BEARERS
Reassemble the carcase with screws only. Using a plywood spacer 10 1/2in high, mark a pencil line round all internal walls. This indicates the top edge of the cornice which should be made next following the profile in Fig 52. Again dismantle the carcase, and glue and pin the cornices in place with their upper edges on the lines just marked and with mitred joints in the corners of the rooms. The outer ends of the cornices on the side walls are cut square and butt behind the thickening strip. The outer ends of the cornices on the outside faces of the partitions are cut square to finish 3/8in short of the back edge of the thickening piece. This allows space for the left- and right-hand front panels. The outer ends of the cornices on the inside

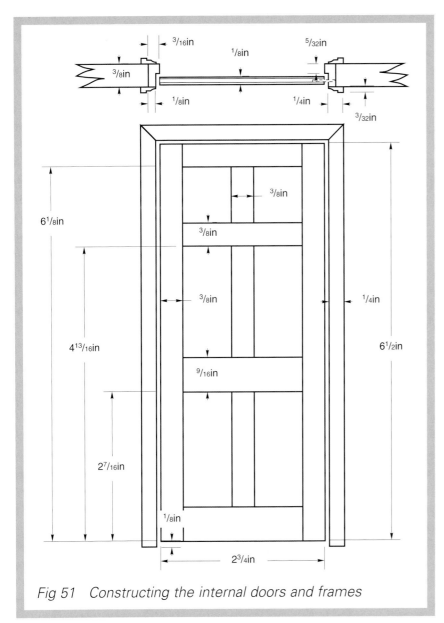

Fig 51   Constructing the internal doors and frames

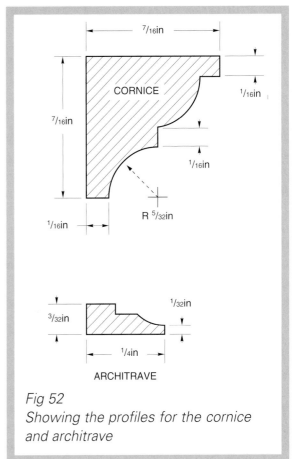

Fig 52
Showing the profiles for the cornice and architrave

FLOORS

The floor in the hall is covered with ready-made parquet strips (Blackwells). Four packets, each containing nine pieces, are needed to cover the whole of the hall floor. Using impact adhesive, start at the front edge of the floor at the left-hand side close against the inside of the routed groove and lay the sections lengthways from front to back. (A sandplate should be used to ease the undersides of the architraves to allow the parquet to fit underneath.) Continue across the front to the right-hand side where a half-width strip will be needed. Continue with a second row behind the first, butting tightly against the inside edges of the sections already laid. Continue to the back and ignore any slight gap at the back wall, as it will later be covered by the landing.

The side sections of ground floor are covered with wood-strip boards of lime or cherry $5/8$in wide and $1/32$in thick, again using impact adhesive. Note that the planking runs from side to side, and should not encroach upon the $3/16$in margins at the outer ends of the base where the side walls will locate. Using an orbital sander, level and smooth the surface of all the ground-

faces of the partitions are cut square and flush with the edges of the partitions. Remember to allow for the $3/16$in inset at the back edges of the end walls and partitions where they are housed in the back wall. A further spacer, this time $9^{3}/4$in high, with its bottom edge resting on the cornice already placed is used to mark the level for the upper cornice which should be applied next in the same manner.

While the carcase is dismantled, make the architraves for the internal doors to the dimensions shown in Fig 52. Glue these round the internal doorways on both faces of the partitions, with mitred joints at the corners, leaving $1/16$in of door frame exposed on the inside. The cornice and door surrounds can now be painted with one coat of Humbrol matt white, and allowed to dry before sanding lightly. This puts a priming coat on before the carcase is assembled.

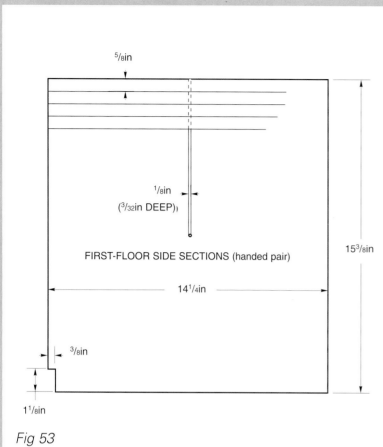

Fig 53
Patterns for the centre and side sections of the first floor

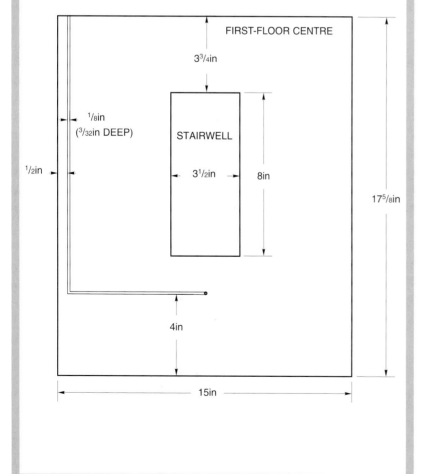

floor sections. They can now have one coat of satin varnish to seal them against glue spills when the carcase is being assembled.

Scribe the upper floor lengthways to represent boards $^5/8$in wide, leaving the two $5^3/16$in wide sections at each end (Fig 49e). Hammer a Cir-Kit canopy connector into each of the tapes under the top floor at the light position. Reassemble the carcase, including the upper floor, using glue this time, but note that one of the side walls must not be fastened in place until the top floor is positioned and pinned down into the tops of the partition walls. Leave to harden overnight, first wiping off all surface glue that has oozed from the joints. Glue in place the front extension to the upper floor.

Following the patterns in Fig 53, cut the three sections of first floor from $^1/4$in plywood. Note that the front edges of the side floors should be inset $^1/16$in from the outer (veneered) edges of the side walls. This allows for the $^1/16$in edge veneer on the floors, which should be fitted now. Check that there is $^1/2$in clearance behind the thickeners on the outside of the partition walls to allow the right- and left-hand front panels to enter. The outer edges of the side floors are notched $^3/8$in x $1^1/8$in to fit round the thickening strips on the inside faces of the side walls. Check that the floors lie evenly on the cornices and adjust with a chisel if necessary. Cut the stairwell from the centre section where shown.

The grooves for wire on the top surfaces of the three first-floor sections should now be routed, still following Fig 53. They are all $^1/8$in wide and $^3/32$in deep. The grooves on both side floors run directly from the light position in the centre, to the back edge. The middle section has the stairwell cut from it near the centre, so the groove must dog-leg round this. Mark the light position centrally 4in back from the front edge and rout a groove from this point, parallel with the front edge of the floor, to a point $^1/2$in from the left-hand edge. From this point, the groove runs directly to the back edge parallel with, and $^1/_2$in from, the left-hand edge of the floor. Floorboards will later be laid from side to side over each of these floors to conceal the wires that will be threaded through the grooves. The short transverse groove on the middle section will be covered by a loose floorboard to provide easier threading. Drill a $^1/_{16}$in diameter hole through each of the floor sections at the light position.

LOWER STAIRS

Referring to Fig 54, prepare sufficient mahogany cut to the profile shown, to produce twelve lower steps, each $3^7/_{16}$in long. At the same time, make twelve upper steps each $3^1/_2$in long and set these aside for the moment. The stairs are made in three stages so that each section can be adjusted to match the previous one. (Stairs are almost impossible to keep within very close tolerances.) None of the three sections will be glued to each other, or to the carcase, to allow removal for access and decoration.

Start by making the handed pair of lower staircases. First cut the triangular outer supports from $^1/_4$in plywood. Reduce the base length to $4^1/_{16}$in by cutting off the point at the lower front corner to produce the profile ABCD. Now, using the upper sloping edge as a guide, cut the two $^1/_4$in x $3^7/_{16}$in plywood carriers to length and bevel the ends to lie vertical and flush with the high back edges and low front edges of the supports. Veneer the outer edge of each with $^1/_4$in x $^1/_8$in mahogany.

Make the combined skirting and inner support XYZD from a laminate of $^1/_8$in mahogany and 0.8mm plywood. The plywood acts as a stiffener to prevent the mahogany from splitting. Remember that these supports must be handed, with their upper and front edges lightly chamfered. Lay the outer support ABCD on top of the inner support XYZD, with points D coinciding and the back and bottom edges flush. Mark the line AB on the inner support.

Still following Fig 54, make a handed pair of bullnosed lower steps and glue the tread on top. There is no need for the spindle holes yet. Take one of the outer supports ABCD and set it up on the bench supported on either side by holding battens from scrap material about $3^1/_2$in long and 1in wide, nailed to the bench top. Add a short stop across one end. With the support thus held, rest the carrier on top and push the bullnosed step against the front edges of both

support and carrier. The block for step 1 can now be placed on the carrier with its bottom edge resting on top of the tread on the bullnosed step. Mark a pencil line on the carrier to show the limits of step 1. Using impact adhesive, glue step 1 to the carrier in this position taking care that it is flush at the edges. Repeat this process for the second staircase.

Cut sufficient mahogany $1^1/_{16}$in wide and $^1/_{16}$in thick, to make twelve treads each $3^9/_{16}$in long ($^1/_8$in longer than each step). With a small plane, bevel the back edge of five of these treads to match the slope of the carrier. Using one of these treads as a spacer, glue the remaining five steps to each carrier leaving a $^1/_{16}$in vertical gap between each successive step. Do not fix the treads yet. Cut two strips of $^3/_8$in plywood $^5/_8$in wide, each the same length as the carriers, and with their ends bevelled to match. Glue one strip under the outer edge of each carrier, inset by $^5/_{16}$in. The outer supports ABCD can now be glued under the carrier against the outside of these plywood strips. When the glue is set, lay this assembly on to the inner support XYZD with the bottom edge of the carrier on the transferred line AB previously marked. Pencil-in the step outline to show the area to be glued. Again using impact adhesive, glue the inner face of the stair assembly to the inner support and put it under pressure in a vice.

The treads can now be fixed to the six plain steps. First, lightly round over the front and outer edges of each tread and then glue in place with impact adhesive, ensuring that the inside edges of the treads are butted square to the inner support/skirting and the back edges are located in the space between the present step and the one above it. It will help in positioning if the area of the tread that fits under the step above it is not glued. The bullnosed step is now glued in place below step no 1.

Following Fig 55, prepare 42in of handrail. This is made by gluing a strip of mahogany $^3/_{16}$in x $^3/_{32}$in on either side of a $^1/_8$in x $^1/_{16}$in centre strip, leaving a channel in the underside $^1/_{16}$in wide and $^1/_{16}$in deep. Round over the top to the pattern shown. Next, make a handed pair of curved handrail ends from a laminate of $^3/_{16}$in mahogany and 1.5mm plywood. Make one additional handrail end, from 0.8mm plywood only, to be used as a drilling template.

The spindles are made next, from mahogany $^1/_{16}$in square. They are $2^7/_8$in long under the

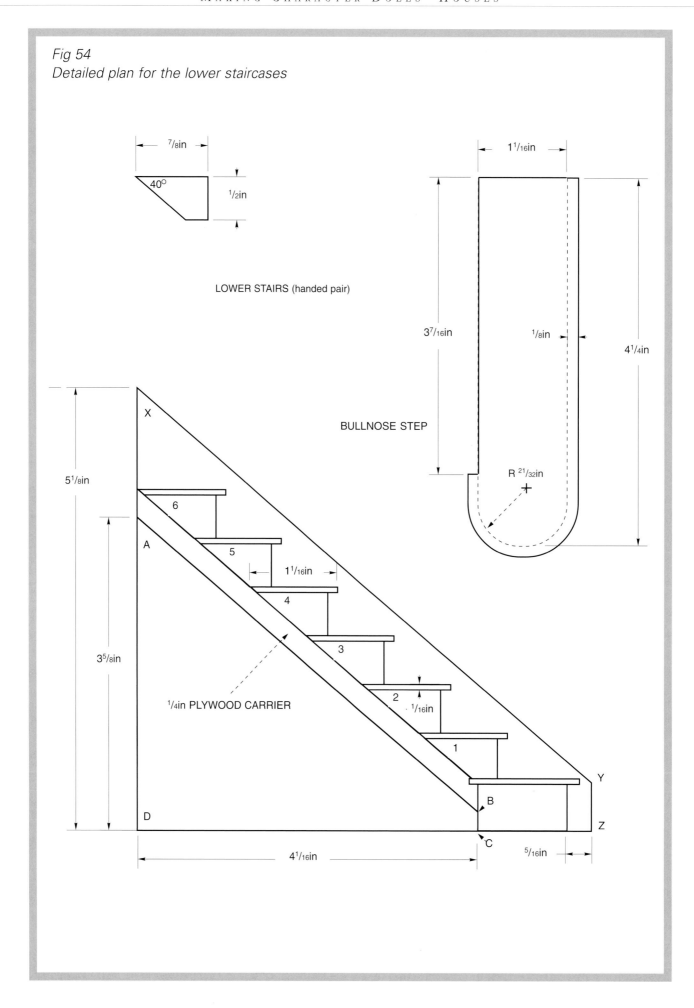

Fig 54
Detailed plan for the lower staircases

LOWER STAIRS (handed pair)

BULLNOSE STEP

¹/₄in PLYWOOD CARRIER

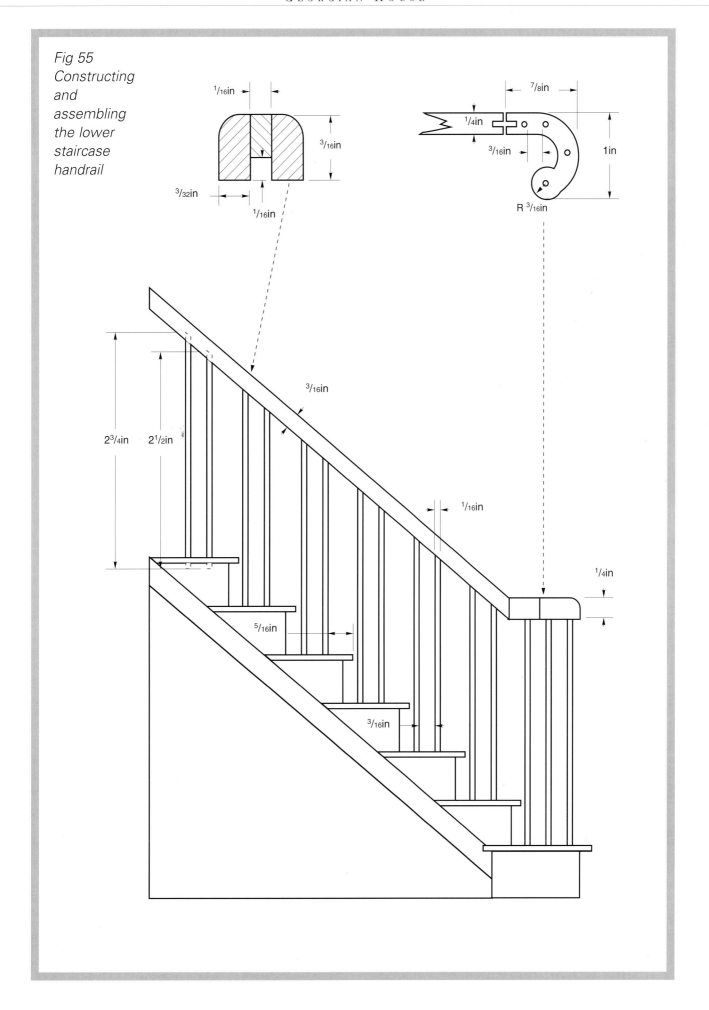

Fig 55
Constructing
and
assembling
the lower
staircase
handrail

Dining-room in the Georgian House

curved handrail section and 2½in long in pairs elsewhere. Drill a pair of holes ¹/₁₆in diameter and ¹/₈in deep, in each of the steps except the bullnose, inset ¹/₁₆in from the outer edge of the step block (*not the tread edge*), and ⁵/₁₆in and ⁹/₁₆in respectively from the front edge of the tread. This will space the pairs of spindles ³/₁₆in apart with the outer spindle ⁵/₁₆in from the front edge of the tread. Cut a 6in length of handrail and bevel the lower end to 50°. Cut a slot ¹/₈in long and ¹/₁₆in wide centrally into this end, and a similar slot in one curved section. Glue these together with a fillet of mahogany in the slots – this is cut back and sanded flush with the handrail when the glue is set.

Still following Fig 55, and using the plywood template with ¹/₁₆in diameter holes drilled through it where shown, drill holes ¹/₈in deep into the underside of the curved section. Repeat this for the second staircase. Now use this template to mark the hole positions on the bullnosed steps (*pencil marks only at this stage*). Round over the bottom end of each spindle using a drawplate, and cut the top ends to conform with the handrail slope.

Dry assemble the structure, and using one spindle cut 2¹³/₁₆in long, with its upper end rounded and fitted successively in each of the holes under the curved handrail end, test the positions previously marked on the bullnosed step. Check that when the spindle is vertical when viewed from both the front and side, its bottom end coincides with the appropriate mark on the bullnosed step. Adjust these positions if necessary and when satisfied drill ¹/₁₆in diameter holes ¹/₈in deep. Reassemble the handrail structure with glue. When set, cut the bevel on the inner end of the handrail to lie flush with the inner face of the stair assembly.

LANDING

This is made from two pieces of ³/₈in plywood, each 15in long, cut to the dimensions shown in Figs 56 and 57, and trimmed at the edges to give a loose sliding fit between the two partition walls at the back of the hall. The lower staircase just made may be a little higher or lower than the target measurements. Adjust the height of the front section of the landing (nominally 3⁷/₈in), so that, with a ¹/₁₆in mahogany facing

Georgian House kitchen

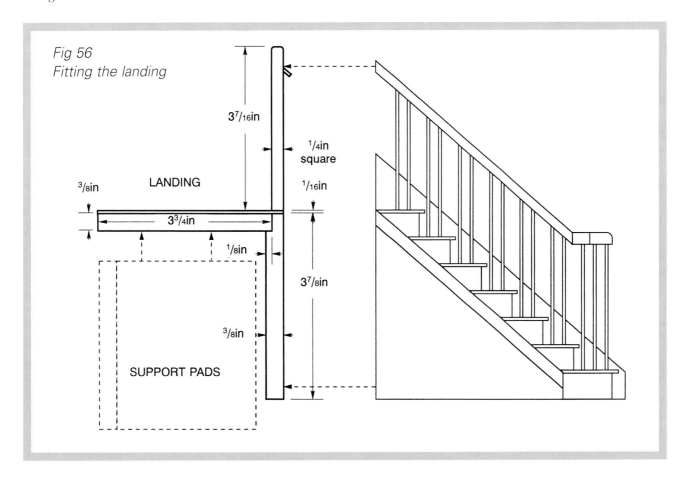

Fig 56
Fitting the landing

3⁷/₁₆in

¹/₄in square

¹/₁₆in

³/₈in

LANDING

3³/₄in

¹/₈in

3⁷/₈in

³/₈in

SUPPORT PADS

Georgian House hall

on the top, its height matches the top face of the tread of the top step. Note that $^1/_{16}$in mahogany was used on this model, but you may wish to use microwood veneer or separately applied floorboards as an alternative. Both of these are thinner than $^1/_{16}$in, so the height of the front landing section should be adjusted accordingly. Rebate the top of the inner face of the front section as shown in Fig 56, and then glue and pin the two sections together. Four support pads of $^3/_8$in plywood, 3in wide and nominally $3^1/_2$in high (depending on the adjusted height of the front), are now glued to the back and side walls in the corners of the hall. The landing will rest on top of these pads. Apply the $^1/_{16}$in mahogany facing (or whatever else you choose), to the top of the landing, with impact adhesive. Set the landing in place and position the two lower staircases against it with their skirting sides against the partition walls. Mark the front edge of the landing where the inner faces of the stairs meet it and glue a strip of mahogany $^1/_4$in x $^1/_8$in

across the front edge of the landing, between the stairs. The top edge of this strip should be flush with the facing on the top of the landing.

Cut two handrail posts from $^1/_4$in square mahogany, each $3^7/_{16}$in long (see Fig 57), and mark their positions on top of the landing flush with its outer edge and with their centres in line with the centres of the sloping handrails of the lower staircases. Lightly chamfer the top edge of each post and drill a hole in the bottom of each $^1/_{16}$in diameter and $^1/_4$in deep. Drill corresponding holes in the landing, $^1/_8$in deep, for bamboo dowels. Drill the spindle holes, spaced as shown in Fig 57, with their centres inset $^1/_8$in from the front edge of the landing. Do not glue the posts or spindles yet. A short length of $^1/_{16}$in mahogany is glued into the front face of each post (drill a pilot hole first), angled downwards to engage in the slot under the lower stair handrail, and projecting $^1/_4$in. A further length of $^1/_{16}$in square mahogany is glued horizontally into the inside face of each post to engage with

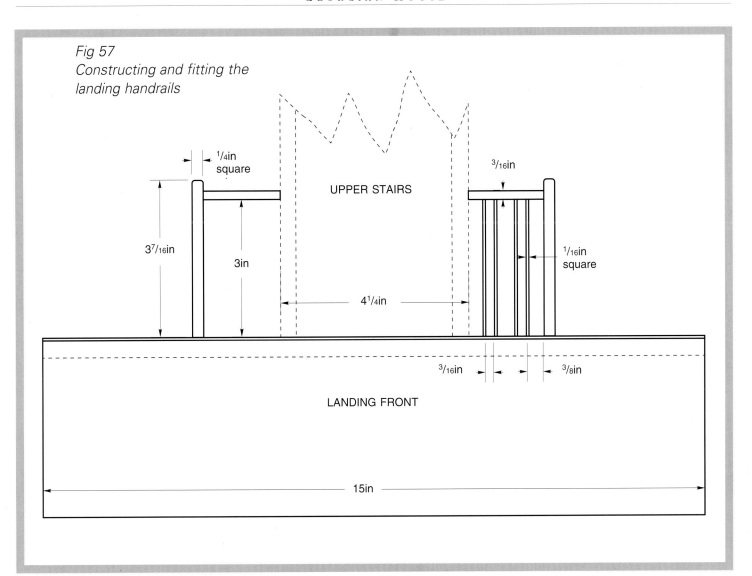

Fig 57
Constructing and fitting the
landing handrails

the slot on the landing handrail. The posts may now be glued in place. Leave the handrail until the upper stairs are completed.

UPPER STAIRS

Referring to Fig 58, make the carrier for the upper stairs from $^1/4$in plywood $3^1/2$in wide with its ends bevelled to rest on the landing at the bottom and against the back edge of the stairwell at the top. (The step blocks were made at the same time as those for the lower stairs.) Make twelve treads from mahogany $1^1/16$in wide, $^1/16$in thick, and $3^1/2$in long. Bevel the back edges of eleven of these as for the lower stairs. Again using one piece as a spacer, glue the blocks to the carrier. Make sure that the lowest block 1 is flush with the bevelled bottom edge of the carrier, and rests evenly on the landing. Continue placing blocks 2 to 11. Before fixing block no 12, check that its height, with a tread on top, will be $^1/32$in (the thickness of the floorboards) above the top surface of the floor. If

necessary adjust the height by decreasing the height of the block or by increasing the thickness of the tread. When satisfied glue all the treads in place, flush with the carrier at each side. Rest the stair assembly so far made, in position between the landing and stairwell.

Again following Fig 58, cut the two side panels ABCD from $^3/8$in plywood, and mark the stair outline on each inside face. Now paint two coats of white emulsion over the inside faces, leaving the marked area clear. Glue these panels, one to each side of the stairs, with impact adhesive taking care that the short, bottom edge CD rests squarely on the landing, and the top edge AB fits snugly under the floor. The sloping lower edge BC should be flush with the underside of the carrier. Compress the assembly in a vice. Glue a facing of 0.8mm plywood to the outside of this assembly to conceal the end grain plywood and plane flush at the edges. Glue and screw these side panels to the underside of the floor. Insert $^3/4$in no 4 screws from the floor into

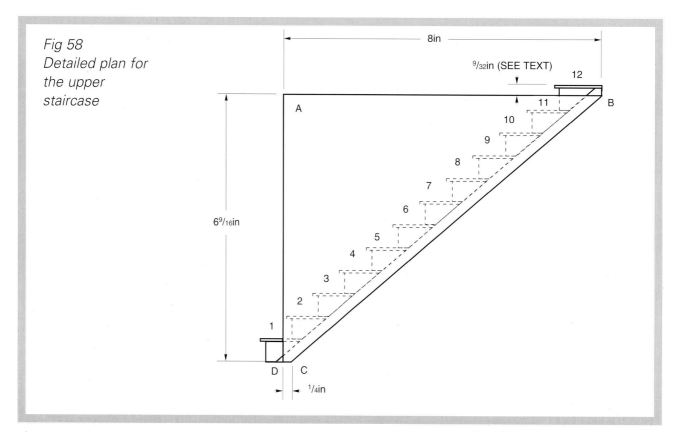

Fig 58
Detailed plan for
the upper
staircase

these panels, 1in from each end and in the centre. The screws will be covered by a moulding to be fitted later.

Cornice moulding should be applied at either side of these stairs against the join between stairs and floor. The inner ends are cut square and the outer ends are angled and mitred at the sloping outer face of the carrier. A further length of moulding, which has been reduced to a thickness of $1/8$in parallel with the sloping moulded face, is glued across the carrier between them. Position the floor in the house and cut two sections of handrail to fit between the posts already fixed on the landing, and the side panels of the upper stairs. This should not be too tight a fit so as not to bind when the floor is slid in and out. In the front edge of the landing, drill holes, $1/16$in diameter, $1/8$in deep, and spaced as shown in Fig 57, to receive the spindles. Cut eight spindles each $1/16$in square and $3^3/16$in long, and glue these into the holes on the landing and the channel under the handrail. At the same time, glue the end of the handrail to the spigot on the post. There is no spigot or glue at the end which meets the upper stairs.

UPPER HANDRAIL AND FLOORBOARDS

Referring to Fig 59, make up sufficient L-shaped mahogany to fit around the back and sides of the stairwell. Mitre the corners and glue in place. This moulding will need to be cut away slightly on the down facing section at each side of the open end to fit over stair no 12. Before proceeding further, support the floor over a Workmate or on blocks on the bench, to protect the staircase which is under it.

Cut sufficient $5/8$in x $1/32$in strips of lime for the floorboards on the three sections of first floor. Starting with the centre section at the inside of the transverse wiring groove, lay and glue these boards across the floor from side to side, cut and butted on either side of the stairwell moulding, and continuing to the back wall. Cut one length of board to the same length as the transverse groove and lay it in place without gluing. Continue to the right by gluing a board from the end of this groove to the right-hand wall. Now work towards the front, finishing flush at the front edge of the floor.

Next, fix the floorboards on the two side sections of the first floor. It will be helpful if lengths of wire are placed in the grooves on the side sections, extending 1in or so at the back of the floor, and from the holes for the lights, before gluing the floorboards in place. These can be used later to pull the wire tails from the lights through the channels in the floor. Sand the floors smooth and apply one coat of varnish, but do not fix them in the house.

Returning to the stairwell and referring to Fig 59, drill the holes for the handrail and posts, each $1/16$in diameter and $1/8$in deep, into the top of the mahogany moulding. Drill the posts where the handrails butt and glue in mahogany spigots as on the landing. Similarly, drill the bottom of the posts for the dowels and glue in place followed by the rail and spindles. All the stair sections should now have two coats of varnish. The complete stair assembly is shown in Fig 60.

ELECTRICS

The tape tabs at the back of the upper floor can now be connected with brads to the tapes across the back wall. Test the circuit and then fit eyelets in pairs for the attic lighting as follows:

In the centre section, 2in to the right of the left-hand partition groove and at the top of the

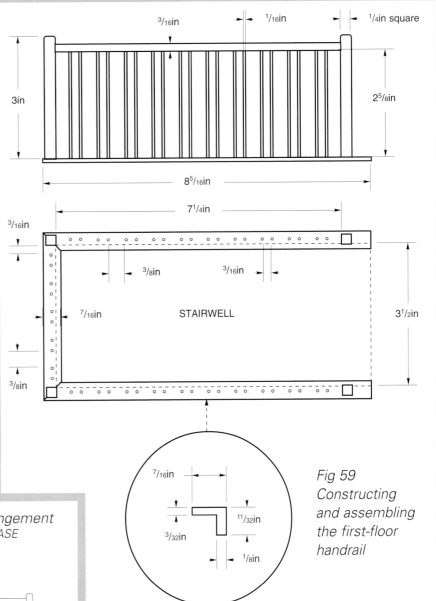

Fig 59
Constructing and assembling the first-floor handrail

Fig 60   Illustrating the stair arrangement (FRONT SECTION OF LOWER STAIRCASE OMITTED FOR CLARITY)

vertical tape just below the slot for the roof support beam; in the left-hand section, 6in to the left of the left-hand partition groove; and in the right-hand section, 6in to the right of the partition groove.

UPPER CARCASE FRAMING

Before cutting out any of the roof or attic components, it is as well to have an overall picture of how everything fits together (see Fig 61). Four partitions are housed in the slots at the back wall and in the floor. The outer partitions have triangular supports, two at the outside of each, on to which the end roof panels are fixed. All partitions are double-thickness at the front edges to provide a land for the portable roof panels. The central gabled roof is supported by a beam run-

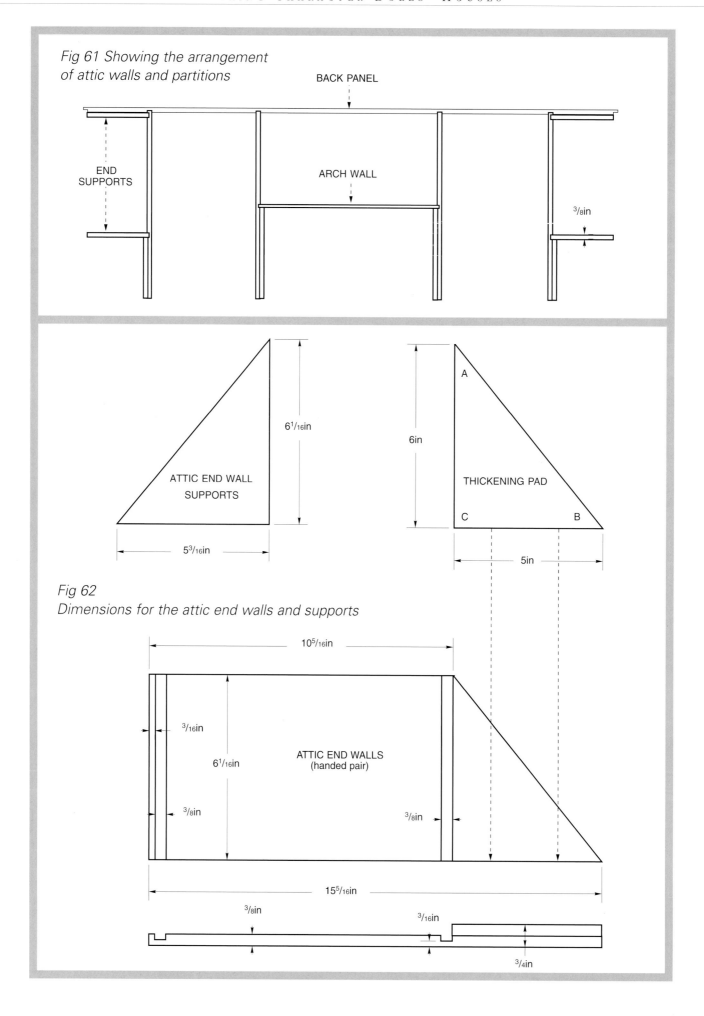

Fig 61 Showing the arrangement
of attic walls and partitions

BACK PANEL

END
SUPPORTS

ARCH WALL

³/₈in

6¹/₁₆in

ATTIC END WALL
SUPPORTS

5³/₁₆in

6in

A

THICKENING PAD

C   B

5in

Fig 62
Dimensions for the attic end walls and supports

10⁵/₁₆in

³/₁₆in

6¹/₁₆in

³/₈in

ATTIC END WALLS
(handed pair)

³/₈in

15⁵/₁₆in

³/₈in

³/₁₆in

³/₄in

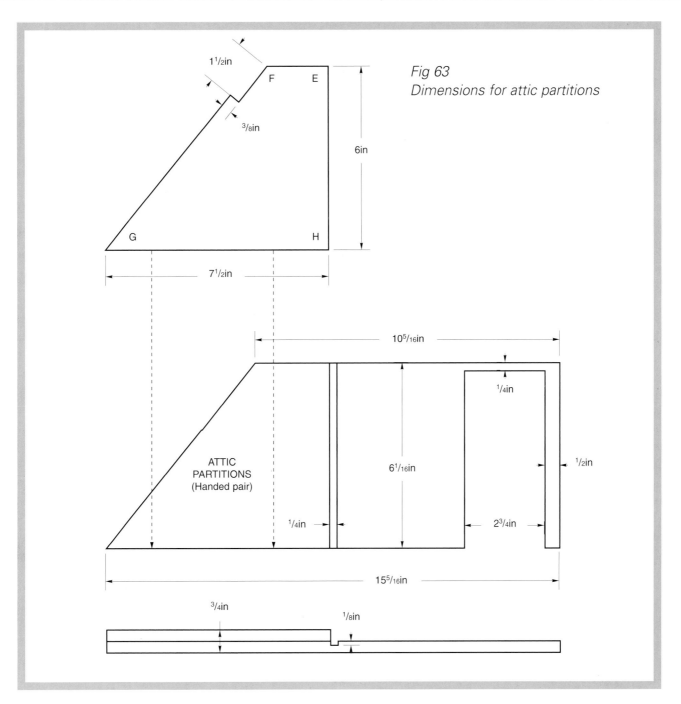

Fig 63
Dimensions for attic partitions

running from front to back which is notched into a support beam, the arched room divider, and the back wall. Two bevelled supports fit under the eaves of the gabled roof. When completed the flat roof is fixed on top.

Referring to Figs 62 and 63, cut, from ³/₈in plywood, two attic end walls and two attic partitions. Rout the grooves on the end walls, where shown, ³/₈in wide and ³/₁₆in deep, remembering that these are a handed pair and that the grooves should be on opposing faces. Cut two triangular thickening pads ABC from ³/₈in plywood, and glue one of these to each end wall outside the outer groove. Note that the base of each pad is ¹/₁₆in above the base of the wall to which it is

glued and that it rests on the floor and not in the groove. Now cut four triangular end roof/wall supports (Fig 62), and glue and screw these into the grooves on the end walls. Check that the bases of these are level with the bases of the walls, as all of them locate in the floor grooves. These two end wall assemblies should be positioned with their bases in the floor grooves, and their back edges in the back wall grooves. In this position, the lower front corner of each wall should be inset ⁵/₁₆in from the front edge of the floor, with its sloping edge rising at 50°.

Take the two partition walls previously cut and rout ¹/₄in wide grooves where shown in Fig 63, but this time only ¹/₈in deep. Mark out and

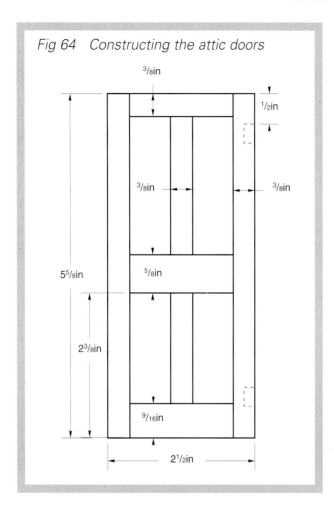

Fig 64   Constructing the attic doors

addition, each partition is held with one 1in panel pin through the lower front corner into the floor and partition below it. Each end wall has a $^3/_4$in panel pin driven upwards through the floor at the same position. After wiping off all surplus glue, allow to harden overnight.

Referring to Fig 65, cut out the transverse attic partition from $^1/_4$in plywood, $15^1/_4$in long to locate at each end in the grooves on the inside faces of the partitions. Cut out the arched opening, and veneer the edge of this with $^1/_{32}$in thick lime. Cut the notch where shown centrally in the top edge, to locate the roof support beam. Still following Fig 65, cut the transverse roof beam support from $^3/_8$in plywood with its top edge bevelled to 50°, and a $^3/_4$in wide notch cut in it. Make the roof beam from lime or beech $^3/_4$in x $^5/_8$in and $18^1/_{16}$in long, noting that the outer part is bevelled to give an included angle of 110° at the top. This bevelled section stops at an angle of 50° with its top edge $10^7/_{16}$in from the inner end. Check that this beam fits snugly in all its locating notches and adjust if necessary. Do not fix any of these items yet. Plane the top edges of the back wall, end walls, partitions, and divider true and fair.

ROOF PANELS

All are cut from $^1/_4$in plywood. Start with the end panels. The dimensions in Fig 66 are the target, but note that any slight variations in the dimensions of the attic walls and supports will affect the angles and dimensions of the end panels. It is advisable to cut a rectangle of $^1/_4$in plywood $8^1/_8$in x $15^5/_8$in (slightly oversize) for each panel, bevel the bottom edge of each to 40°, and notch the back edge, as shown in Fig 66, $^3/_8$in deep and $2^7/_8$in high with the top of the notch again bevelled to 40°. This allows the panels to fit over the back wall of the house, with their bevelled bottom edges fitting against the upstands of the carcase end walls.

Place the panels in position, bearing on the triangular roof supports at the outside of the attic walls, and carefully mark the inside face of each where it overlaps the attic end wall at the top of the front edge, and at a point $^5/_{16}$in in from the outer edge of the floor at the bottom. A pencil line joining these two points will give the slope (nominally 58°). Now plane a bevel at 65° along the sloping edges, and test with a batten, laid across the slopes of the other walls, until the slope and bevel of the end panel are

cut the door openings. *Extreme care is needed to avoid breaking the $^1/_4$in deep section over the door.* Alternatively, leave the partition uncut and fit dummy doors.

If opening doors are to be fitted, they should be made next, to the dimensions in Fig 64. The framing follows the method used for the other internal doors, and should be glued in place on the wall, together with the architraves. Put the doors aside for now.

Referring to Fig 63, cut the two thickening pads EFGH and glue these to the inside faces of the partitions, outside the $^1/_4$in grooves, again noting that the bases are $^1/_{16}$in above those on the partitions. Cut a $1^1/_2$in x $^3/_8$in notch at position F on each partition. The doors should now be removed and put aside and the frames and architraves painted with two coats of Humbrol satin white. Check that these assemblies locate correctly in the floor grooves.

Remove both end and partition wall assemblies and give the upper floor surface one sealing coat of satin varnish. When dry, both walls and partitions can now be fixed to the carcase with glue and $^3/_4$in no 4 screws driven from the back (two screws to each wall or partition). In

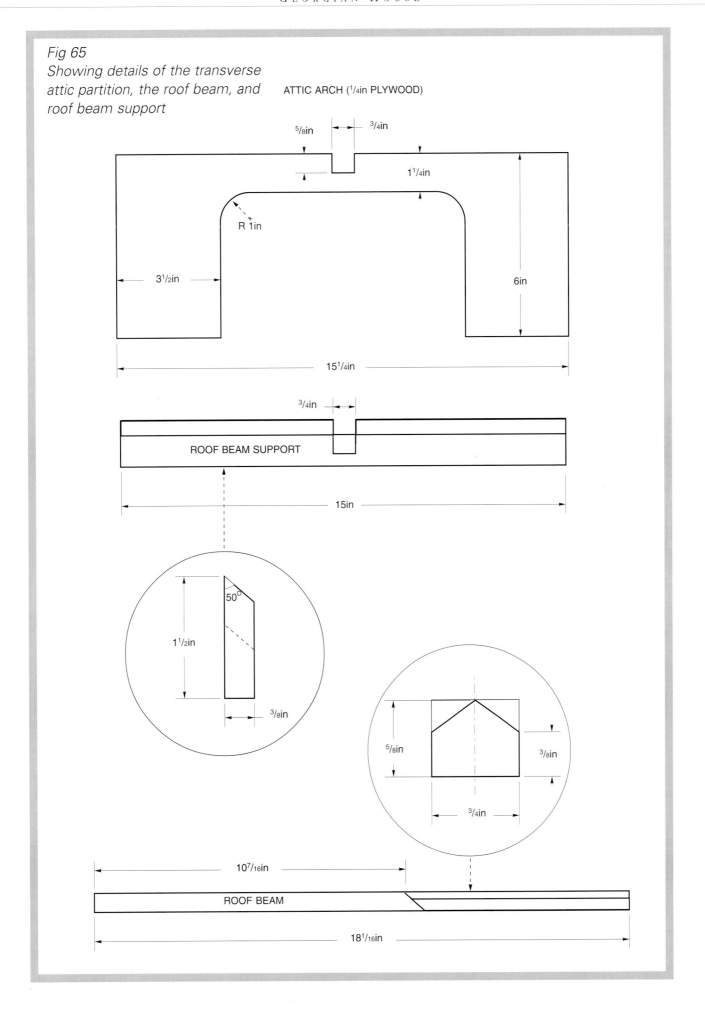

Fig 65
Showing details of the transverse
attic partition, the roof beam, and
roof beam support

ATTIC ARCH (¹/₄in PLYWOOD)

⁵/₈in   ³/₄in

1¹/₄in

R 1in

3¹/₂in

6in

15¹/₄in

³/₄in

ROOF BEAM SUPPORT

15in

50°

1¹/₂in

³/₈in

⁵/₈in   ³/₈in

³/₄in

10⁷/₁₆in

ROOF BEAM

18¹/₁₆in

fair. Glue and pin these end panels in place with three panel pins in each of the end roof/wall supports (see Fig 62), and the sloping section of the carcase back wall. Plane the top edges of each end panel flush with the top of the attic and back walls, and also plane the back edge of each panel flush with the carcase back wall.

Cut two triangular front panels from $^1/4$in plywood to fill the space between the end roof panels just fitted, and the attic walls. Again, it is better to cut a little oversize and then trim to fit. The bevelled lower edge should lie on the floor, flush at the front when bearing on the sloping front of the attic wall, with the 65° bevel on the sloping outer edge making that edge flush with the surface of the end panel previously fixed. The vertical inner edge should lie on the centre-line of the thickened attic wall, leaving a $^3/8$in wide section of this sloping wall end exposed. This will form a land for the portable section which fits between here and the next partition wall.

When the panels fit satisfactorily, they can be glued and pinned in place using PVA adhesive and $^3/4$in panel pins. *Note that both end roof panels and the small triangular front roof sections are handed, and remember to bevel opposing faces.* Take care when pinning the sloping edges which butt, that the pins do not break through to the outside face. The joint should be fair, but slight irregularities can be smoothed with a sandplate, once the glue has set. Any slight overlap at the top should be planed flush with the tops of the walls. The transverse roof beam support can now be glued and pinned into the notches on the partition walls (Fig 63), ensuring that its bevelled top edge is flush with the tops of these walls.

GABLE ROOF

Rest the roof support beam in the notches previously cut and temporarily fasten it into the top of the back wall with a 40mm panel pin driven partway home. (Leave enough of the head projecting to ease removal.) Referring to Fig 67,

Unfurnished interior of the Georgian House, showing right-hand section of lower staircase, and partly open garden drawer

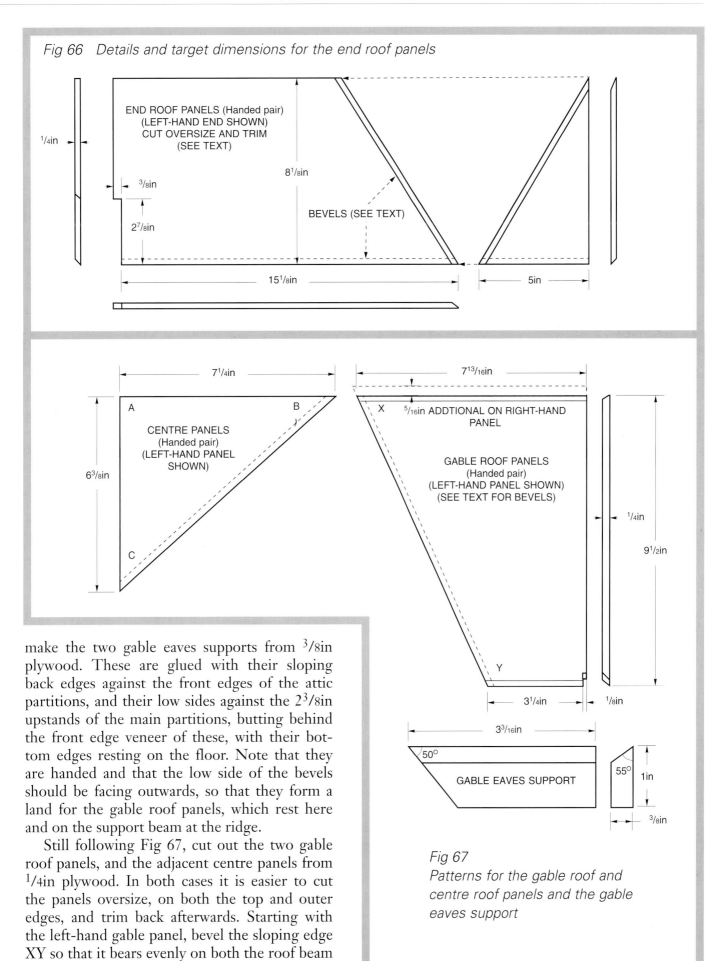

Fig 66 Details and target dimensions for the end roof panels

END ROOF PANELS (Handed pair)
(LEFT-HAND END SHOWN)
CUT OVERSIZE AND TRIM
(SEE TEXT)

1/4in

3/8in

2 7/8in

8 1/8in

BEVELS (SEE TEXT)

15 1/8in

5in

7 1/4in

CENTRE PANELS
(Handed pair)
(LEFT-HAND PANEL
SHOWN)

A   B

6 3/8in

C

7 13/16in

X   5/16in ADDTIONAL ON RIGHT-HAND PANEL

GABLE ROOF PANELS
(Handed pair)
(LEFT-HAND PANEL SHOWN)
(SEE TEXT FOR BEVELS)

1/4in

9 1/2in

Y

3 1/4in   1/8in

3 3/16in

50°

GABLE EAVES SUPPORT

55°   1in

3/8in

make the two gable eaves supports from 3/8in plywood. These are glued with their sloping back edges against the front edges of the attic partitions, and their low sides against the 2 3/8in upstands of the main partitions, butting behind the front edge veneer of these, with their bottom edges resting on the floor. Note that they are handed and that the low side of the bevels should be facing outwards, so that they form a land for the gable roof panels, which rest here and on the support beam at the ridge.

Still following Fig 67, cut out the two gable roof panels, and the adjacent centre panels from 1/4in plywood. In both cases it is easier to cut the panels oversize, on both the top and outer edges, and trim back afterwards. Starting with the left-hand gable panel, bevel the sloping edge XY so that it bears evenly on both the roof beam support and the front of the attic partition.

Fig 67
Patterns for the gable roof and centre roof panels and the gable eaves support

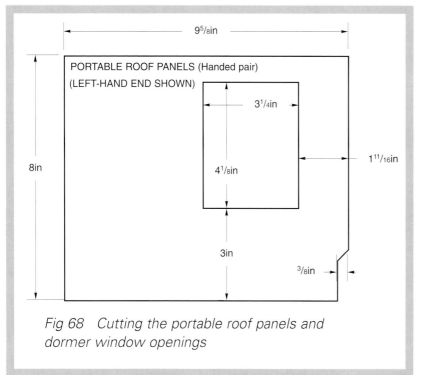

9⁵/₈in

PORTABLE ROOF PANELS (Handed pair)
(LEFT-HAND END SHOWN)

3¹/₄in

1¹¹/₁₆in

8in

4¹/₈in

3in

³/₈in

Fig 68 Cutting the portable roof panels and dormer window openings

Next, bevel the bottom edge to 55° so that, when resting on the eaves support, it bears against the upstand of the partition wall. Cut the notch in the outer bottom corner. When satisfied that the panels fit at these specified points, mark the top edge along the roof beam, and plane a 70° bevel here to bring the top edge flush with the opposing face of the roof beam. Draw a line on the underside of the outer edge from the outside of the carcase partition to the outside of the roof beam. The edge should now be cut ¹/₁₆in inside this line, and veneered with ¹/₁₆in lime. Repeat this for the right-hand gable panel, remembering that its top edge will be ⁵/₁₆in higher to allow for the overlap at the ridge.

With these components lightly tacked in place, fit the centre roof panels. The bevel should be planed first on the sloping edge BC, to bear on the gable roof. This should be done very carefully as this joint will be glued later. The top edge AB will be trimmed off after fixing, and the vertical edge AC will lie on the seam between the two ³/₈in wide sections at the front of the attic partitions, to leave a ³/₈in wide land for the portable panels. Mark where the centre panel line BC rests on the upper face of the gable roof at its edge XY, remove the gable roof panels, and glue this joint with impact adhesive. This is not a particularly strong joint, but the instant grab is useful for holding the parts together while panel pins are inserted

along the joint. *Take care that these do not break through to the surface.* The joint is now adequately strong.

Replace the gable roof and tack the triangular centre roof panels temporarily to the front of the attic partitions. Drill, and insert two ¹/₂in no 4 screws from the gable roof into the roof beam on each side, about ¹/₂in from each end. Do not glue yet. Next, from ¹/₄in plywood cut two portable panels, each 8¹/₈ x 9³/₄in (Fig 68). These dimensions are oversize and the panels need to be trimmed in length to ¹/₈in less than the gap between the roof panels previously fixed. The heights should be adjusted with bevelled edges (50°) at the tops which lie fair with the tops of the attic partitions. Take care when doing this not to plane a flat on top of the gable ridge whose apex will be flush with the top of the ¹/₄in thick flat roof when fitted. Glue an edge veneer of ¹/₁₆in lime to each vertical edge of each panel, to fill the gap and provide a harder rubbing surface. Note that bevelled notches will be required to fit over the gable roof at the lower inside corners of these panels, and the bottom edges are bevelled to 50° to fit against the floor. Fig 69 shows the arrangement of the roof structure.

FLAT ROOF

Cut this from ¹/₄in plywood, 35¹/₈in long and 11in wide. This is slightly oversize to allow for the bevelled edge. Assemble this temporarily with ³/₄in no 4 screws driven into the tops of the attic partitions and back wall, allowing a slight overlap all round. Mark round the underside of this roof panel inside each of the three rooms, to show the areas to be left as bare wood when the ceilings are painted. Do not plane the bevelled edge fair with the roof slope yet.

Before fixing the flat roof, arched partition, and any other loose components, the decorating in the central attic room must be completed as it becomes inaccessible once the roof sections are in place. The three back walls should now be faced with thin card with a rectangular cutout over the eyelets to match the overall size of the plug to be used. When the card has dried, the central room can be painted, including the door frames and architraves.

Carefully mark the back wall where the

Fig 69   Showing the arrangement of front roof panels

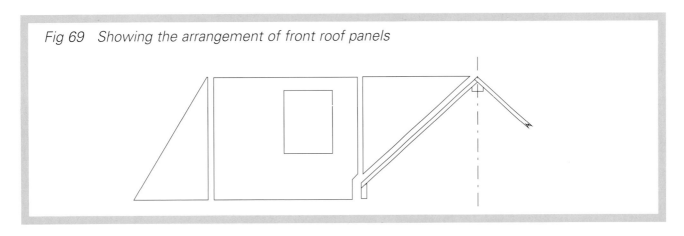

Fig 70   Showing details of the skirting

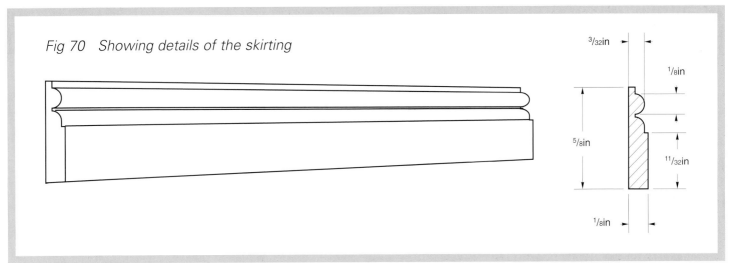

Right-hand attic bedroom in the Georgian House

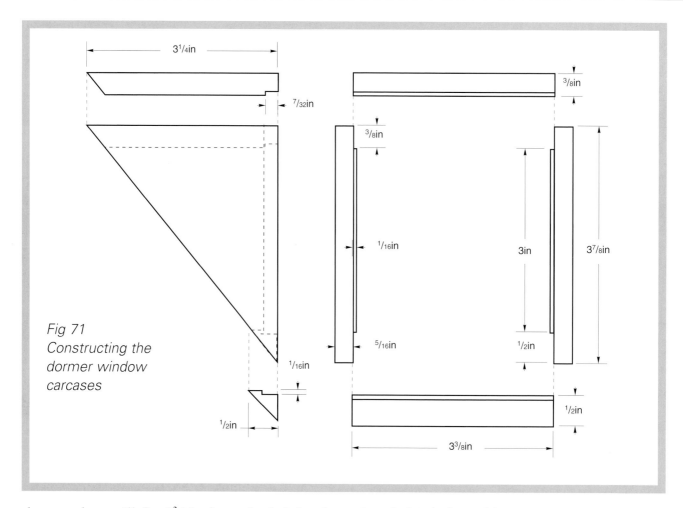

*Fig 71
Constructing the
dormer window
carcases*

dummy door will fit, $2^3/4$in from the left-hand wall, and glue the door in place with either PVA or impact adhesive, having first fitted the brass door knob. The skirting should now be fitted to the area behind the transverse partition. This can be bought ready-made or constructed to the dimensions shown in Fig 70. Now paint the ceiling areas under the flat roof panel and the gable roof, with three coats of white emulsion. Note that if opening doors have been fitted to the attic rooms, small fillets should be glued in the floor grooves under the doors. The attic floors should now have a further coat of satin varnish. Note: the decorating in the side rooms is best left until the roof is in place, to avoid possible damage to the wallpapers.

Fix one small screw-eye or hook at the right-hand side of the roof support beam $1/2$in from the back wall, and another halfway between this and the back of the arched partition. Cut a $1/8$in square notch at the top of the arched partition just outside the right-hand side of the $3/4$in x $5/8$in notch already there. These are to carry the lighting wire from the upper socket on the back wall to a Cir-Kit Fluorette lamp which will be positioned at the back of the transverse roof sec-

tion, behind the gable extension on the right-hand side of the front attic room.

Now fix the two attic partition doors in place with knobs on either side of each. Lightly glue the edges of the arched partition, and slide this into place in the grooves at either side. Glue the roof support beam in position with a 40mm panel pin driven through its top edge into the back wall. Glue alone will suffice in the remaining slots. The gable roof sections can now be fixed in place with glue, $1/2$in no 4 screws into the roof beam, and panel pins into the eaves and through the small triangular sections into the sloping edges of the partition walls.

Glue and screw the flat roof in place adding panel pins between the screws. When the glue has set, plane the ends and front flush with the roof slope. Take care, and use a chisel in the area close to the inner end of the gable. Plane the back edge flush with the outside of the back wall.

PORTABLE ROOF PANELS
Referring to Fig 71, make up two dormer carcases. These are made from $3/8$in plywood rebated at the front for both window and

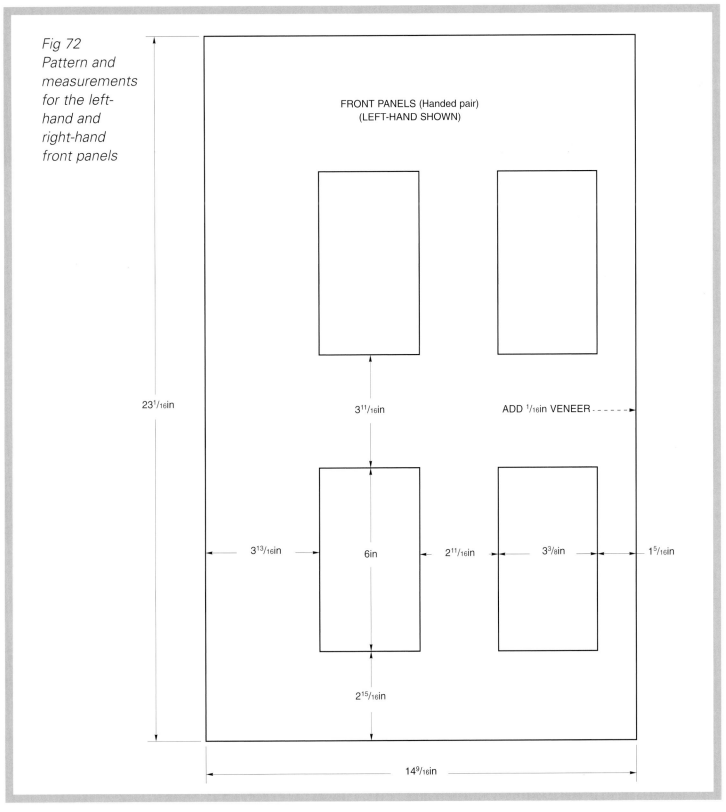

*Fig 72
Pattern and
measurements
for the left-
hand and
right-hand
front panels*

FRONT PANELS (Handed pair)
(LEFT-HAND SHOWN)

23¹/₁₆in

3¹¹/₁₆in

ADD ¹/₁₆in VENEER - - - - - - -

3¹³/₁₆in   6in   2¹¹/₁₆in   3³/₈in   1⁵/₁₆in

2¹⁵/₁₆in

14⁹/₁₆in

glazing. Referring to Fig 68, mark the position of the dormer on the portable roof panels where shown, and cut out the opening in the panels. Glue and screw the dormer carcases in place, and when the glue is dry, clean up the inside of the openings with a sandplate. Make the dormer roofs from ¹/₈in plywood, to overhang the dormer carcase by ¹/₈in at the front and sides

and with their back edges bevelled to butt the portable roof panel. Glue these in place.

PORTABLE FRONT WALLS

Cut the three front panels from ³/₈in plywood and rout the window and door openings as shown in Figs 72 and 73. Cut the 2¹/₈in diameter hole in the gable section. Note that each of

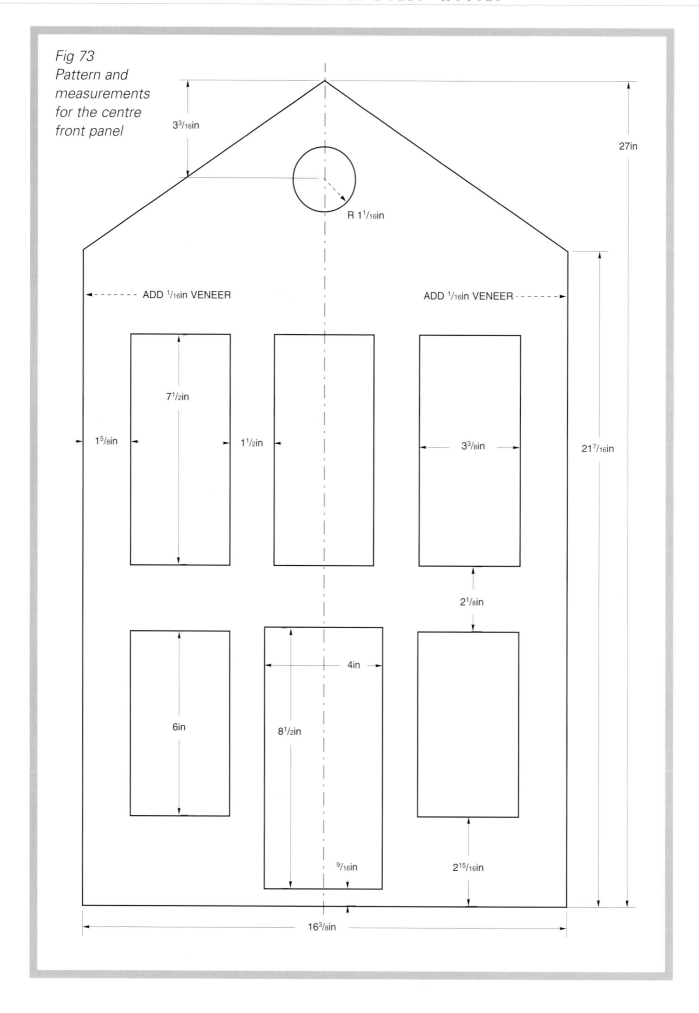

Fig 73
Pattern and
measurements
for the centre
front panel

Georgian House drawing room

these components is best cut a little larger than the measurements given, and then trimmed back where necessary to obtain a good fit. The inner edge of each side panel, and both edges of the centre panel, should be veneered with $^1/_{16}$in lime before proceeding further. It is important that the gable slope on the centre panel corresponds exactly with the gable roof behind it. Note also that the front panels are $^3/_{16}$in less in height than the side carcase panels as their bases slide in a $^3/_{16}$in deep groove. The doorway cutout starts $^9/_{16}$in up from the bottom edge of the panel, to allow for the porch base which will be fitted later.

FRONT DOOR AND FRAME

Referring to Fig 74, make about 2ft of door frame and header moulding, or use any left over from the internal doors. Frame the door opening and make the front door which opens inwards, and is hinged on the left-hand side when viewed from the front. The core is 1.5mm plywood and the applied framing on the inside

of the door is from 0.8mm plywood, while the framing on the outside is 1.5mm plywood. The fielded panels are made from 1.5mm plywood, and glued in afterwards, having first had their edges chamfered. Plane the frame flush on both faces of the panel.

PARAPET AND GABLE PEDIMENT

Referring to Fig 75, make up 12ft of moulding. Starting with the centre panel, lay an 18in length of moulding across the gable with its top edge at the intersection of the vertical side edges and the gable slope. Mark and mitre the ends of this moulding at the back to accept the two short returns to be fixed to the panel edges. Glue the long length in place with impact adhesive and then glue and pin the short return pieces to the panel edges, this time using PVA adhesive, and noting that the inner ends of these returns finish square and flush at the back of panel. Cut two further lengths of moulding, mitred at the joints, to fit from the top of the horizontal moulding to the apex flush with the sloping edges of the panel. Glue these in place.

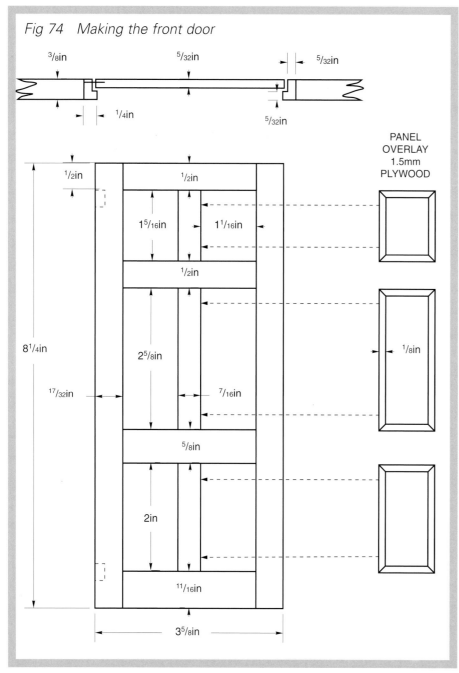

Fig 74 Making the front door

PANEL
OVERLAY
1.5mm
PLYWOOD

Position the two side panels with their inner ends tight in behind the thickening strips on the partition walls. Cut two further lengths of moulding to fit the remainder of the return wall from the centre panel. Mitre the inner ends where they touch the side panels, leaving a plain edge at each outer end to butt the returns on the front panel edges. Glue these in place. When the glue has set, the horizontal moulding can be continued across the side panels, having been mitred to fit behind the return sections. This joint should not be glued. Note that the inner mitred ends of the horizontal mouldings on the side panels are inset $3/8$in from the inner edges of the panels, which are behind the thickening pieces, and are mitred again at their outer ends for the return sections on the end walls. Glue this horizontal moulding in place with impact adhesive. Further short return sections are mitred and one fixed at the outer edge of each side panel, trimmed square and flush at the back. The remaining section on each end wall is left square ended and fitted so that it butts the plain end of the return, and finishes flush at the outside face of the back wall of the house.

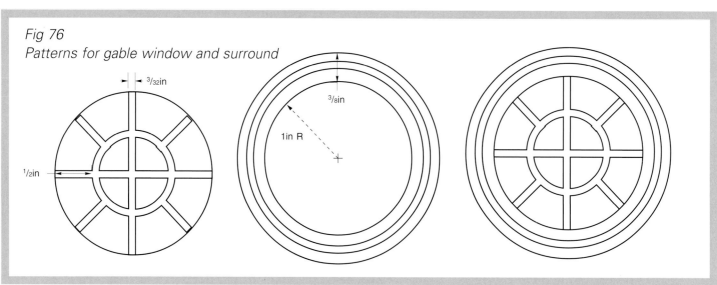

Fig 76
Patterns for gable window and surround

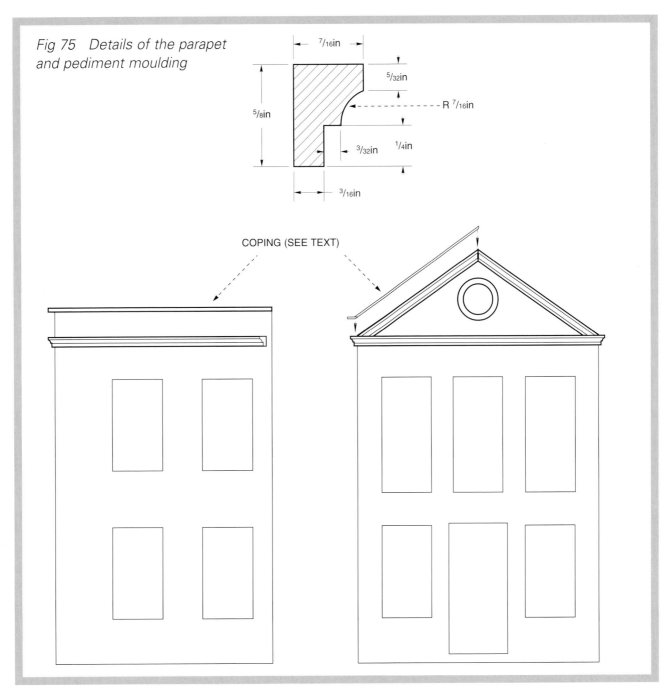

Fig 75 Details of the parapet and pediment moulding

COPING (SEE TEXT)

Now cut two triangular fillets of $3/8$in plywood to fill the gap between the gable roof and the top of the upward extensions of the thickening pieces at each side (see colour illustration page 100). Trim tops of these fillets flush with the top edges of both the side panels and the upward extensions. Glue them in place so that the outer faces of the fillets are flush with the outer edges of the thickening pieces.

COPING

A coping of $1/2$in x $1/4$in lime is now glued and pinned to the top edges of the end walls, sliding side panels, triangular parapet fillets, and the short section of parapet at each end of the back wall. This should be mitred where there is a fixed turn, but left square ended at the front of the end walls and on the removable front sections. It should be flush at the inside faces of each panel, and should overlap $1/8$in at the outside.

GABLE COPING

Cut 2ft of 1in x $1/8$in lime. Referring again to Fig 75, glue and pin two short lengths on top of the horizontal pediment moulding at each end, overhanging the moulding by $3/16$in at the sides and front. The ends which fit against the sloping gable moulding should be bevelled accordingly. Cut the remainder to make the two sections which are fixed on top of the sloping pediment

Fig 77   Patterns and details for the windows and sash overlays

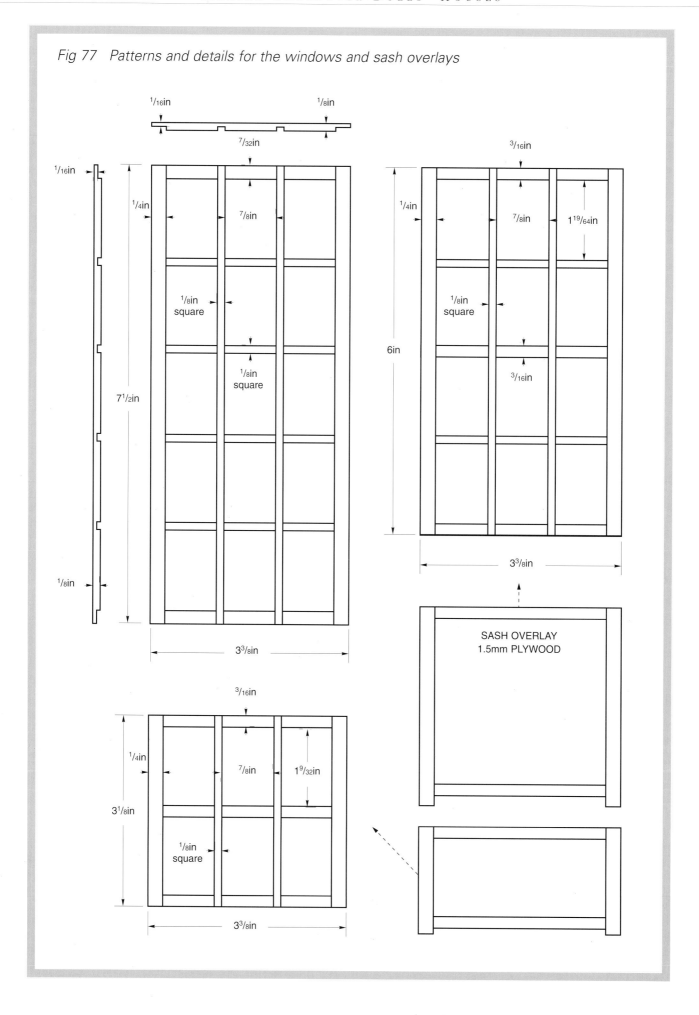

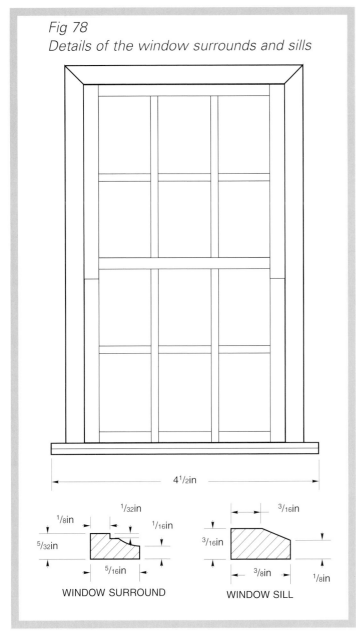

Fig 78
Details of the window surrounds and sills

4¹/2in

¹/8in
¹/32in
¹/16in
⁵/32in
⁵/16in

WINDOW SURROUND

³/16in
³/16in
³/8in
¹/8in

WINDOW SILL

moulding. These are bevelled at the top and bottom ends, and glued and pinned in place flush at the back and overhanging at the front. The coping on the two short sections of parapet at either side of the centre panel must be notched to fit round the coping on the gable pediment.

GABLE WINDOW

Using either a lathe or a router, make the circular surround for the window from ¹/4in plywood. The inside diameter should be 2in and the outside diameter 2³/4in. The outer face should be moulded to match the window surrounds. Glue this in place with an even ¹/16in overlap all round the 2¹/8in diameter hole (Fig 76). The scrolls are available from most DIY shops. They start one third of the way up the

surround and run downwards and outwards to finish level with the bottom of the surround at their outer ends.

WINDOWS

Referring to Fig 77, make all the windows and their sash overlays, and trim as necessary to fit snugly in the openings. Do not glue. The windows should be marked on one edge with their respective positions, and painted. Three coats are recommended, two of Humbrol matt white, followed by one of Humbrol satin white.

Referring to Fig 78, make sufficient mouldings for the window surrounds. Cut these to fit round the openings at the sides and top, with mitred joints at the top and square ends at the bottom. Glue these in place round the openings so that they overlap the hole by ¹/32in all round, and provide a land for the windows which will be pushed in from the inside. Again referring to Fig 78, make the window sills and glue these in position beneath the window surrounds, overhanging equally at either side of the windows. Note that the ground-floor windows at each side of the front door have sills only. There is no room for surrounds between the windows and the half columns. The sills here may need to be trimmed back slightly when the columns are fitted.

BALCONY

Referring to Fig 79, turn six columns from lime, tapering from 1¹/4in diameter at the bottom to 1in at the top, each with a ³/8in x ¹/4in spigot at each end. Carefully saw two of these columns in half lengthways to produce four half columns. Alternatively, make up blanks from two pieces of lime 1¹/2in x ³/4in glued together with water soluble glue with a brown paper insert between them. After turning, the halves can be separated easily. You should now have four full, and four half columns. Again referring to Fig 79, make six each of the top and bottom plinths from ¹/4in plywood. Halve two of each to leave four full, and four half plinths of each size. While using the lathe you should now turn thirteen balusters from lime to the pattern in Fig 80. Note if you do not have access to a lathe, these parts can be made for you by a specialist wood turner.

The construction of the porch starts with the base which is cut from ³/8in plywood, 16³/8in long and 3¹⁵/16in deep. Veneer the ends and front edge of this with ¹/16in lime to bring its measurements to 16¹/2in x 4in. Set the centre

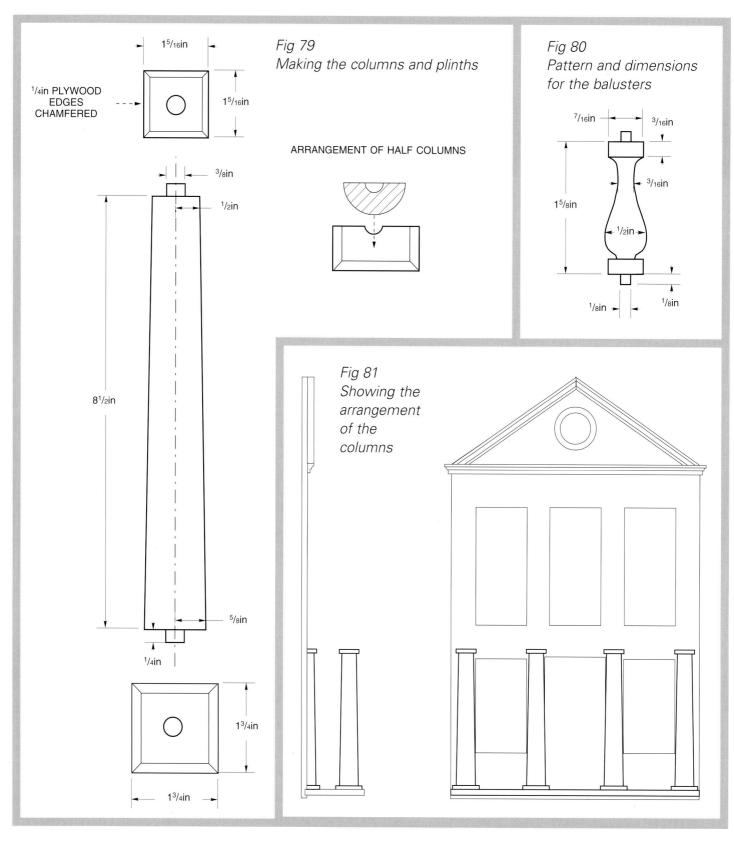

1⁵/₁₆in

¹/₄in PLYWOOD
EDGES
CHAMFERED

1⁵/₁₆in

Fig 79
Making the columns and plinths

ARRANGEMENT OF HALF COLUMNS

³/₈in

¹/₂in

8¹/₂in

5/₈in

¹/₄in

1³/₄in

1³/₄in

Fig 80
Pattern and dimensions for the balusters

7/₁₆in   ³/₁₆in

³/₁₆in

1⁵/₈in   ¹/₂in

¹/₈in   ¹/₈in

Fig 81
Showing the arrangement of the columns

front panel in place with its bottom edge resting in the groove, and lay the porch base in front of it. Mark the centre panel where the top of the porch base rests against it. Now remove the centre panel and rout a ³/₈in x ¹/₈in groove right across its outer face where marked to locate the porch base. This can now be glued and screwed

in position, taking care that the angle between the panel and the porch base is truly square. Lay the front panel flat on the bench, place the half columns on it (Fig 81), with a half plinth at the top and bottom of each, and position them so that the outer edges of the lower plinths on the outer columns are ¹/₈in inside the base edge.

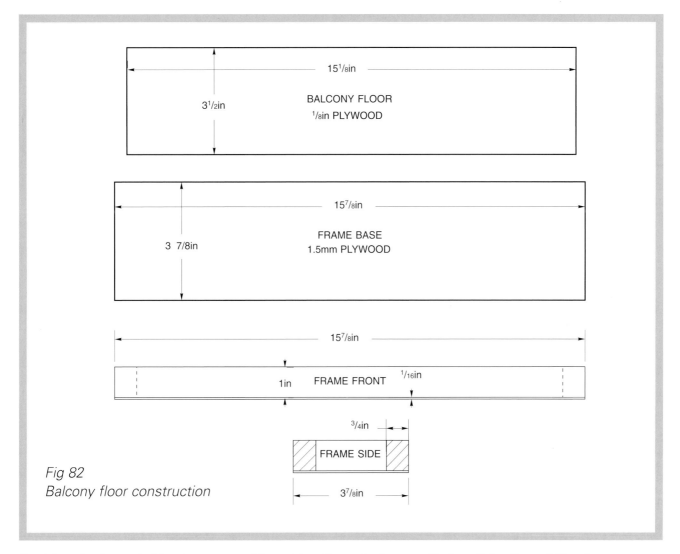

15¹/₈in

BALCONY FLOOR
¹/₈in PLYWOOD

3¹/₂in

15⁷/₈in

FRAME BASE
1.5mm PLYWOOD

3 7/8in

15⁷/₈in

1in   FRAME FRONT   ¹/₁₆in

³/₄in

FRAME SIDE

3⁷/₈in

Fig 82
Balcony floor construction

Position the inner half columns on either side of the doorway so that the plinths do not encroach on the door opening and the two pairs of columns are evenly spaced either side of the lower windows. When satisfied, mark round the profile of the columns and glue them to the panel with impact adhesive.

The lower half plinths are now glued with PVA adhesive and pushed under the half columns to butt the wall. Insert one ³/₄in no 4 screw through the panel into the back of each half column about halfway up. Cut a piece of 1.5mm plywood, 15⁷/₈in long and 3⁷/₈in deep. To the top of this, using impact adhesive, glue a frame of 1in x ³/₄in lime or pine (1in is the vertical measurement, see Fig 82). Plane this assembly fair at the edges. Loosely place the upper half plinths on the half columns, and lay the box assembly in place inset by ⁵/₁₆in at each end of the panel. Mark the positions of the plinths on the underside of the box and fasten with impact adhesive, ensuring that they are flush at the back. Now mark the positions for

the lower plinths of the front full columns on to the porch base, in line with those already glued at the back, and inset ¹/₈in from the front edge of the base. Glue these in place. Mark the positions of the upper plinths for the full columns on the underside of the box, ensuring that the hole centres correspond with those on the base. Glue them in place.

Reassemble with the front columns loosely in place, and using three ³/₄in no 4 screws equally spaced, fasten the box section to the front panel from the back. Dismantle this assembly.

The front and sides for the balcony are now cut from ³/₈in plywood following the pattern in Fig 83. Note that the upstanding edges of the side sections that locate in the rebate behind the front section are ³/₁₆in narrower than those at the back. Assemble the balcony front and sides with panel pins and PVA glue. Mark and drill the three equidistant holes in the bottom of each cutout on the front section, and the two holes in each side section. These holes are ¹/₈in diameter and ¹/₈in deep. The centres are spaced at

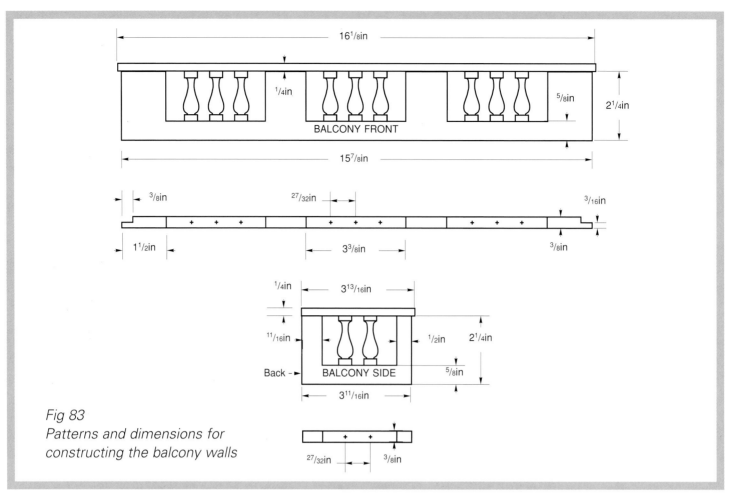

16¹/8in

¹/4in

5⁵/8in

2¹/4in

BALCONY FRONT

15⁷/8in

³/8in

27²⁷/32in

³/16in

1¹/2in

3³/8in

³/8in

¹/4in

3¹³/16in

11¹¹/16in

¹/2in

2¹/4in

Back -

BALCONY SIDE

⁵/8in

3¹¹/16in

Fig 83
Patterns and dimensions for
constructing the balcony walls

27²⁷/32in

³/8in

²⁷/32in. Cut a balcony floor from ¹/8in plywood, ³/4in shorter and ³/8in narrower than the box (Fig 82). Glue and pin this to the top of the box, inset ³/8in at each end and at the front.

Make a capping rail from lime ³/4in wide and ¹/4in thick, long enough to overhang ¹/8in at each end, mitred at the two front corners, and overhanging the plywood balcony walls equally at the inside and outside edges. This is cut square and flush at the back of the side walls. Drill ¹/8in holes ¹/8in deep on the underside of the capping, to correspond with those on the wall sections. Now glue the balusters, which were made previously, into the lower holes, and then glue and pin the capping on top, with the upper spigots of the balusters engaged in the holes in the capping. The balcony wall assembly can now be glued in place on the box. Its walls should fit in the rebate outside the balcony floor.

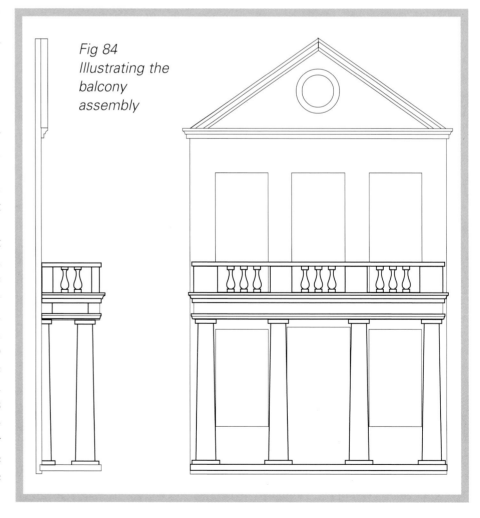

Fig 84
Illustrating the balcony assembly

Front of the Georgian House, showing fully open garden drawer

BALCONY MOULDINGS

Following Fig 84, a 3ft length of the moulding used for the pediment and parapet is now cut, mitred, and glued round the outside of the porch with its top edge level with the bases of the balusters. A further 3ft length of moulding, this time similar to that used for the window surrounds, is mitred and fixed round the porch with its bottom edge flush with the underside of the porch. Both these mouldings should be trimmed flush and square at the back. The complete assembly, including the loose front columns, should now be refastened to the front panel, without glue, as it will be helpful if it can be taken off when decorating.

QUOINS

Prepare 14ft of $^1/_8$in plywood in strips 2ft long and $^3/_4$in wide. Bevel both long edges to half the thickness of the plywood. This is best done with a router and a V-cutter, as the same setting will be needed later to bevel the cut edges. Cut these strips into short pieces as follows:

Centre front panel – ten pieces 1in long, and ten pieces $^5/_8$in long; edge of side panels – twenty-six pieces $1^1/_8$in long, and twenty-four pieces $^5/_8$in long; front of side panels – twenty-four pieces $1^1/_4$in long, and twenty-six pieces $^3/_4$in long; stringers – two pieces each 15in long. Bevel one end only of each quoin to match the bevel on the sides. The lengths of stringer are

Fig 85
To show the arrangement of the quoins

left square-ended with no bevel.

Referring to Fig 85, and starting on the right-hand side of the centre front panel, using impact adhesive glue a 1in quoin immediately below the horizontal pediment moulding with its bevelled end towards the centre of the panel, and its plain end flush at the panel edge. Add a $^5/_8$in quoin below it, and then continue downwards with alternate lengths until the balcony capping rail is reached. Repeat this on the left-hand side. The bottom quoin on each side may need to be a little narrower or deeper to fit exactly. Sand the outer edges smooth and flush with the panel edge. No quoins are fitted to the return walls.

As quoins will be required on the end return walls, a different method is used for the side panels. Cut two strips of 0.8mm plywood each $1^1/_8$in wide and $20^5/_8$in long. Adjust the length to fit from the lower edge of the parapet moulding to $^3/_{16}$in above the lower edge of the panel. Using the $1^1/_8$in and $^5/_8$in quoins, glue these to the 0.8mm plywood strip, starting with a $^5/_8$in quoin at the top of each strip. These two strips should be assembled as a handed pair, with all quoins on one strip flush with its left-hand edge, and all the quoins on the other flush with the

right-hand edge. Counting downwards from the top, for quoin no 13 use a piece $1^1/_8$in long with no end bevel in place of a short quoin. This plain quoin will form one end of the stringing course. Use a craft knife to cut away the 0.8mm plywood in the spaces between the longer quoins. Now glue and pin one of these prepared strips to the outer edge of each side panel with its indented edge towards the back. Plane the other edge flush with the front face of the panel.

Referring again to Fig 85, and starting immediately below the parapet moulding on the front face of each side panel, glue a long quoin in place with its outer edge flush with the face of the short quoin on the edge return. Alternate downwards to quoin no 13. At this point, instead of a long quoin, take a 15in length of stringer and glue this across each panel, stopping $^3/_8$in from the inner edge where the panel fits behind the wall thickener. Continue alternating to the bottom, where once again a narrower quoin may be needed. Note that there should be $^3/_{16}$in clear space below the bottom quoin, to allow the panel to enter the base groove. Trim off the surplus stringing course at the outside edge, plane the edges flush and sand smooth. With both front panels in place, cut the remaining 15½in lengths of stringer to reach from the short lengths on the edges of the front panels, to the back edge of the end walls. Both these strips should be backed with 0.8 plywood before being glued to the walls, to bring them level with the short lengths and quoins which already have a 0.8mm backing.

Although the depth of each quoin is given as ³/4in the slightest variation up or down can make a considerable difference to the running measurement and to the positions of the quoins towards the bottom of the panel. For example, with twenty-six quoins, a difference of plus or minus ¹/32in in depth will result in a difference of plus or minus ¹³/16in (approximately one quoin more or less) overall. This makes very little difference except to the positioning of the stringer. You should therefore, lay the first twelve quoins loosely on the panel before starting to glue and check that the stringer will lie between the upper and lower windows, approximately midway up the panels. If necessary, make a plus or minus adjustment to the first quoin. Next, add a strip of ³/8in x ¹/8in lime across each end wall to cover the seam between the base frame and the wall. This should start behind the ³/8in base groove for the front panels.

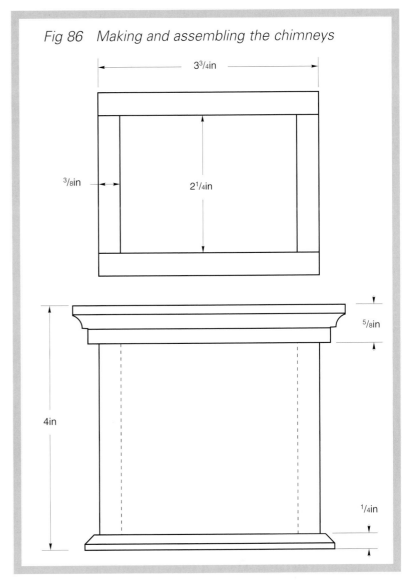

Fig 86   Making and assembling the chimneys

CHIMNEYS

Referring to Fig 86, make two chimneys from ³/8in plywood, in a box section, each 4in high. The mouldings are mitred at the corners, the upper one being the same as that used for the pediment and parapet, the lower moulding being made from plain edged material ¹/4in square, with its top edge lightly chamfered. Make two locating blocks from ³/8in plywood 3in x 2¹/4in and glue these to the top of the flat roof. Each should be inset ³/4in from the back, and 1³/4in from the side. There is no need to glue the chimneys in place, as the locating blocks hold them firmly.

The roof can now be painted with grey emulsion to represent a lead covering.

DRAWER/GARDEN

The drawer front will be hinged at the bottom and allowed to fold forward when the drawer is fully open to reveal the iron railings which are mounted on it. The drawer will be a loose sliding fit in the space between the house base and the carrier. Before making the drawer, bearers of ³/4in x ¹/2in pine should be fixed under the base frame at the front and back, and in line with the centre transverse member, inset ³/8in at the sides.

Referring to Figs 87 and 88, construct the drawer from ³/4in x 3¹/2in pine. The back of the drawer is rebated ³/4in wide and ³/8in deep on the inside face at the ends to locate the two sides, and all three sections are rebated ³/8in x ³/8in on the inside of their bottom edges to receive the ³/8in plywood drawer bottom. The drawer bottom has a rebate ⁵/8in wide and ¹/8in deep on the underside of its front edge to locate the piano hinge. The rebate is made to this depth so that the barrel of the hinge will not project. The drawer so far constructed should now be assembled with PVA glue and screws or nails.

The front is cut from pine 45in long, 3⁷/8in

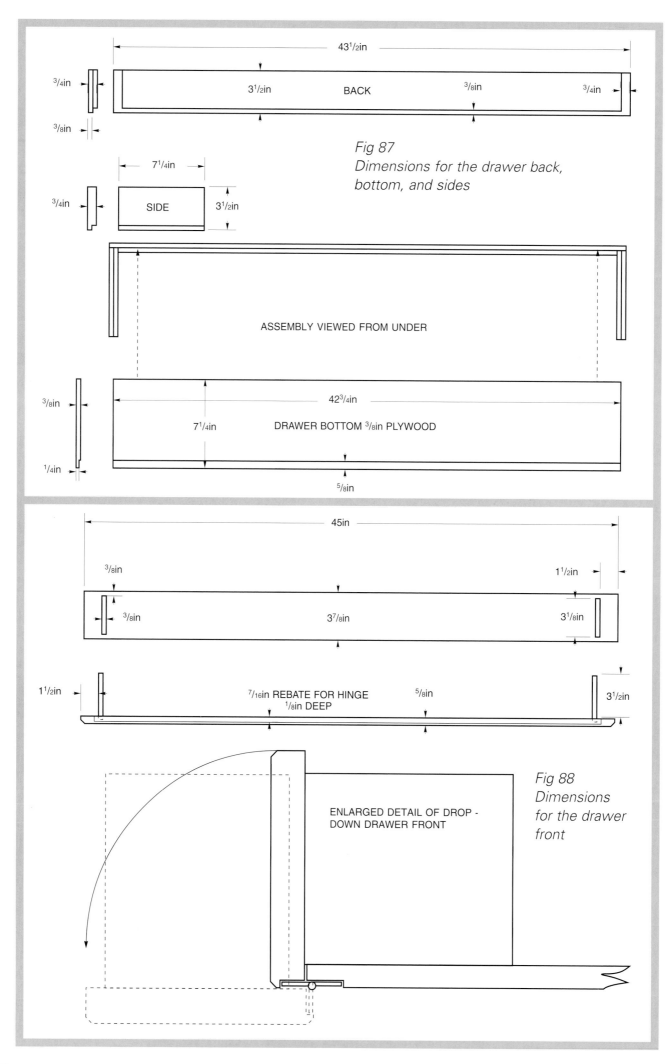

43¹⁄₂in

³⁄₄in

3¹⁄₂in   BACK   ³⁄₈in   ³⁄₄in

³⁄₈in

Fig 87
Dimensions for the drawer back,
bottom, and sides

7¹⁄₄in

³⁄₄in   SIDE   3¹⁄₂in

ASSEMBLY VIEWED FROM UNDER

³⁄₈in

7¹⁄₄in   42³⁄₄in

DRAWER BOTTOM ³⁄₈in PLYWOOD

¹⁄₄in

⁵⁄₈in

45in

³⁄₈in   1¹⁄₂in

³⁄₈in   3⁷⁄₈in   3¹⁄₈in

1¹⁄₂in   ⁷⁄₁₆in REBATE FOR HINGE   ⁵⁄₈in   3¹⁄₂in
¹⁄₈in DEEP

ENLARGED DETAIL OF DROP -
DOWN DRAWER FRONT

Fig 88
Dimensions
for the drawer
front

wide, and $5/8$in thick. A rebate is cut $7/16$in wide and $1/8$in deep at the inside of its bottom edge for the piano hinge which is $42^3/4$in long. The inside face of the drawer front has two $3/8$in wide and $1/4$in deep housings, each $3^1/8$in long, routed across the ends inset $1^1/2$in, and stopped $3/8$in from both the top and bottom edges. Two small rectangles of $3/8$in plywood each $3^1/8$in x $3^3/4$in are now cut and glued, one into each housing at the back of the drawer front, with the $3^3/4$in edges standing vertical and inset into the housings by $1/4$in, so that they project $3^1/2$in upwards. These form a garden wall extension when the drawer is open, and they must be set square to avoid binding when the drawer front is folded. The outside face of the drawer front has its edges chamfered to $45°$. Turn the drawer upside down and screw on the piano hinge. The $1/2$in no 3 brass screws will break through to the inside of the drawer bottom, and should be cut off and filed smooth. Use only three screws in each section at first (middle and ends), and check for alignment before proceeding further. When satisfied insert the remaining screws.

Fit the drawer in the recess on the base frame and with it tightly closed drill $1/8$in diameter holes through the house base into the top of the drawer sides. These holes are $1/2$in back from the front edge of the base frame, and in line with the centreline of the drawer sides – they are $3/4$in deep. Now fully open the drawer so that the inside face of the drawer back is flush with the outside edge of the base frame. Drill again into the drawer sides through the holes already made in the base frame.

Four urns should now be turned from beech or lime (see Fig 89), with a 1in length of $1/8$in diameter brass rod glued centrally into the underside of each of their bases, and projecting $3/4$in. These urns will be used to lock the drawer in the open or closed position by inserting them into the holes just drilled. Two are required to hold the drawer, and two more to fill the extra holes that are visible when the drawer is open. With the drawer open, and the front folded down, check that the height of the two small walls glued at the back of the drawer front, matches the height of the drawer sides. Adjust if necessary by planing a little off the top edge or by adding a thin strip of wood on top.

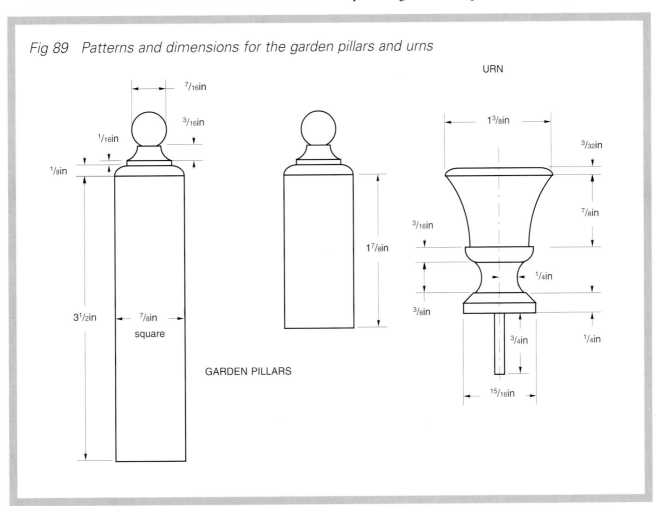

Fig 89   Patterns and dimensions for the garden pillars and urns

URN

GARDEN PILLARS

Left-hand attic bedroom in the Georgian House

STEPS

These are made as shown in Fig 90, from stacked blocks of $^3/4$in thick pine, each 6in long. The bottom step is $6^3/4$in deep and the others are each reduced by $1^{11}/16$in in depth to finish with the top step $1^{11}/16$in deep. After assembling the blocks, glue a facing of $^3/8$in plywood ABCDE at either side, noting that these are only $5^7/8$in long to leave room for the $^7/8$in square pillars at the front. The short pillars (see Fig 89), are made from $^7/8$in square hardwood with the moulded top, excluding the ball, machined with a router. A holding jig will be needed for this. The balls are $^7/16$in diameter wooden beads, fixed with bamboo dowel. While making the short pillars, it is as well to make the six long pillars for the front of the garden (see Fig 89).

Glue the short pillars at each side of the lower step butted tightly against the front edge of the facings ABCDE. A stonework panel of 1.5mm plywood, again cut to the profile ABCDE, will be added to each outside face of the steps behind the pillars. As similar panels will be needed elsewhere in the garden, a total of eleven should be made, following the pattern in Fig 91, each $6^3/16$in long and $3^3/16$in high. The length is governed by the maximum reach of the router from its fence. In this case, a Bosch POF 500 A was used in a stand, with a V-cutter, set to half the thickness of the plywood. Two of these stonework panels should now be trimmed as a handed pair to the profile of the step facing ABCDE, and glued in place against the steps. A $^1/2$in x $^1/8$in capping should be added on the top edges of the step facings flush at the inside, and with the overlap to the outside of the steps. The step assembly should now be set in position centrally against the inside of the back face of the drawer. Do not glue.

Next, cut two pieces of $^3/8$in plywood each $3^1/16$in wide and $7^1/4$in long. Veneer one long edge of each with $^1/16$in lime to bring the width to $3^1/8$in. These two pieces are now trimmed to fit snugly between the drawer back and the back edges of the $^3/8$in wall that is glued into the drawer front, thus bringing the inside face of the drawer sides flush with the inside face of the small walls at the front. Glue a stonework panel of 1.5mm plywood on the inside face of each piece. These two wall sections remain portable,

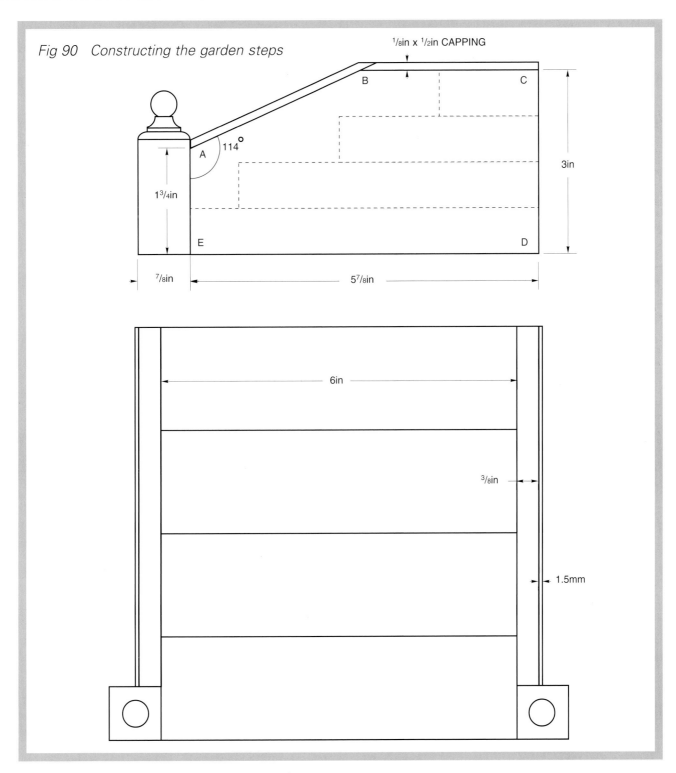

Fig 90   Constructing the garden steps

as they must be removed to enable the drawer front to close. Joins in the stonework are made by cutting out the half blocks from the ends of the panels and interlocking them like a jigsaw.

Three sections of stonework should be fitted to the back of the drawer, reaching from the portable side walls to the steps on either side. Further sections of stonework panel should be glued on the small walls at the back of the drawer front. If these walls were increased in height, a narrow strip of stonework should first be added at the bottom. In any case, the stonework applied here must leave a $^7/_8$in wide space at the front where the front pillars will be glued. The six long front pillars previously made are now drilled at the bottom, $^1/_8$in diameter and $^3/_8$in deep for the $^1/_8$in diameter bamboo spigots that will be used to locate them. Corresponding holes are drilled in the back of the drawer front, three at each end, at $7^1/_8$in centres, starting $^7/_{16}$in inside the walls and $^{13}/_{16}$in from the front edge. The end pillars will eventually be glued to

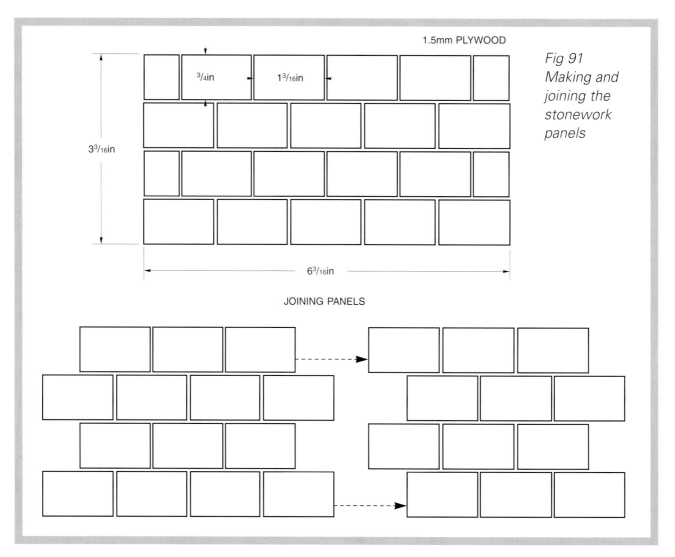

1.5mm PLYWOOD

³/₄in

1³/₁₆in

3³/₁₆in

6³/₁₆in

*Fig 91
Making and
joining the
stonework
panels*

JOINING PANELS

the walls, but none of these components should be fixed until the painting is completed. The railings shown here are from John Watkins and are fixed to the pillars by their extended horizontal rails which locate in holes drilled in the pillar sides.

Paint all the posts and the step facings with Humbrol pale stone. Scribe paving 2in square on the base in front of the house, and also on the balcony base. This should be painted a more sandy colour than the pillars (Humbrol desert sand). Similar colour should be applied to the steps and the garden wall stone panels. Paint the inside of the drawer front dark grey and glue either a grass flock paper or apply model railway powders to the bottom of the drawer inside the hinge. Paint the outside of the drawer and the sides of the base frame with light grey emulsion.

KITCHEN CHIMNEY BREAST

Make the kitchen chimney breast following Fig 92. The range has been made from a Phoenix Kit. If any other make is used the inter-

nal opening must be adjusted accordingly. The shell is made from ³/₈in plywood with a backing of 1.5mm plywood. Cornice moulding is glued round the top edge, mitred at the corners, but cut at the back ends to fit neatly against that already applied in the kitchen. A facing of lime with a moulded edge is applied round the opening, and a shelf fitted above it. The inside of the opening is covered with a tile paper and the drying rack, constructed from three lengths of ¹/₁₆in brass rod fitted into end blocks of ¹/₈in square lime, each 1¹/₄in long, is glued into the opening 4¹/₈in above the floor.

ELECTRICS

Thread a length of Cir-Kit twin wire through each of the channels under the floorboards at first-floor level. Take the wire down through the hole in the floor at each light position. Bare the ends and wrap them round the pins of a Cir-Kit canopy connector before hammering this into the underside of the floor – a special punch, supplied by Cir-Kit for this purpose, is available

Attic centre school-room in the Georgian House

from Dijon. The lights in the hall and library, and the candlesticks in the dining-room are from Peter Kennedy, the others are from Wood 'n' Wool. All are fitted with replaceable bi-pin bulbs. The lights in the attic rooms are all of the plug-in type from Wood 'n' Wool, and are fitted with grain-of-wheat bulbs. Moulded ceiling roses are available for the ceiling lights and, if used, they must be drilled out in the centre to accommodate the canopy connectors.

Glue the roses, if required, to the ceiling with quick-setting epoxy adhesive. Set the side floors in place, and mark the horizontal tape on the back wall where the wires emerge from the floor. Insert a pair of eyelets at each point. A further pair of eyelets is inserted in the tape at the back of the centre section (library), 6½in from the left-hand wall. On the floor of this section, which remains portable, gouge a groove along the back edge from the point where the wire emerges to the position of the eyelets. This houses the wire when the floor is pushed right in. A two-pin plug should be fitted to this wire.

This model has glowing embers in the drawing-room fireplace (Dijon). If these are required add a further pair of eyelets at the back of the fireplace opening.

The windows can now be glued in place in the end walls, flush with the outside faces to leave a rebate for the glazing, and the surrounds and sills can be glued to the outside of the walls. Following this, the side floors are glued and pinned to the cornice.

Now shorten the wire tails at the back of the side floors, bare the ends, and solder them into the eyelets. The wire will be hidden later behind the skirting which will be notched accordingly.

SKIRTING

This can either be bought ready-made, or you can make it yourself following the pattern in Fig 70. It should now be dry-fitted, mitred in the corners, and butted against the door surrounds and fireplaces. Mark all the loose sections on the back with their respective room positions, and paint them with two coats of Humbrol satin

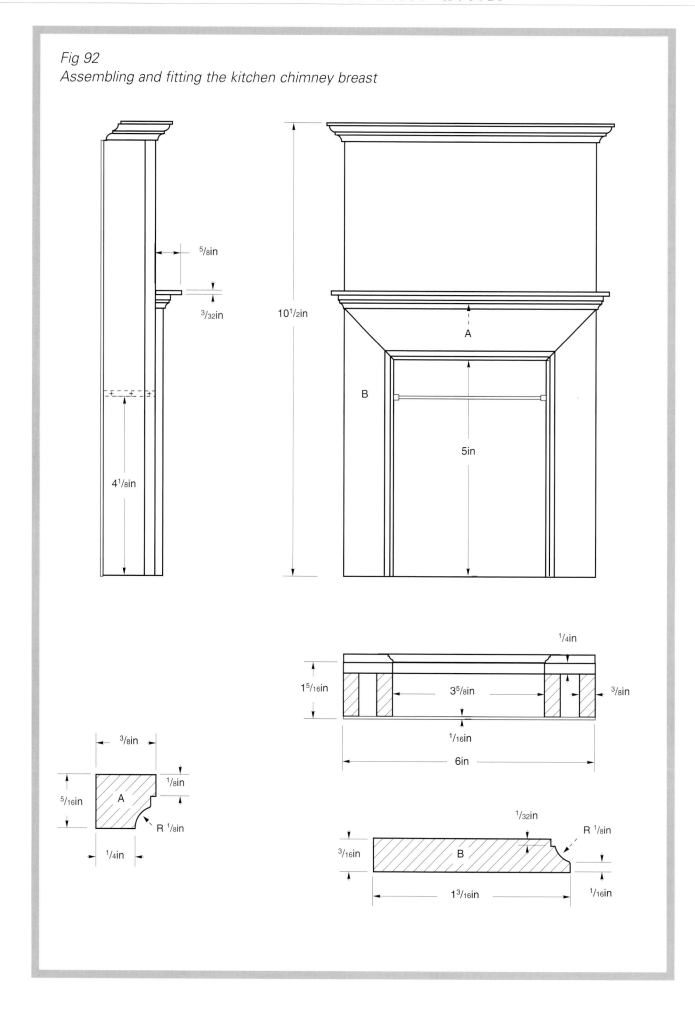

Fig 92
Assembling and fitting the kitchen chimney breast

Georgian House landing / library

white. They can now be put aside ready to be glued in place when the decorating and wallpapering is completed. A mahogany skirting, 1/8in thick with a backing of 0.8mm plywood, 1³/16in high, is required for the landing. It forms a continuation from point X at the top of the combined skirting and support XYZD on the lower stairs.

DECORATING

The remaining internal doors, including the two dummies, should now be painted with two coats of Humbrol satin white. When the paint is dry the door knobs can be fitted, and the doors put aside until decoration is complete. The floors at all three levels have already had one priming coat of varnish. Lightly sand them all, and apply one more coat. Stop in any gaps between the ceiling and cornice, sand smooth and then apply two coats of white emulsion to cornice and ceilings. The interior walls can now be papered. The wallpapers in the hall, library, and dining-room are from The Singing Tree, and those in

the three bedrooms and drawing-room are by Mini Graphics, available through Dijon. The central attic rooms are painted with magnolia emulsion, and the kitchen with white emulsion. When the wallpaper has dried, the dummy doors in the library can be glued in place, each ⁷/8in from the wall beside it, together with the skirting throughout the interior. Replace all the interior doors in their respective positions, lightly gluing the exposed hinge flaps on each with a very small amount of epoxy resin before pushing the hinges into the slots in the door frames. The interior is now complete.

EXTERIOR

The windows on the three front panels are now glued in place, all flush with the outside faces, the surrounds and sills having already been glued on the outside. All wall surfaces on the outside of the house are painted with two coats of emulsion. The colour used here is peanut butter from Sanderson's Spectrum range. The balcony mouldings, balusters, capping, and

Main bedroom in the Georgian House

columns, together with the parapet and pediment mouldings and capping, and the quoins, stringing courses, and window surrounds on the remainder of the building are painted with two coats of Humbrol pale stone. The balcony can now be fixed in place, and the screw holes stopped over at the back of the panel. The glazing can now be carried out using 2mm glass held in place with narrow strips of white card glued to the sides of the window openings behind them. When glazing the front panels, wood strip should be used in place of card, as it can be planed flush with the inside of the panels without causing damage to the wallpapers. Note that

on the dormer windows, the glass is inserted first, followed by the window, and a facing of 1.5mm plywood, 5/16in wide, mitred at the corners, is glued to the outside of the dormer carcase round the outside of the window. The facing should be painted pale stone. The gable window has its glazing bars cut from card (see Fig 76). Insert these from the back, followed by the glass which again is held in place by a strip of card. The inside faces of the front panels can now be painted or varnished – varnish is preferable as it will not show fingermarks. It only remains to connect each of the lights to its canopy connector, and set them in place.

GEORGIAN HOUSE – LIST OF SUPPLIERS

Lucy Askew: Dining-room fireplace and mirror.
Avon Miniatures: Dining-room and kitchen crockery, drawing-room vases and jug, wash basin and pot in left-hand attic bedroom.
Peggy Birrell: Flower arrangement in hall.
Carol Black: Servants' bells and sheet music.
Gordon Blacklock: Silver wine coaster, toast rack, and condiment set.
Blackwells: Dining-room carpet, parquet flooring in hall, oval picture frames in main bedroom.
Patricia Borwick: Needlepoint footstool (kit).
Bryntor Miniatures: Kitchen storage jars.
Irene Campbell: Kitchen jug, jug and wash basin in right-hand attic bedroom.
Cassel's: Egg cups, joint of lamb.
C & D Crafts: Basket.
Crafts & Collectables: Library steps.
Terry Curran: Kitchen storage jars.
Dijon: Cir-Kit twin tape, canopy connectors, Mini Graphics wallpapers in bedrooms and drawing-room; hall sideboard, bed (re-painted) and mirror in right-hand attic bedroom, spinet and display cabinet in library. Bed (adapted), bedside cabinet, chair and carpet in main bedroom, fireplace, glowing embers, foot-stool, striped wing chair, sofa, small table and carpet in drawing-room, garden seat (kit).
The Dolls' House (Covent Garden): Suit of armour, pictures, globe, music stool, wardrobe in main bedroom.
Dolphin Miniatures: Silver coffee set, dining table, chairs, semi-circular tables, wine cooler, kitchen dresser, wheelback chair, salt box, candle box, table, plate rack, and worktops. Copperware (Bodo Hennig), circular hall table, silverware, washstand, bedside chest, chest of drawers, and chair in right-hand attic bedroom, chair, chest of drawers, mirror and slop-pail in left-hand attic bedroom, sewing machine (Bodo Hennig), desks, stools, rocking horse, toy box, chair, books and blackboard in attic centre room, bookcase and books in library, mirror and upholstered chair in main bedroom, plain upholstered chairs, bureau and bookcase in drawing-room.
Dorking Dolls' House Gallery: Child's slate and chalk, small spaniel in the garden.
David Edwards: Silver brushes.
Marie Theresa Endean: All the dolls.

Escutcheon: Corner what-not in hall, dressing table in main bedroom.
Fantasie: Linen basket in right-hand attic bedroom, and high chair in attic centre room.
Hobby's: Door knobs and hinges, open atlas and rug in library, carpet in attic centre room.
Isobel Hockey: Crochet pot holder in kitchen, and sampler in attic centre room.
C.A. & B.A. Hooper: Curtain rails throughout. Coffee grinder and water carrier in the kitchen, fire irons and door stop in drawing-room, and front door knob and knocker.
Carol Lodder: Kitchen crockery and storage jars.
Stuart McCabe: Silver chamberstick in main bedroom, and candlesticks in the drawing-room.
Miniature Curios: Glass bottles in dining-room.
Miniature Dreams: Pot of stew in the kitchen, dressing-table set and picture frame in right-hand attic bedroom.
Lynne Mitchell: Roses in main bedroom.
Ottervale China: Vase of flowers in right-hand attic bedroom.
Leo Pilley: Glass demi-john in kitchen.
Phoenix Model Developments: Small clock in dining-room, kitchen range and pump, bed and fireplace in left-hand attic bedroom, fire basket in drawing-room.
The Pram Collection: Baby carriage with sunshade.
Quaintways: Dunces cap, satchel, bell and pencils in centre attic room, butterfly-display table in library.
The Singing Tree: Wallpapers in hall, library and dining-room.
Terence Stringer: Silver shoe pincushion in main bedroom, small firescreen in drawing-room.
Sussex Crafts: Bucket and housemaids' box in kitchen, fireplace in right-hand attic bedroom.
Thames Valley Crafts: Tea and flour, jar and pill bottle in right-hand attic bedroom.
Bernardo Traettino: Tilting pedestal table in dining-room.
Warwick Miniatures: Toys in central attic room.
John Watkins: Garden railings.
Wood 'n' Wool Miniatures: Chandeliers in bedroom, drawing-room, dining-room and kitchen, oil lamp and candlesticks in attic room.
The chandeliers in the hall and library, and the candlesticks in the dining-room, made by Peter Kennedy, are from the author's collection. The porcelain figurines are also from this collection.

WATER MILL

This is not a copy of any particular building, but the workings follow as closely as possible those traditionally used. An undershot water-wheel, which is chain-driven from a small electric motor, operates all the essential features such as millstones, sack hoist, and flour dresser. A small, one up, one down, cottage is attached to the mill, with access over the millstream by a plank bridge.

Fully fitted interior of the mill and cottage

TIMBER REQUIREMENTS – WATER MILL

WOOD	THICKNESS	AREA sq ft	
Birch plywood	1.5mm	5	
	1/8in (3mm)	1	
	1/4in (6mm)	5 1/2	
	3/8in (9mm)	23	

WOOD	THICKNESS in	WIDTH in	LENGTH ft	in
Elm	1/32	7/16	2	6
		1/2	1	-
		17/32	6	-
	1/8	1/4	4	-
		1/2	4	-
	1/4	1/4		8
		3/8	22	-
		1/2	12	-
		5/8	3	-
		1 1/8		10
	9/32	1 1/8		10
	5/16	5/16	3	-
		3/8	1	1
	3/8	1/2		8
		5/8	1	8
	1/2	3/4	2	-
		1 1/8		6
		2	2	6
	9/16	9/16	5	-
	5/8	7/8		10
		1 1/8		6
	11/16	3/4	3	-
	3/4in	1		4
	13/16in	1 1/8	2	-
Pine	7/8	2 1/8	18	-
Lime	1/8	1/8	8	-
		3/8	3	-

Although this building is a freelance design, the workings follow fairly closely those traditionally used. An undershot wheel is featured, and the gearing has been adapted, as far as possible, to use stock items. Some purists may feel that the considerable expense of having gears specially cut is worthwhile. The 'works' are made at a very early stage, and are removable for adjustment and attention if required.

Note the framing is wood and a certain amount of movement is likely due to atmospheric changes. Also the joints in parts of the Hurst Frame are designed to be slack and are held by screws only. This enables small adjustments to be made with wedges or strips of veneer.

If you decide to motorize the model, the Crouzet mains motor, running at 10 rpm, is the most convenient (see colour illustration page 137). Although double-insulated and fitted with only two supply wires, it should be earthed as a safety precaution. This is arranged simply by adding a wire from the junction box to one of the motor mounting screws. The mains supply should be by a 3-core cable with its earth

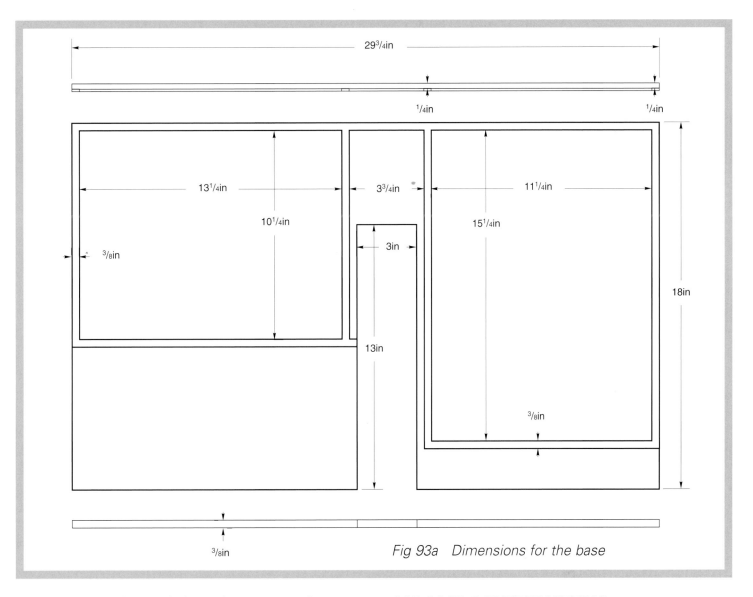

Fig 93a   Dimensions for the base

nected to the earth from the motor at the junction box. *Take care not to confuse the wiring.* For example, the lighting is 12v DC, and should on no account come into contact with the 240v AC motor system. The Clearbox motor from Hobby's (illustrated on page 181) is a useful alternative, but is 6v DC and rather noisy unless fitted on rubber mountings. Transmission to the water-wheel in both cases is arranged by sprocket wheels and chain, both of which are available from Hobby's.

The Hurst Frame is the most complex part of the model and the more care you can give to its construction the better as it will save a lot of time and trial and error when getting gears to engage properly, and the machinery to run smoothly.

Note that throughout construction, very little mention is made of varnishing. This is deliberate as most of the timberwork looks better when left with a natural finish.

CARCASE CONSTRUCTION

Following Figs 93a–93g, cut the base, back panel, end and partition walls for the cottage, two side walls for the mill, and the small arched front wall over the water-wheel from $3/8$in plywood. Note that the partition wall for the cottage extends at its front edge $1/8$in further than the end wall so that it can engage in the groove at the back of the arch wall. These are all the fixed carcase components.

Cut out the window and fireplace openings, and rout the $3/8$in x $1/8$in rebates and grooves where shown. It will be easier to work if the long 3in wide cutout in the base for the water-wheel and the $3^3/4$in x $6^1/2$in cutout in the back panel for motor access are both left until the routing is completed. The triangular pad of $3/8$in plywood, corresponding to the upper 6in of the partition wall, shown on the outside of the inner mill wall, can be cut out, but not fixed until the top edge of the wall has been bevelled.

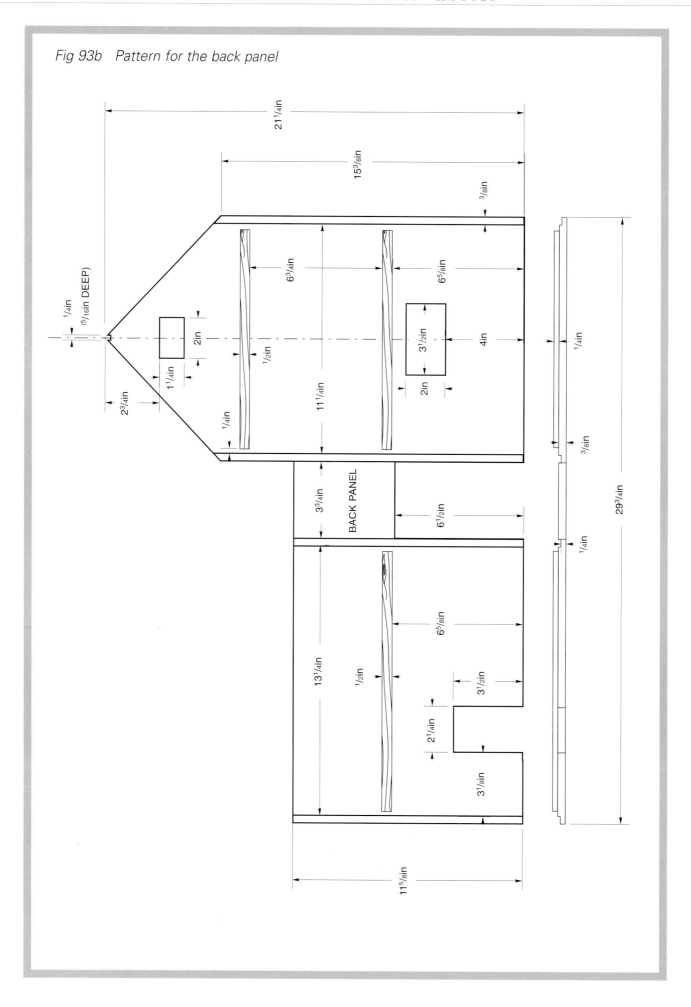

Fig 93b   Pattern for the back panel

Drill the $3/16$in diameter holes for the water-wheel shaft through the inner mill wall and cottage partition wall where shown in Figs 93d and 93e. Cut notches $1/4$in wide and $5/16$in deep at the tops of all gables, including the triangular pad, to accept the ridgeboards which will be made and fitted later. Assemble the carcase with three $3/4$in no 4 screws in each joint line, ensuring that all bottom edges are level, *but do not glue yet*. Now fix the carcase to its base. Using spacers of scrap plywood, mark a pencil line on each inside wall at the height of the top edge of the floor bearers (Figs 93b–93f). Using the cottage end wall and the gabled back wall of the mill as a guide, bevel the tops of the remaining wall sections to the appropriate roof slope. Dismantle the carcase and veneer the outer edges of the mill side walls and the cottage end wall, with elm $3/8$in wide and $1/16$in thick. Still following Figs 93b–93f, cut sufficient $1/2$in x $1/4$in elm for all the floor bearers. Texture the outer and bottom faces of the bearers, using a Minicraft disc sander and a saw-blade (see page 187), and glue all the bearers in place, noting that those on the

mill side walls and cottage ends are stopped $1/8$in from the back edge of the panels to allow them to fit into the back panel. The bearers on the back walls are stopped $1/4$in in from each end so that they will fit between the bearers on the side walls.

Glue and screw the triangular pad to the outside of the inner mill wall so that it conforms with the gable on the cottage partition wall, having first removed $1/8$in from its short vertical back edge so that the wall can enter the groove in the back panel. Frame the room side of the cottage partition wall with $5/8$in x $1/4$in elm at the roof slopes, and $3/4$in x $1/4$in elm at the front edge (Fig 93e). Note that this latter framing is inset by $1/2$in at the front to fit behind the arched waterwheel wall, which has a length of $3/8$in elm or plywood, $1 1/8$in wide, glued behind it flush with the outside of the groove. This will form a land for the inner end of the sliding cottage front. Both the top edge of this strip and the top edge of the arched wall, should now be bevelled to the roof slope of the cottage partition wall.

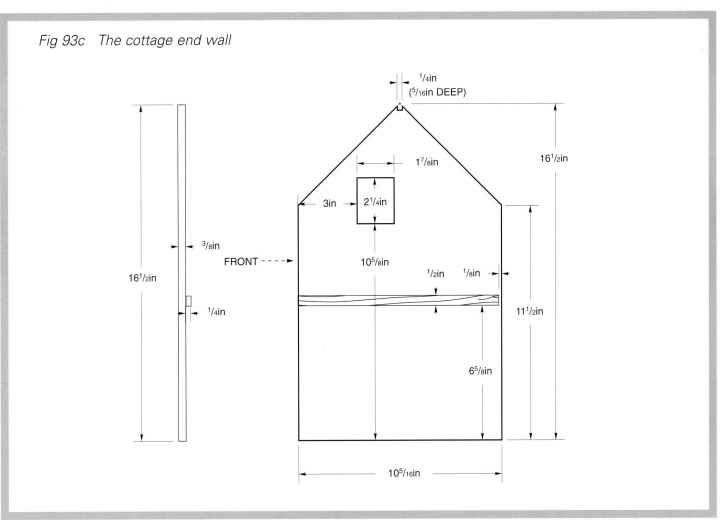

Fig 93c   The cottage end wall

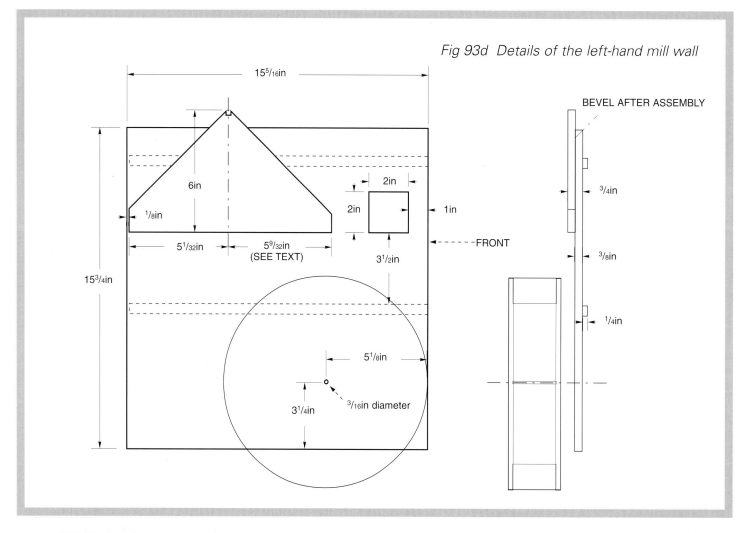

Fig 93d *Details of the left-hand mill wall*

WINDOWS

Referring to Fig 94, make all the windows for the mill, except that on the front panel. Note that the openings are lined at the top and bottom with $^3/_8$in x $^1/_8$in elm, having mullions of $^3/_{16}$in square elm glued between them and set obliquely. Lintels and sills of $^1/_{16}$in thick elm, waned and textured, with an average depth of $^1/_4$in, are now glued to both the insides and outsides of the windows – the lower edges of the lintels, and the upper edges of the sills, should conform with the open edges of the linings. A suitably textured lintel, $^1/_2$in deep, $^1/_8$in thick, and $3^3/_4$in long, is glued over the fireplace opening. The windows for the cottage are identical to those on the Swan Inn. There are two small four-pane windows and one double six-pane window. These can now be made and painted with two coats of Humbrol satin white. Having first lined the opening with $^3/_8$in x $^1/_8$in elm, glue one small window in place in the end wall of the cottage. The others should be put aside for later use on the cottage front. All the mill windows and the linings of the cottage window,

should now be painted with one coat of vinegar mix (see page 18) to achieve a weathered look.

MOTOR MOUNTING

This should now be made to the dimensions in Fig 95, and the guides fitted to the carcase base. The guides are made from a laminate of $^3/_8$in and $^1/_4$in plywood, glued and screwed to the base, one lying against the side wall of the mill, and the other at right angles to it, across the edge of the base cut-out. Screw Meccano double-arm cranks (part no 62 B), bored to $^3/_{16}$in, to the inside of the inner mill wall, and to the outside of the cottage partition wall, to coincide with the holes previously bored through these sections. Screw a junction box for the motor, and a connector block for the lighting, to the outside face of the left-hand mill wall close to the back edge and 3–4in above floor level.

FINAL ASSEMBLY

The carcase can now be reassembled with glue, apart from the small arched front wall, which is best left portable for now. Because the water-

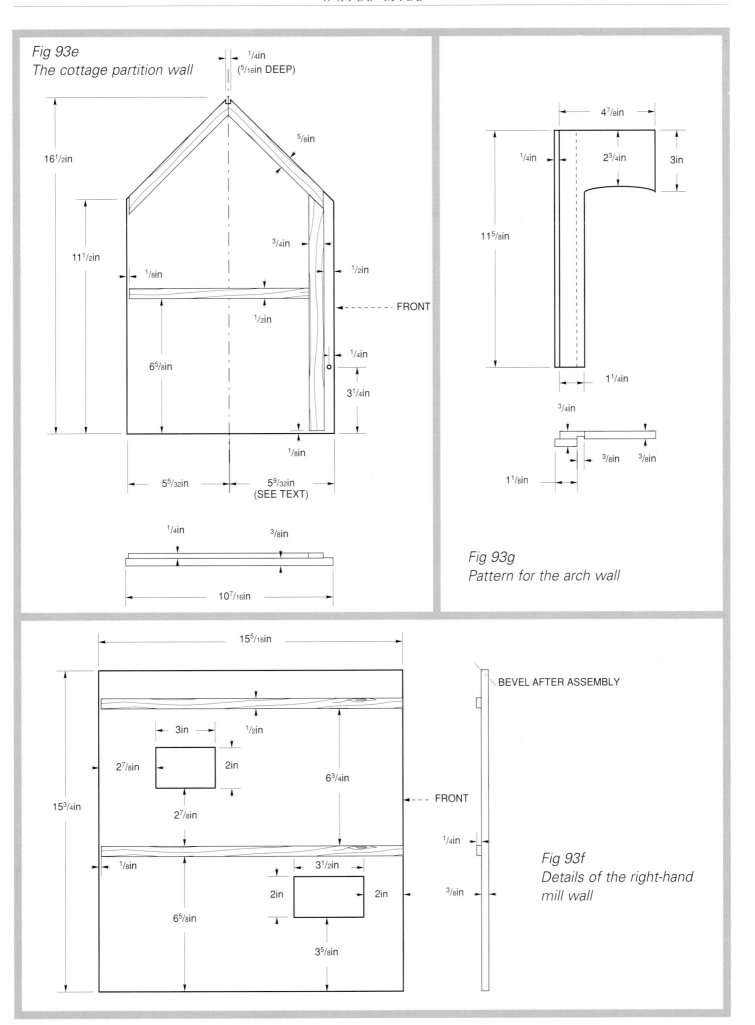

Fig 93e
The cottage partition wall

¹/₄in
(⁵/₁₆in DEEP)

16¹/₂in

⁵/₈in

11¹/₂in

³/₄in

¹/₂in

¹/₈in

FRONT

¹/₂in

6⁵/₈in

¹/₄in

3¹/₄in

¹/₈in

5⁵/₃₂in

5⁹/₃₂in
(SEE TEXT)

¹/₄in

³/₈in

10⁷/₁₆in

Fig 93g
Pattern for the arch wall

4⁷/₈in

¹/₄in

2³/₄in

3in

11⁵/₈in

1¹/₄in

³/₄in

³/₈in

³/₈in

1¹/₈in

15⁵/₁₆in

BEVEL AFTER ASSEMBLY

3in

¹/₂in

2⁷/₈in

2in

6³/₄in

15³/₄in

2⁷/₈in

FRONT

¹/₄in

¹/₈in

3¹/₂in

Fig 93f
Details of the right-hand
mill wall

2in

2in

³/₈in

6⁵/₈in

3⁵/₈in

Fig 94 Constructing the mill windows

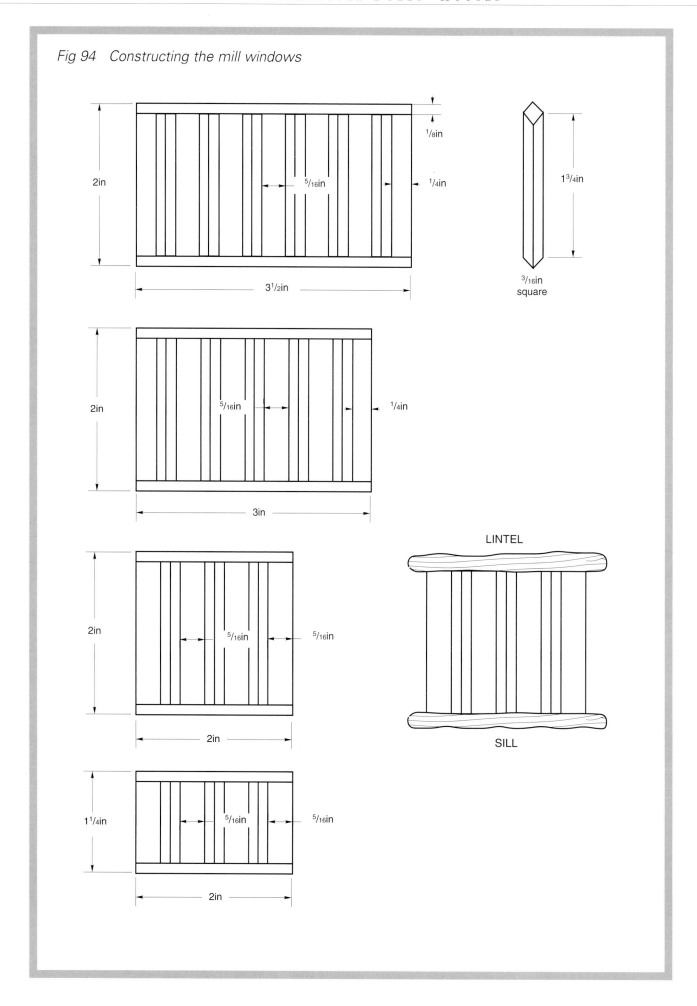

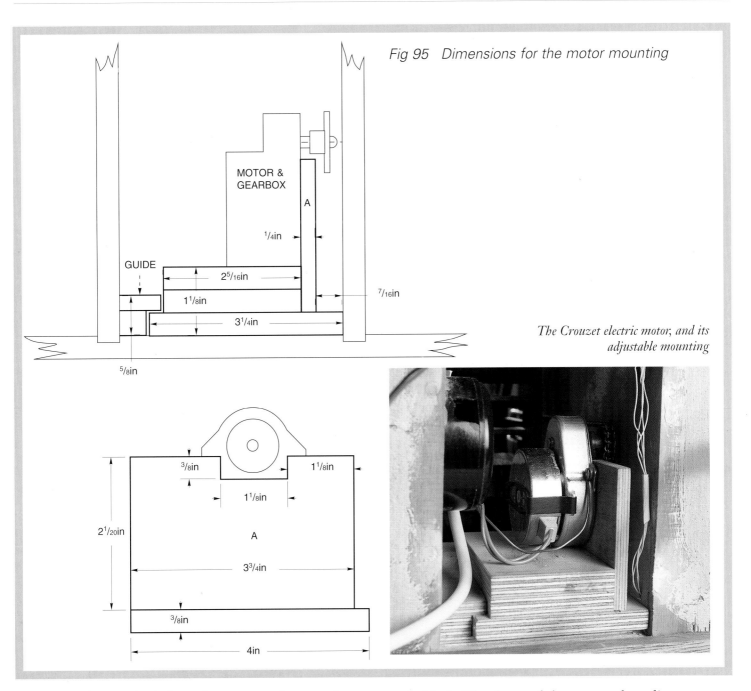

Fig 95   Dimensions for the motor mounting

MOTOR & GEARBOX

A

GUIDE

1/4in

2⁵/₁₆in

1¹/₈in

3¹/₄in

7/16in

5/8in

3/8in   1¹/₈in

1¹/₈in

2¹/₂₀in

A

3³/₄in

3/8in

4in

The Crouzet electric motor, and its adjustable mounting

wheel extends below the carcase base, a base frame is required to give clearance. This also provides the groundwork for a landscaped area in front of the buildings and should be made next.

Referring to Fig 96, make the base frame from mahogany or good-quality pine 2¹/₈in wide and ⁷/₈in thick. All joints should be glued, and either screwed or nailed. The joints at the centre should be made first, as they become inaccessible later. The fastenings should be well countersunk, or punched below the surface and stopped over. When the glue has set, rest the carcase on top of the frame so that its outside edges are on the centrelines of the frame members that support them (⁷/₁₆in inset at the back

and sides). The front of the carcase base lies on the centreline of the two transverse members near the front of the frame.

Cut sufficient mahogany or pine, ⁷/₁₆in wide and ³/₈in deep, to make a border round the base frame. Starting at the back, glue and pin a strip across the top of the base frame flush with its back edge. Continue along each side of the carcase base, and beyond it, to a point ⁷/₁₆in short of the front edge of the base frame. A further strip will be added across the front of the base frame later. The exposed area of frame in front of the carcase base is now covered with ³/₈in plywood, cut to fit between the border strips already fitted at the sides and with its front edge inset ⁷/₁₆in from the front of the base frame.

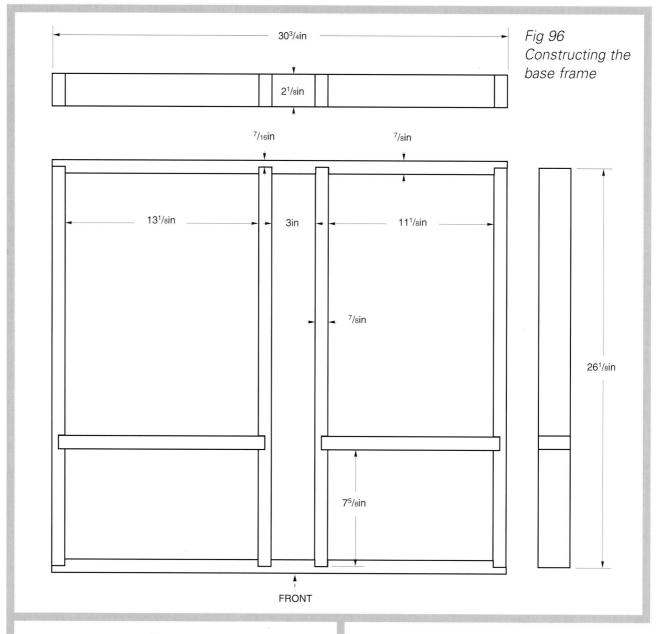

*Fig 96
Constructing the base frame*

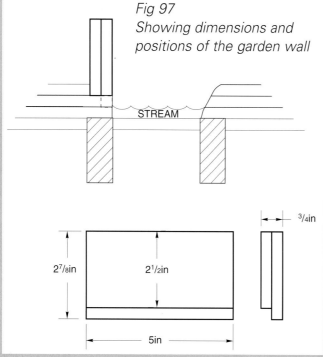

*Fig 97
Showing dimensions and positions of the garden wall*

Lightly tack this in place, and mark the cutout for the millstream as follows:

At the right-hand side, mark a line from the water-wheel slot in the carcase base to run in a sweeping curve to a point about 9$\frac{1}{2}$in from the left-hand end of the front edge. A similar line is drawn from the left-hand side of the wheel slot to a point 2$\frac{1}{2}$in from the left-hand end at the front. This should run roughly parallel to the first line (see colour illustration page 129). Cut away the area between the lines and, using their cut edges as guides, increase the thickness of the river banks by gluing two additional sections of $\frac{3}{8}$in plywood at each side (Fig 97). The right-hand sections are roughly triangular in shape, running from a width of about 2in at the inside end to 11in at the outside end.

Fully equipped mill interior

Fig 98 Constructing the water-wheel

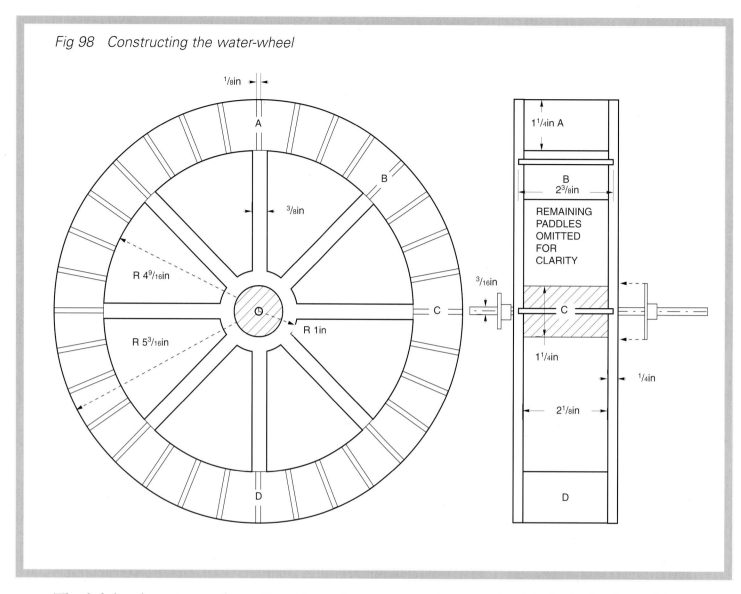

The left-hand section is about 4in wide at the inside, running out to a width of about $^1/_2$in at the front. Further pieces are glued to the top surface of the carcase base to continue this raised section back to the outside edges of the grooves for the building fronts, each finishing about 1in wide at this point. *This measurement is particularly important at the front of the mill as space must be left for the lower door to fold back.* The lower section, to the left of the stream, is notched $^3/_8$in for a distance of 5in from its inner end and a wall $2^1/_2$in high and $^3/_4$in thick (Fig 97), is screwed to its edge.

Glue and pin these raised sections in place and add the remaining $^7/_{16}$in wide strip across the front of the base frame. Using a larger disc sander (3–4in diameter), lightly round over the river banks, and feather the outer edges so that they flow and blend into the remaining single-thickness covering. Take care when cutting that the front edges of the contour pads fixed to the carcase base match with the back edges of those fixed to the base frame and that neither overhangs the groundwork under it. This will ensure that the buildings can be separated easily from the base frame for ease of transport. Do not fix the carcase to the base frame. Fill in the open river bed area with scrap plywood, cut and fitted between the frame members and glued to the underside of the $^3/_8$in base covering. Seal the edges with masking tape.

MILL WORKINGS

All the machinery should now be made and fitted before proceeding further with the buildings. First, following Fig 98, make the water-wheel from $^1/_4$in plywood. Cut out the two $10^3/_8$in diameter discs, using the router or jigsaw, and then rout the slots round the perimeter on one face of each. Take care that the slots on one disc will match those on the other when the discs are placed together. The slots are $^1/_8$in

Unfurnished interior of the mill, showing the joint between the building and base, and the profile of the contour pads

wide and $^1/_8$in deep, extending inwards for $1^1/_4$in. Drill a $^3/_{16}$in diameter hole through the centre of each disc. Now, using a fretsaw or jigsaw, cut away the area between the spokes on each disc and sand smooth. The hub is turned from hardwood $1^1/_4$in in diameter and $2^1/_8$in long, with a $^3/_{16}$in diameter hole bored through its centre. *This must be accurate, to ensure that the wheel will run truly*. Cut thirty-two paddles from $^1/_8$in plywood, each $2^3/_8$in wide and $1^1/_4$in deep.

Before assembly, cut a $7^1/_2$in length of $^3/_{16}$in mild steel rod, for the water shaft. Glue the hub between the wheel discs, using the shaft to centre them and ensuring that the paddle slots are all in line. Four paddles, inserted at 90° to each other but not glued, will hold this alignment. Additional fastening is provided by pinning through the central section of each wheel disc into the end of the hub. When the glue has set, all the paddles should be glued in place between the discs, and additionally secured with a pair of

railway track pins driven into them from the wheel disc at either side. These pins are positioned $^1/_4$in from each edge of the paddles. When set, the wheel should be sprayed with matt or satin black. A Meccano bush wheel (part no 24), bored to $^3/_{16}$in is screwed to one side of the wheel, centred on the shaft. This provides a means of fastening the wheel to the shaft. Tilt the carcase back on the base frame, and insert the shaft through the wheel and the bearing plates on the walls. Test that it revolves freely. If it binds, adjust the position of the bearing plate on one wall. The shaft should extend 3in into the mill building at one end, and $^1/_4$in into the cottage wall at the other.

Remove the wheel and shaft and, after trimming the shaft to length, if necessary, reassemble with a sprocket to the left of the wheel (cottage side), and the screwed Meccano bush wheel to the right. Add one or two $^3/_{16}$in washers between the wheel and the mill wall. Fasten the

141

Fig 99
Details and dimensions for the lower Hurst Frame front

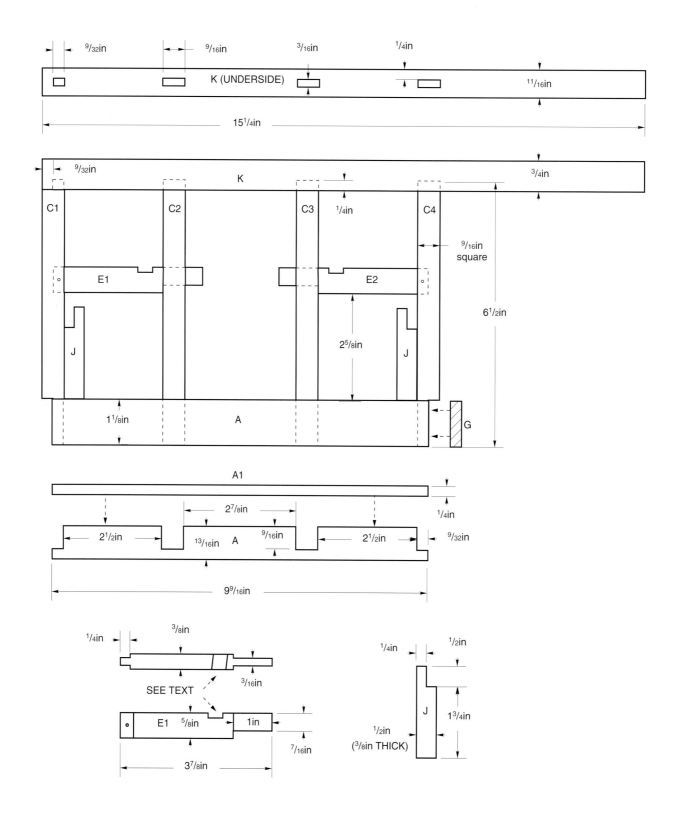

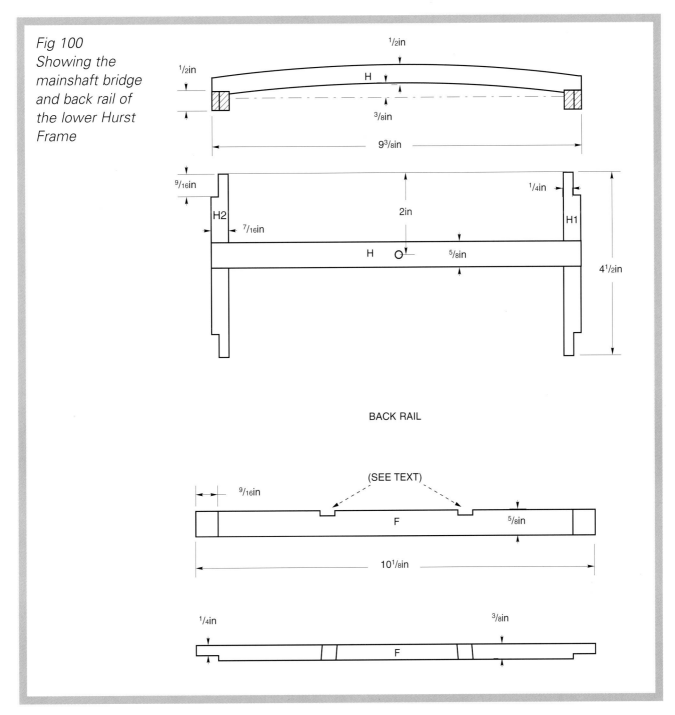

*Fig 100
Showing the
mainshaft bridge
and back rail of
the lower Hurst
Frame*

BACK RAIL

(SEE TEXT)

motor to its mounting block, and add a further sprocket on its shaft. With the motor pushed fully forward (the base of the mounting block fully engaged with the transverse slide), cut and fit a length of sprocket chain to fit loosely around both sprocket wheels. This chain can be tensioned by sliding the motor mounting block towards the back of the building.

Connect the motor and earth wires to the junction box provided, and make a further connection here to a length of 3-core cable, terminating in a square-pin plug fitted with a 3 amp fuse. The length of this cable will be governed by the position of the building in relation

to the nearest outlet socket in your house. Test the assembly so far for free running, adding or subtracting washers as required, and adjusting the position of the wheel and sprockets on the shaft as necessary.

HURST FRAME

This is the timber framework which supports the remainder of the mill machinery, and will be made next, following Figs 99–102 and the illustration on page 144. The lower frame, from ground floor to first floor should be made first. Cut the two base beams A and B from elm $1\frac{1}{8}$in x $\frac{13}{16}$in, each $9\frac{9}{16}$in long. The front

Left: Hurst Frame assembly, showing main shaft, line shaft, mill-stone spindle, and watershaft bearing block

Above: Spout floor with Hurst Frame removed to show pit wheel, watershaft and water-wheel

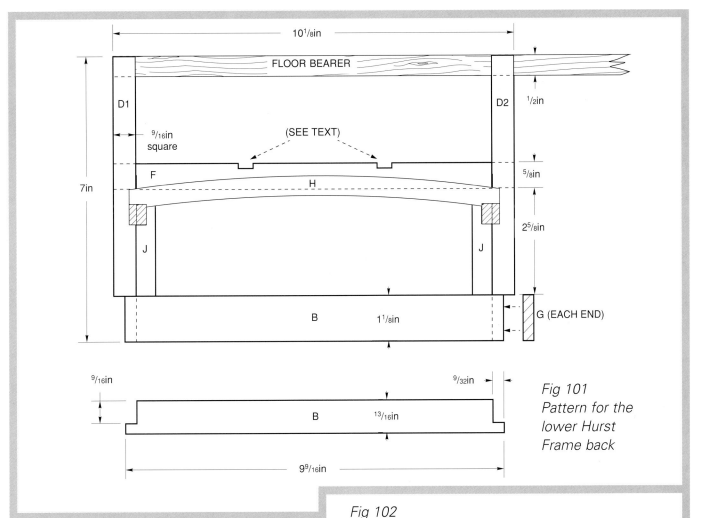

Fig 101
Pattern for the lower Hurst Frame back

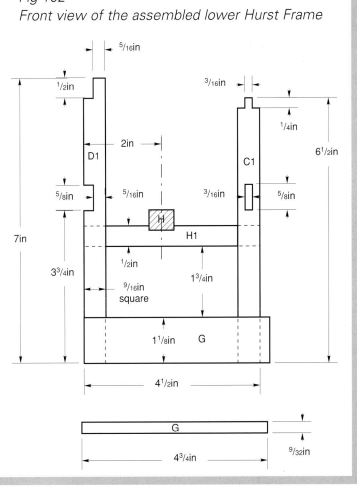

Fig 102
Front view of the assembled lower Hurst Frame

beam A has two slots, each $^9/_{16}$in wide and $^9/_{16}$in deep, routed across the $1^1/_8$in wide face, and a rebate cut at each end, $^9/_{32}$in wide and $^9/_{16}$in deep. The back beam B has only the rebates at its ends. Now cut the four front posts, C1,2,3, and 4, each $^9/_{16}$in square and $6^1/_2$in long, and the two back posts D1 and 2, again $^9/_{16}$in square, but 7in long. C1 and C4 have their outside faces cut back at the bottom to leave a tenon $^9/_{32}$in thick, for a height of $1^1/_8$in. C2 and C3 have their bottom ends left square at $^9/_{16}$in. The top of C1 has a tenon formed on it, $^9/_{32}$in x $^3/_{16}$in to a depth of $^1/_4$in. The tops of C2,3, and 4 have $^9/_{16}$in x $^3/_{16}$in tenons, again $^1/_4$in deep. The back posts, D1 and D2 have their bottom ends reduced to $^9/_{32}$in as for the front posts, and a $^5/_8$in x $^1/_4$in slot cut into the back face $3^3/_4$in above the bottom. The tops of the back faces of these posts are notched $^1/_2$in x $^1/_4$in, to fit over the floor bearer, when the frame is positioned in the building. The four front posts C are slotted in the same plane as the tenons as follows:

C1 and C4 have a slot $5/8$in x $3/16$ x $1/4$in deep with its lower edge $3^3/4$in above the bottom of the posts; C2 and C3 have a similar slot at the same height, but cut right through the posts.

The two adjustable bridge supports, E1 and E2, should be made next from elm $5/8$in x $3/8$in, each $3^7/8$in long. The short tenons should be slightly rounded at their outer ends so that they can pivot inside the slots on C1 and C4. The ends with the long shouldered tenons will fit into the through slots on C2 and C3. The lower frame components can now be assembled.

First, fit the adjustable bridges E1 and E2 between C1 and C2, and C3 and C4. No glue is required but a $1/16$in pivot pin of brass wire should be inserted centrally through the short tenons on posts C1 and C4. The bottom ends of C1,2,3, and 4 are now glued into the appropriate slots at the back of base frame A, and a facing piece, A1, $1^1/8$in x $1/4$in, $9^9/16$in long, glued over them. The back posts D1 and 2 are now glued into the back base beam B, where no facing is required.

Following Fig 102, cut the two base ends G from elm, $1^1/8$in deep, $13/16$in thick, and $4^3/4$in long. The inside faces at both ends of each are rebated for a distance of $13/16$in from the ends to leave a residual thickness of $9/32$in. These ends should now be glued and pinned across the bottom of the front and back frames, with their outside faces flush with the outsides of C1 and C4, and D1 and D2. You should now have a framework looking like that in the lower section of the illustration on page 144, with a distance between the front and back posts, C and D, of $3^3/8$in. The back rail F should now be made from elm $5/8$in x $3/8$in, $10^1/8$in long, with each end shouldered down to $1/4$in thick, for a length of $9/16$in, (see Figs 100 and 101). Ignore the angled slots on the top edge for the present. This rail fits in the slots cut at the back of posts D1 and 2, and should not be glued. When the gearing is added later, this rail passes behind the bevelled pit wheel, and needs to be loose, so that the entire Hurst Frame can be removed for maintenance or adjustment.

You should now set the Hurst Frame assembly, so far completed, into the ground floor of the mill, against the left-hand wall. Check that it fits snugly against the wall, with the notches at the tops of D1 and D2 fitting round the floor bearer. Post D1 should be flush with the outer edge of the wall, and the front base end G flush with the inside of the groove in the carcase base provided to locate the front panel of the mill. With the frame held in this position, drill a $3/32$in diameter hole through D1 and the mill wall and the floor bearer where they cross at the top, and insert a bolt 1–$1^1/8$in long, threaded either M2 or 8BA. Drill and fit a similar bolt through D1 and the mill wall, $1/2$in above the top of the base end G. There is no need to repeat this on D2. Insert two $3/4$in no 4 screws from the underside of the carcase base into base beam A, about 1in from each end. Now remove all the fastenings, and put them aside – they will ensure that on future assembly the frame is located in the identical position.

Remove the Hurst Frame and the back rail. Referring to Fig 101, make four support posts J from elm $3/8$in x $1/2$in, each $2^1/4$in long, with their tops notched $1/2$in x $1/4$in. Bolt one of these to the inside face of C1, C4, D1, and D2, using M2 or 8BA bolts. You should now make the main bridge beam H and its transverse end supports, H1 and H2 following Fig 100. This assembly will provide the support for the bottom end of the vertical main shaft. Cut the long beam H from elm $5/8$in thick and $7/8$in deep, then cut the deep face to the curved profile shown so that it finishes $1/2$in deep in this plane and $9^3/8$in long. Now cut the two ends H1 and H2 from $1/2$in x $7/16$in elm, with the ends shouldered as shown to finish $1/4$in thick for a distance of $9/16$in from each end, and with notches in their top edges $5/8$in wide and $1/8$in deep at a distance of $1^{11}/16$in from the ends nearest the mill wall. This measurement, when added to half the thickness of H, will place the vertical main shaft centre exactly 2in from the mill wall.

The bridge beam H is now set on top of H1 and H2, in the notches, flush at the ends, and secured with a bolt (M2 or 8BA), vertically through the centre of the joint at each end of the beam. The bridge beam assembly fits inside the Hurst Frame, with the end supports H1 locating in the notches on the supports J (Fig 101). No fastening is required here.

With the bridge beam now assembled as part of the Hurst Frame, re-position the whole structure on the ground floor of the mill, and replace the fastenings. The water-wheel shaft passes

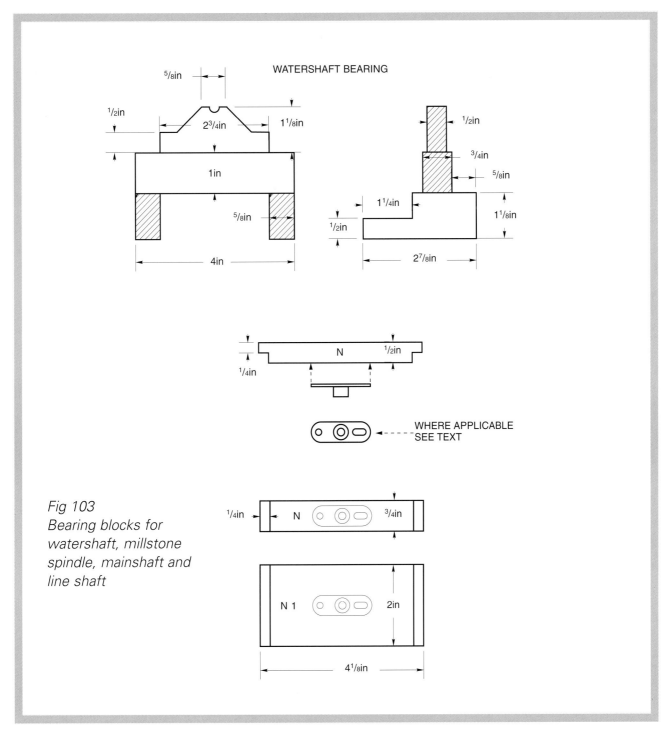

WATERSHAFT BEARING

Fig 103
Bearing blocks for
watershaft, millstone
spindle, mainshaft and
line shaft

under the bridge, which should be marked on the centreline of its top face to coincide with the crossing point. Once again, unfasten and remove the Hurst Frame and drill a $^3/_{16}$in diameter hole into the top of the bridge beam, where marked, to a depth of $^1/_4$in. A Meccano double-arm crank (part no 62 B), bored to $^3/_{16}$in, is screwed on top of the beam and a small ball-bearing, about $^1/_8$in diameter, is dropped into the hole to provide a crude but effective thrust bearing for the vertical shaft. Take care not to lose this ball-bearing when removing or replacing the Hurst Frame.

Before proceeding further, refer to Fig 103, and make the watershaft bearing block from elm. This rests loosely on the floor between the front and back base beams of the Hurst Frame, and is for appearance only. The half round notch at the top should clear the shaft, not rub on it. Before adding the vertical shaft, the Hurst Frame has to be extended upwards, by the addition of the long first-floor support beam K, two more posts L1 and L2, and then the top-floor support beam M.

These components are now cut from elm following Fig 104. First make the two beams K and

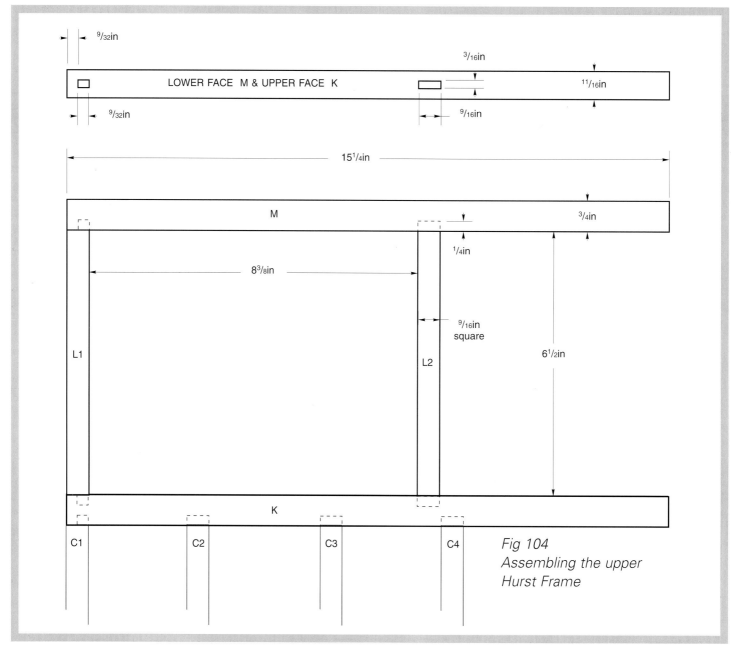

Fig 104
Assembling the upper
Hurst Frame

M, each $3/4$in deep, $11/16$in wide, and $15\frac{1}{4}$in long. Take beam K and cut the four mortises on the underside and the two mortises on the top, where shown, all $1/4$in deep. Cut the two mortises on the underside of beam M to match those on the top of K. Posts L1 and L2 are both cut from elm $9/16$in square and 7in long. Shouldered tenons are cut at the top and bottom of L1, and full tenons on L2, to engage with the mortises on K and M. *Take great care in cutting these joints as accurately as possible, as they will be assembled as a push fit, without glue or any other fastening.*

Now replace the Hurst Frame and refasten to ensure correct location. Add the support beam K, having first cut away the floor bearer on the back wall to accept it. The upper frame members L and M can be put aside for now.

Five bearing blocks N should now be made. Two will be required for the main shaft at first- and top-floor levels. Note that the upper one of these, N1, is 2in wide, and the other, $3/4$in wide. The other three are also $3/4$in wide. Of these, one is required at first-floor level for the mill-stone spindle, and the others for the upper transmission. Following Fig 103, and noting the widths just mentioned, make the five blocks from elm each $1/2$in deep and $4\frac{1}{8}$in long, and then halve the ends to $1/4$in where shown. Place one narrow block on top of the first-floor bearer and the support beam K, so that the halved ends rest on the floor bearer and beam, with the body of the block fitting between them.

Now cut the main shaft from $3/16$in mild steel rod, $11\frac{1}{2}$in long. Rest one end of this in the bearing on the bridge beam and, using either a small set square or a spacer from the mill wall, set the shaft truly vertical. Mark where it crosses the bearing block N (2in from the mill wall), and drill a $^3/_{16}$in diameter hole through the centreline of the block at this position. Remove the bearing block and replace it over the shaft. Slide it back and forth until the shaft is vertical in the other plane. Now mark round the halved ends where they rest on the bearer and beam, and cut out this area to a depth of $^1/_4$in so that the bearing block drops down with its top edge flush with those of the beam and bearer. Remove the block and add a Meccano double-arm crank (part no 62 B), drilled $^3/_{16}$in, on the underside to coincide with the existing hole. Note that the notches cut to house the bearing block N can be a little oversize to allow for fractional adjustment with veneer strips.

When satisfied that the position is correct, drill down through each end of the block and insert a $^3/_4$in no 4 screw, which must be well countersunk. Add the upper posts L and the beam M, which is also slotted into the back wall floor bearer at this level. Fit the 2in wide bearing block N at upper-floor level by the same method as that used for the lower block. The remaining blocks can be put aside for now, but note that two of them will not be drilled as they are for the line shaft support.

GEARS

Traditionally, all the gears in a water mill have names. For ease of reference later on, a brief description of each is included here:

The water-wheel drives the watershaft, on which is mounted the *pit wheel*, whose name derives from its large diameter which necessitated digging a pit in the floor to accommodate it. This is a bevelled gear which engages with the wallower. The *wallower* is mounted at the lower end of the main shaft. Above this is the *spur wheel* which drives the millstone spindle via a small gear called a *stone nut*. At the top of the main shaft, just below the ceiling on the first, or *stone floor*, is the *crown wheel* which drives the line shaft. This in turn provides drive to the sack hoist by a loose belt, which is tensioned by a lever, as a form of primitive clutch. Other pulleys on the line shaft drive machinery such as flour dressers and cleaners.

The three floors of a mill are named as follows:

The ground floor is called the *spout floor*, as it has all the shutes from the millstones and cleaning and dressing machinery at this level. The first floor has the millstones, hence its name, *stone floor*. The *bin floor* at the top of the building houses all the grain bins. Grain for milling enters the building at the spout floor, and is taken up to the bin floor by the sack hoist, which passes through self-closing trap-doors at each level. The grain is emptied into the bins from where it travels down by gravity to the hopper over the millstones for grinding, or to one of the cleaning machines, emerging again through a shute on the spout floor. Fig 105 shows the arrangement of the mill workings.

The bevel gears connecting the watershaft and the main shaft should now be added (pit wheel and wallower). These can be obtained from Bonds (see list of suppliers), with a ratio of 2:1 (catalogue no C130). Alternatively, you could use the bevel gears from an old hand drill. The gears from Bonds will probably be bored $^3/_8$in, and will need to be bushed down to $^3/_{16}$in. If you do not have a lathe, this will have to be done for you. In reality the pit wheel was quite large, usually 6ft or more in diameter, while the gears mentioned above are proportionately rather on the small side, around $2^1/_2$in diameter, but they are available from stock at reasonable cost, whereas the price for specially made gears of a larger size is prohibitive, unless you have the skill and equipment to make them yourself. In practice, there is so much timberwork in front of the pit wheel that its small size is not obvious. For the same reason, Meccano gears have been used wherever possible on the remainder of the workings. The shaft used is $^3/_{16}$in diameter to provide more rigidity than the standard Meccano size of $^5/_{32}$in, so all the gears used will need to be bored out to $^3/_{16}$in.

Remove the Hurst Frame, and slide the pit wheel on to the watershaft, ensuring that the teeth face outwards. Replace the Hurst Frame, remembering to insert the back rail behind the pit wheel, and temporarily locate the wallower on the main shaft about 1in from the bottom. All gears are held in place on their respective shafts with grub screws. Replace the bearing blocks N at stone- and bin-floor levels. Slacken the grub screws, and adjust the position of the gears until they mesh evenly. Test under power from the motor. If the gears bind at just one spot when rotated, this probably means that one or

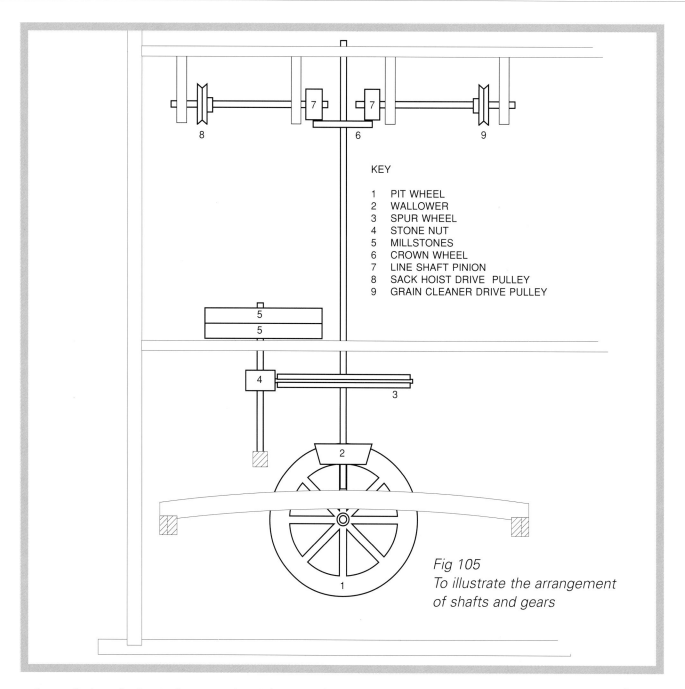

KEY

1   PIT WHEEL
2   WALLOWER
3   SPUR WHEEL
4   STONE NUT
5   MILLSTONES
6   CROWN WHEEL
7   LINE SHAFT PINION
8   SACK HOIST DRIVE PULLEY
9   GRAIN CLEANER DRIVE PULLEY

Fig 105
To illustrate the arrangement
of shafts and gears

other of the shafts is bent – discard it, and replace with a new length. When satisfied, further gears can be added. Note that on the model, the watershaft, mainshaft, and stone spindle have octagonal wooden casings fitted over the shafts, to simulate the wooden shafts in a full-size mill. This can be done on a lathe, or by gluing four strips of wood in a box section round a spare length of $^3/_{16}$in rod. Plane the flats afterwards to finish approximately $^3/_8$in in diameter. This casing is best ignored for now, and added if required after all the shafting and gears have been set up and tested, when the exact length of each section can be determined.

The spur wheel is added next, and is made from a large Meccano gear $3^9/_{16}$in in diameter

(part no 27 B). It should be bored out to $^3/_{16}$in, and have a disc of $^1/_8$in plywood bolted on each face, to increase its apparent thickness. These discs should be $3^7/_{16}$in diameter, so that the gear teeth are kept clear. The spur wheel is now added to the main shaft, approximately $^3/_4$in above the wallower.

Referring to Fig 106, the millstone spindle will be added next, but first the two spindle bridges O should be made from $^3/_8$in square elm, each $4^1/_2$in long. Only one set of millstones is fitted on the model, so the back bridge is inoperative. Position one bridge across the Hurst Frame, resting on top of the back rail F at one end, and the pivoting support E1 at the front. Mark the centre of the top edge of the

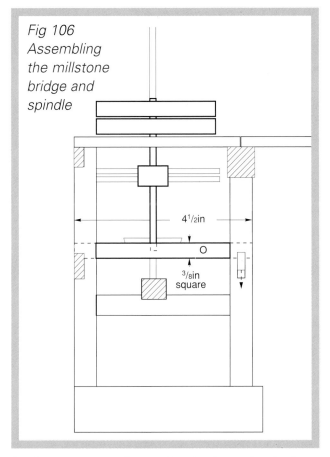

Fig 106
Assembling
the millstone
bridge and
spindle

4¹/₂in

3/8in
square

bridge 2in out from the back end which is against the mill wall, and adjust its position so that this mark lies approximately 2¹/₈in from the centre of the vertical mainshaft, and 2in from the wall of the mill, whilst keeping the front end close against the side of C2. This will place the bridge at a slight angle, with its back end fairly close to the pit wheel. Now adjust the mark on the bridge if necessary, so that it remains 2in from the wall of the mill. Drill a ³/₁₆in diameter hole in the top, where marked, ³/₁₆in deep, and screw a Meccano double-arm crank (part no 62 B), bored to ³/₁₆in, over it.

The third bearing block N should now be drilled ³/₁₆in in diameter, and fitted with a Meccano crank, as for those on the mainshaft. Set the millstone spindle in position with its lower end in the bearing hole on the bridge, and its top end passing through the bearing block N which rests on top of the floor bearer and beam K.

The stone nut can now be positioned on the spindle, and its height adjusted to mesh with the spur wheel. This stone nut is a ³/₄in Meccano pinion, and the spindle is ³/₁₆in diameter, nominally 4¹/₂in long – its length will be adjusted later. Adjust the positions of the bridge O, and bearing block N, to give even meshing, with the spindle remaining vertical.

Now mark round the bearing block and house it into the top of the floor bearer and beam K, as for the mainshaft. Similarly mark the back rail and support E1, and notch each of these ³/₈in wide and ¹/₈in deep, to locate the bridge. The bridge is secured to E1 at the front by a 10BA bolt, and at the back by a panel pin driven through the top, and cut off underneath to leave a ¹/₈in projection. This locates in a ¹/₁₆in diameter hole, to be drilled in the centre of the notch on the back rail. The support beam E1 is now free to pivot with about ¹/₄in movement at the free end. This is sufficient to disengage the stone nut, or to adjust the space between the millstones when fitted. For this purpose, a small wedge is cut to fit in the slot on C2, under the shouldered end of E1. The millstone spindle should project 1¹/₈in above the bearing block N. Cut to length, and with a hacksaw and file, form a slot in the top end ¹/₁₆in wide and ³/₁₆in deep. This slot will later locate the upper, running, millstone. Test again under power, and adjust if necessary.

UPPER TRANSMISSION

The crown wheel (1¹/₂in diameter Meccano contrate gear, part no 28), should now be fitted to the main shaft, about 1in below the 2in wide upper bearing block N1. Remove this bearing block, and mark across its top face through the centre of the shaft hole.

Following Fig 107, make four hangers P from ¹/₂in x ¹/₄in elm, each 1⁷/₈in long, and drilled on the centreline of a ¹/₂in face, ³/₁₆in diameter ¹/₄in from one end. Glue and pin one of these at either side of the bearing block N1 so that they project downwards with the holes in line with the mainshaft. Repeat this on the two remaining ³/₄in wide blocks, which each have a hanger on one side only. A short Meccano plate (3 holes), should be fitted to the face of each hanger which

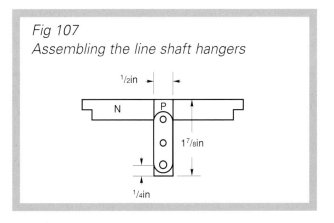

Fig 107
Assembling the line shaft hangers

¹/₂in

N   P

1⁷/₈in

¹/₄in

lies nearest to the crown wheel. Notch these last two blocks into the top of the floor bearer, and beam M. The outer one is fitted so that it lies flush with the outer end of the floor bearer and beam, with the hanger on the inside, and the second is fitted so that its hanger lies $3^{1}/2$in behind the rearmost hanger on the middle block.

Cut two lengths of $3/16$in rod, one long enough to reach from the mainshaft to the outside face of the front hanger, and the other to reach from the mainshaft to the outside face of the back hanger. The front section has a 1in diameter Meccano pulley and a collar fitted between the hangers, and a $9/16$in diameter gear on the crown-wheel end. The back section is similar, but has a $1^{1}/2$in diameter pulley.

Adjust the height of the crown wheel, and the position of the line shaft collars to give even meshing of the gears, and test again under power.

The remainder of the workings (sack hoist, flour dresser, and millstones), will be made and fitted later when the building has progressed further.

LADDERS AND FLOORS

Three ladders are required, one in the cottage, and two in the mill. All are identical and should be made from elm as shown in Fig 108, with the steps glued into routed slots on the stringers. It will be helpful if the timber for the stringers is left about 2in wide when routing the slots for the handed sides, and then reduced to $1/2$in wide afterwards on a circular saw.

Following Fig 109, cut out the first floor for the cottage from $1/4$in plywood, with its grain running from end to end. Scribe $3/4$in wide planking on the top surface in the same direction. Cut out the stairwell and the notches at the front right-hand corner. The front edge should now be veneered with $1/16$in thick elm. Line the stairwell opening with lime or elm $5/16$in deep and $1/16$in thick, to leave a $1/16$in coaming above the floor edge.

Six $3/8$in x $1/4$in elm or lime joists are now glued under the floor, approximately $1^{9}/16$in apart – note that joist no 1 passes under the outside edge of the stairwell, and must be flush with that edge. All the joists stop $1/4$in from the back

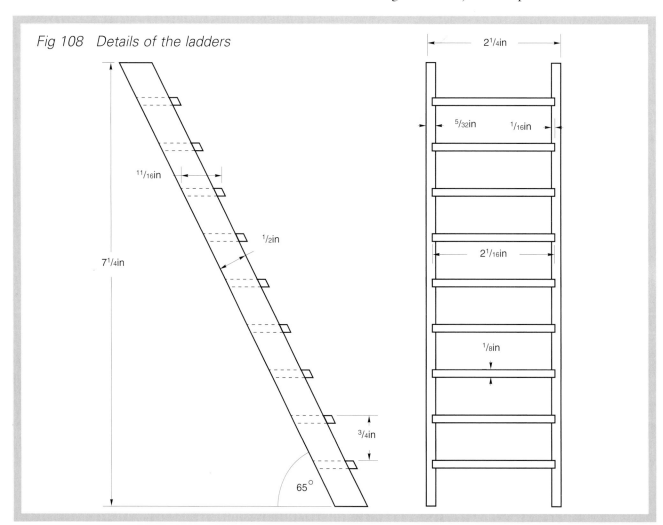

Fig 108   Details of the ladders

Fig 109   Pattern and dimensions for the cottage first floor

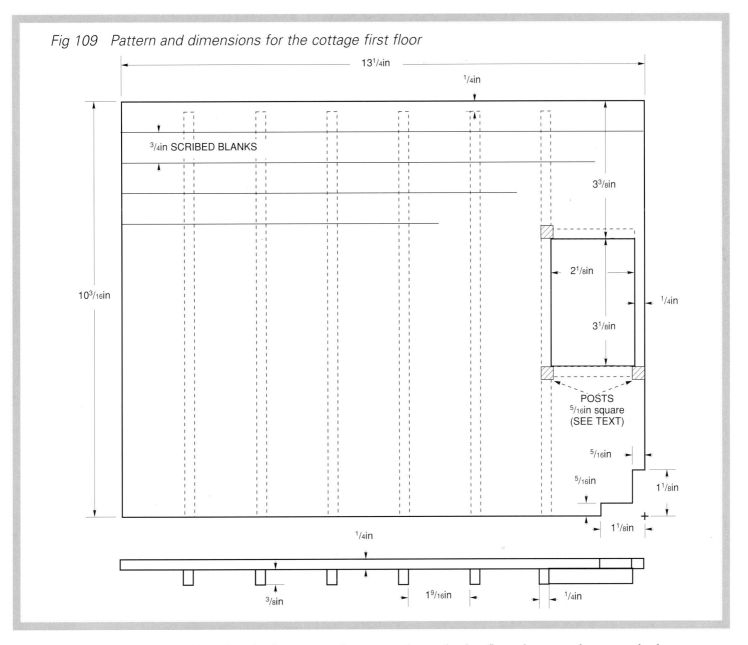

edge of the floor, to allow for the bearer on the back wall. Two further short joists are glued under the front and back edges of the stairwell, fitting from joist no 1 to a point ^{1}/4in inside the right-hand edge of the floor.

Position the floor in the cottage, resting on the bearers, and mark the right-hand floor bearer in line with the inner end of the stairwell. Remove the floor and place a ladder against the floor bearer in this position, with its back/underside against the mark. Ensure that the ladder is positioned so that it is angled downwards from the top at 65° towards the front of the ground floor. Use an angled plywood template to achieve this. Mark the ground floor where the bottom ends of the two stringers rest, and also mark the side of the floor bearer where the ladder crosses it. Remove the ladder

and notch the floor bearer where marked to a depth of ^{1}/8in. A corresponding notch is cut into joist no 1 on the face inside the stairwell. These notches will locate the top of the ladder.

Three handrail posts are made from elm, ^{5}/16in square and 2^1/2in long. Drill ^{3}/32in diameter holes centrally in one end of each, ^{1}/4in deep, and glue in ^{1}/2in lengths of ^{3}/32in bamboo dowel. This is made from barbecue skewers, reduced with a drawplate. Drill three corresponding holes in the floor at the positions shown. Rails of ^{3}/16in square elm are drilled at the ends, and pegged between the posts with their top edges ^{1}/8in below the tops of the posts. Lightly chamfer the tops of both posts and rails, and glue in place.

Rather than scribe the carcase for the cottage ground floor, it is preferable to fit a floor cover-

Fig 110 Pattern for the stone floor

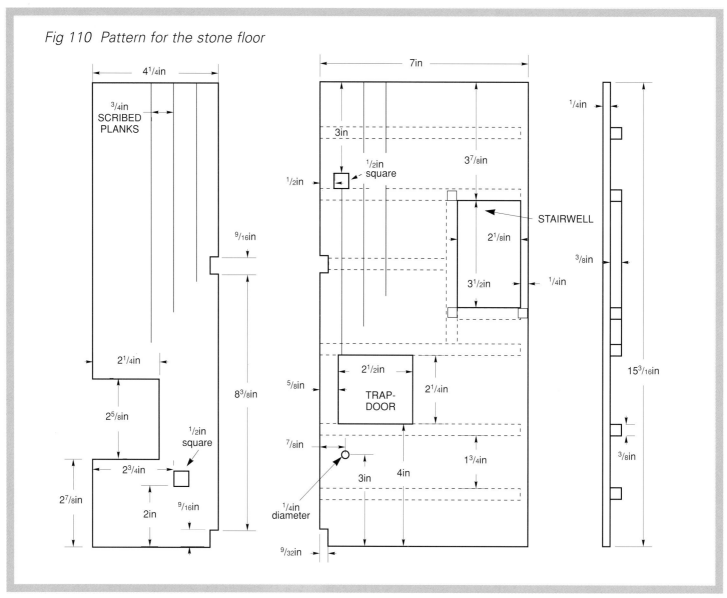

ing of 1.5mm plywood, which is scribed with $3/4$in wide planking, and slotted in the appropriate position to locate the bottom ends of the ladder. This covering should be removed until the inside walls have been painted.

STONE FLOOR

This is cut from $1/4$in plywood in two sections, with the grain running from front to back (see Fig 110). The left-hand section should be made first. This is only $4^1/4$in wide and reaches from the left-hand wall of the mill to the centreline of the support beam K on the Hurst Frame – $9/16$in x $9/32$in notches are cut into the outer edge to fit round the two posts L. An area $2^5/8$in x $2^1/4$in is cut from the left-hand edge, starting $2^7/8$in from the front of the floor. This clears the mainshaft and millstone spindle and will be filled later with a loose-fitting section of $1/4$in plywood notched to fit round the shaft and spindle. A $1/2$in square

hole for the flour shute should be marked on the floor, but is best left uncut until the shute is fitted later as the hole needs to be cut at an angle to allow the shute to run from under the lower millstone (bedstone), over the pivoted beam E1.

Next, cut out the right-hand section 7in wide, again with the grain running from front to back, but this time notched on the left-hand edge for the posts L. Cut out the openings for the stairwell and trap-door. Drill a $1/4$in diameter hole through the floor just in front of the trap-door opening, where shown in Fig 110. This is for the sack hoist operating chain. A hole $1/2$in square is cut through the floor, 3in from the back edge and $1/2$in from the left-hand edge, for a vertical shute which will be made and fitted later. The stairwell should now be lined, as in the cottage.

Line the trap-door opening with $3/16$in x $1/8$in lime or elm, leaving 1.5mm clear at the top to provide a land for the trap-door, (see Fig 112).

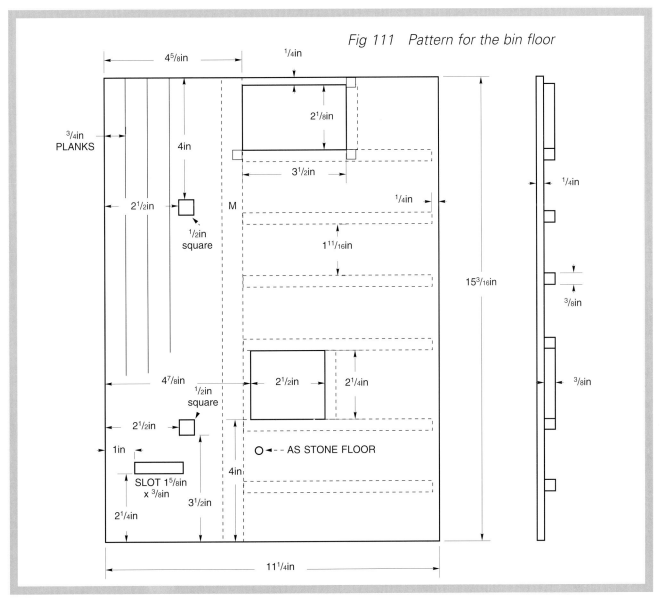

Fig 111   Pattern for the bin floor

The trap-doors can now be made and fixed. Cut two pieces of 1.5mm plywood, $2^1/4$in long and $1^1/4$in wide. File a half round slot into the edge of each piece where they meet in the centre, to form a $^1/4$in diameter hole for the sack hoist chain. The outer edges are hinged to the top of the floor with $^1/4$in wide strips of thin leather. Both floor sections can now be scribed with $^3/4$in wide planks, starting either side of the seam over beam K. Veneer their front edges with $^1/16$in thick elm.

Joists of $^3/8$in square elm are now glued under the right-hand section only. They fit across the floor between beam K and the floor bearer on the right-hand wall. Six are required, as shown in Fig 110. The ladder should now be fitted as in the cottage with the stairwell side and the floor bearer notched to locate its upper end, and the ground floor marked where the bottom rests.

A further handrail on three posts should now be made and glued in position on the floor. Construction is identical to that on the cottage, but note that the stairwell is $^3/8$in longer.

SPOUT FLOOR
The floor area outside the Hurst Frame is covered with flagstones made from Formica as in the Swan Inn (Fig 33 page 62). Take care when fixing these not to glue the frame to the floor. The area inside the base of the frame is painted dark grey. Remember to leave slots in the flagstone covering, where the floor was previously marked, to locate the bottom of the ladder.

BIN FLOOR
Following Fig 111, this floor is cut in one piece from $^1/4$in plywood, again with the grain running from front to back. Cut out the stairwell at the back, ensuring that the left-hand side of the

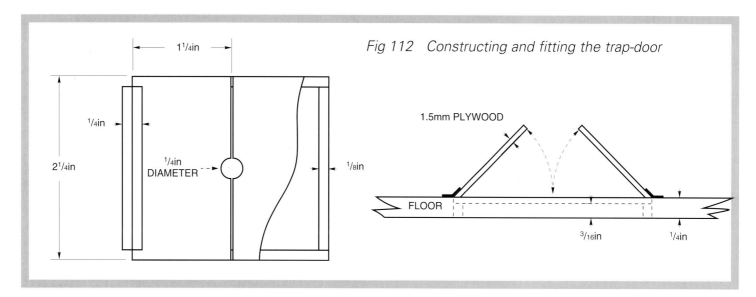

Fig 112   Constructing and fitting the trap-door

Bin floor in the mill

cutout (2^1/8in long), exactly corresponds with the outside face of the support beam M. Cut out the trap-door opening, using the right-hand section of the stone floor as a template to ensure that both trap-door openings coincide. There are two further ^{1}/2in square holes for shutes which should be cut out next, together with the 1^5/8in x ^{3}/8in slot for the sack hoist driving belt.

Drill a ^{1}/4in diameter hole in front of the trap-door opening, where shown, to coincide exactly with the one on the stone floor below. Scribe the ^{3}/4in planking, and veneer the front edge, before lining the stairwell and the trap-door opening, as for the stone floor. Make and fit the trap-door. Elm joists ^{3}/8in square are glued under the right-hand section only (the area to the right of support beam M). Six are required, reaching from M to the floor bearer on the right-hand wall as shown in Fig 111.

Note that these joists should not fit too tightly between the support beam M and the floor bearer, as this floor needs to slide in and out.

The ladder to the bin floor can now be fitted as for the other floors, but a pad of 1.5mm plywood suitably slotted, should be glued to the stone floor to hold the bottom of the ladder. Make the handrail round the stairwell to the same dimensions as that on the stone floor.

In order to thicken the walls at the eaves for better fastening of the roof panels, a skirting strip of ^{3}/8in plywood, 1^1/2in high, is glued along the inside of both the right-hand and left-hand walls above the bin floor, to reach from the back wall to ^{7}/16in short of the front edge of the floor. This left-hand strip should be cut away where it passes over the upper shaft bearing and hanger blocks, to provide access to the screws. When the roof is fixed, this access is limited, but can be achieved with a very short screwdriver. Bevel the top edges of these strips to the roof slope. The ^{7}/16in space at the front is for location of the roof truss which will be made with the roof.

SACK HOIST

The supports are cut from ^{3}/8in thick elm to the profiles in Fig 113, with ^{3}/16in diameter holes drilled through them for the hoist spindle. Note that the front support is wider, to allow for the pivoted operating lever, and that its hole should be more in the form of a slot. It needs to allow about ^{3}/32in up-and-down movement at the spindle end. A slack driving belt of string or, preferably, a spring band as sold for model steam engines, will connect the hoist pulley with the pulley on the line shaft below, passing through

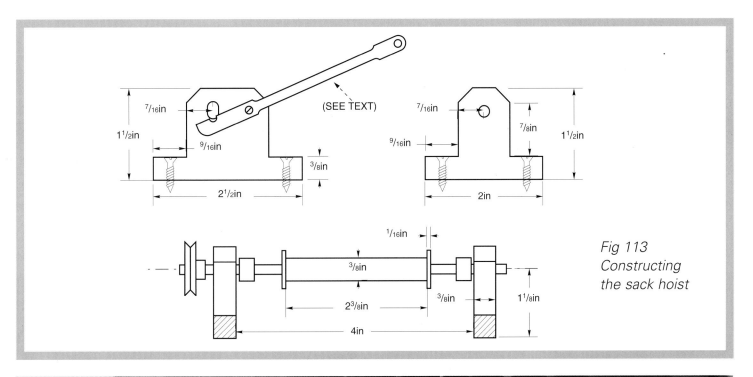

Fig 113
Constructing
the sack hoist

Stone floor in the mill

Mill interior, showing the millstones, sack hoist, and trap-doors

the slot in the bin floor. A downward pull on the operating lever tensions the belt and provides drive to the hoist spindle. A chain will be connected to this lever on completion of the building, and will pass down through the $1/4$in diameter holes in the bin and stone floors to the spout floor at the bottom. The drum is turned from wood to finish $3/8$in diameter, with a $3/16$in hole bored through from end to end. This drum should have a $1/2$in diameter washer glued at each end. Both the supports should be pre-drilled and countersunk for $3/4$in no 4 screws.

Assemble the winding drum on its $5 1/2$in long spindle, with a Meccano collar at each end, and add the support block at each end. A 1in diameter Meccano pulley is positioned close outside the front support.

The structure should now be screwed to the bin floor with the supports 4in apart, the spindle in line with the transmission shaft below the floor, and the pulley adjusted to be centred over the floor slot. Adjust the collars to provide just enough end-to-end movement for free running.

Make the operating lever from a $3 1/2$in length of $5/32$in copper tube (Hobby's). Flatten the inner end of the tube so that it is about $1/4$in wide for 1in from one end. Drill a $1/8$in hole through it $5/8$in from the end. Flatten the outer end for $1/2$in and drill a further $1/8$in diameter hole just inside the end. A semi-circular slot is filed on the top of the inner end to engage the spindle. This lever can now be screwed to the front support block with a small round headed screw.

A 14in length of light chain (12–14 links per inch), is attached to the lever with a jump ring, and led to the ground floor. A 24in length of similar sized chain is wired on to the winding drum and will pass over a pulley under the ridgeboard, when fitted, down through both trap-doors to the spout floor. The winding drum is secured to the spindle with a small dab of epoxy adhesive at each end.

GRAIN CLEANER

This should be made next following Fig 114. Cut the two sloping sides and the

long and short ends from either $1/8$in lime or plywood, to the dimensions shown. The sloping face nearest the front of the mill is scribed with $3/8$in wide margin boards and planking – the back face cannot be seen, so scribing is unnecessary. Glue these components together as a box, and add a top cover over the sloping section only, again from $1/8$in thick material. Drill a $3/16$in hole through both side panels, for the spindle, in the position shown. A $3/16$in diameter spindle $3 1/2$in long should now be inserted with a 1in diameter Meccano pulley at the front, and a collar at the back. Now cut a piece of $1/4$in plywood, $5 1/2$in long. Its width should be a tight fit inside the bottom of the box. Cut this in half to form two pieces each $2 1/4$in long and trim these so that both halves, when butted together, fit snugly inside the bottom of the box. These two

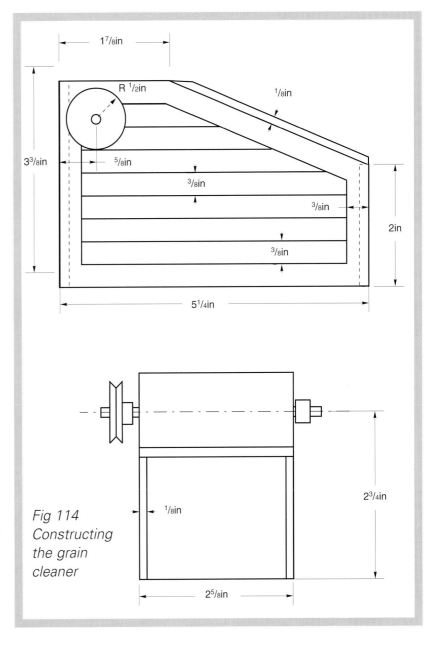

Fig 114
Constructing
the grain
cleaner

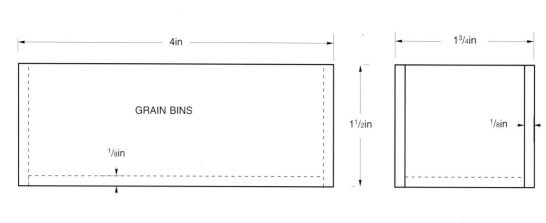

Fig 115
Details of the grain bins and the millstone shute

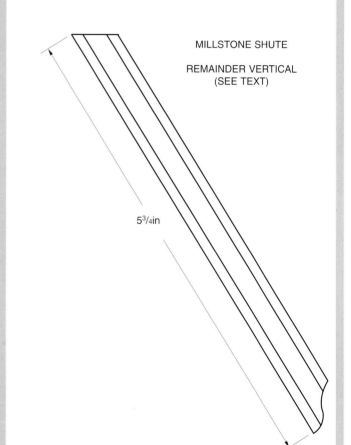

MILLSTONE SHUTE

REMAINDER VERTICAL
(SEE TEXT)

pads are now glued on top of the stone floor, one either side of the seam in the floor over beam K, with their back edges 3in from the back edge of the floor. They now form a tight push location for the cleaner. Connect the pulley on the cleaner to the 1¹/₂in diameter pulley on the line shaft with a spring band.

GRAIN BINS

Two of these should be made as boxes to the dimensions given in Fig 115. The bottoms, which are also ¹/₈in thick, are inset. These two bins are loosely placed on the bin floor, one in front of the sack hoist, and the other further back so that its back edge just covers the shute hole in the floor.

MILLSTONES

These are both 3in diameter discs of ³/₈in plywood. The lower one (bed stone), is drilled ¹/₄in diameter in the centre, so that the spindle can revolve inside it. The upper running stone is drilled ³/₁₆in diameter and has a ¹/₂in length of ¹/₁₆in diameter wire or brass rod set into the top face, and glued, as shown in Fig 116, across the centre of the hole. This engages with the slot previously cut in the top of the spindle, to provide drive. The upper face of the running stone, and the edges of both stones should be painted with Humbrol pale stone. The bedstone just rests on the floor, and should not be glued.

TUN

This is the cover over the millstones. Its top surface supports the horse which is the frame holding the hopper and shoe, which in turn channel the grain into the hole through the centre of the running stone, where it is then ground between the stones to emerge through the shute on the spout floor. Ideally the tun should be

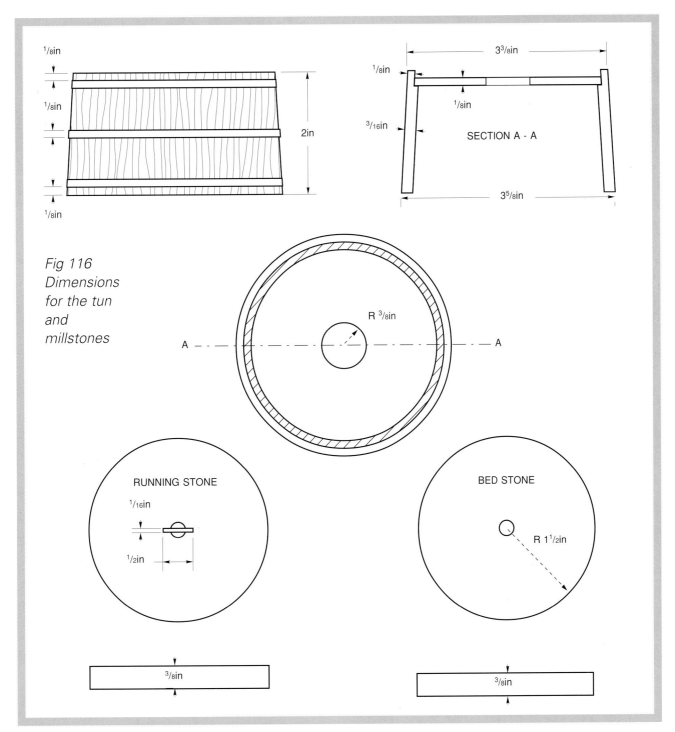

SECTION A - A

Fig 116
Dimensions
for the tun
and
millstones

RUNNING STONE

BED STONE

made as a hollow turning to the dimensions given in Fig 116, with an inset lid having a 3/4in diameter hole at the centre. If you do not have a lathe, it can be made in the following manner:

Cut a disc of plywood 1/8in thick and 31/4in diameter. Drill a 3/4in hole through the centre. Now glue a continuous strip of card 2in wide around its circumference for at least two roundings, allowing the card to project downwards for 2in. When finished, the card skirt should not exceed 35/8in in diameter, nor be less than 31/4in diameter at the bottom edge – too large, and it will not fit against the mill wall; too small, and it

will bind on the millstones. When the glue has set, paint the outside to represent timber, and add one 1/8in wide band of black card round the centre of the skirt, followed by two more, 1/8in from the top and bottom edges respectively. This addition of card bands is also used on the timber version.

HORSE

This is made simply from 1/4in square hardwood, and 1/8in dowel, drilled and fitted together following the dimensions in Fig 117. The finished horse should be painted dull black.

Fig 117 Showing dimensions and assembly for the horse, shoe, and hopper

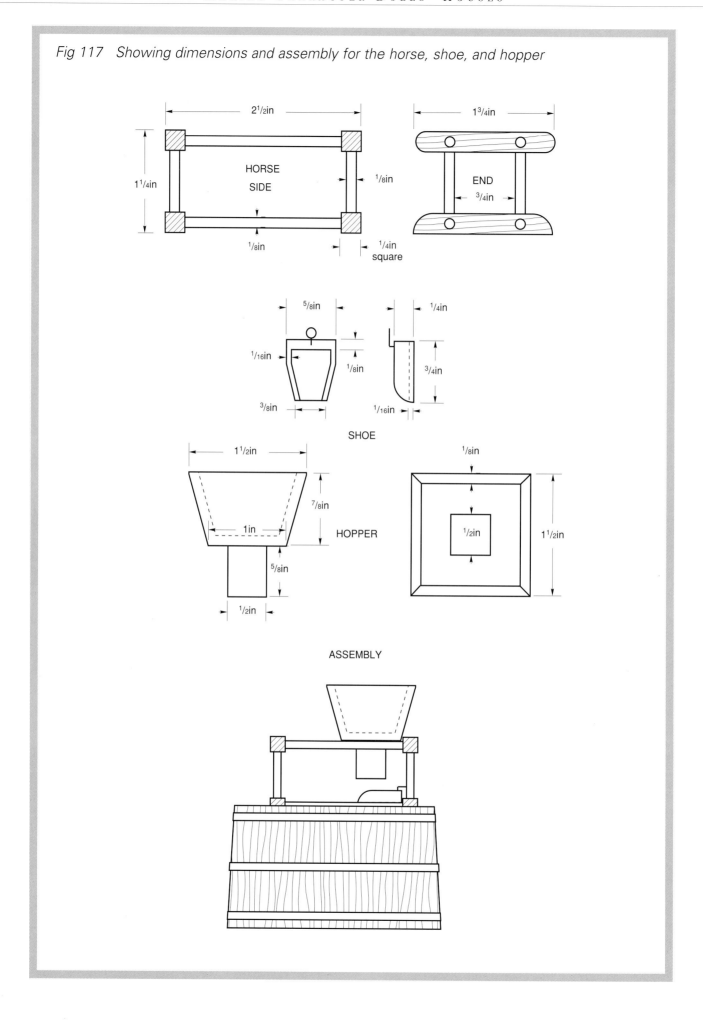

Spout floor in the mill

SHOE

Still following Fig 117, the shoe is best carved at the end of a strip of elm $^5/8$in x $^1/4$in, about 6in long to provide a handle. The shaped shoe is cut away afterwards, and fixed to the inside of one end of the horse by a pair of eyes formed from brass wire. It is supported by the tun and can pivot from side to side within the frame of the horse.

HOPPER

Again referring to Fig 117, carve this from solid wood, again left long enough to provide a handle or, alternatively, make the hopper from card. Note that there must be a flat area around the $^1/2$in square spout for it to rest on top of the horse.

SHUTES

Four of these are needed, all finishing $^1/2$in square in section, but differing in length. Refer again to Fig 115, and make them from strips of $^1/4$in x $^1/8$in elm glued between strips of $^1/2$in x $^1/8$in elm, to form a box. The shute illustrated is that from the millstones to the ground floor. It is angled at the top, and has a shaped spout. The hole previously marked on the stone floor should now be cut out at an angle to receive the top end of the shute, the lower end of which rests against the top of the pivoted beam E1. The remaining three shutes are all square-ended at the top and bottom, and are pushed into their respective holes so that they hang vertically. The lengths are as follows:

Under the flour dresser – 4$^3/4$in; back bin to

Fig 118   Making the chimney

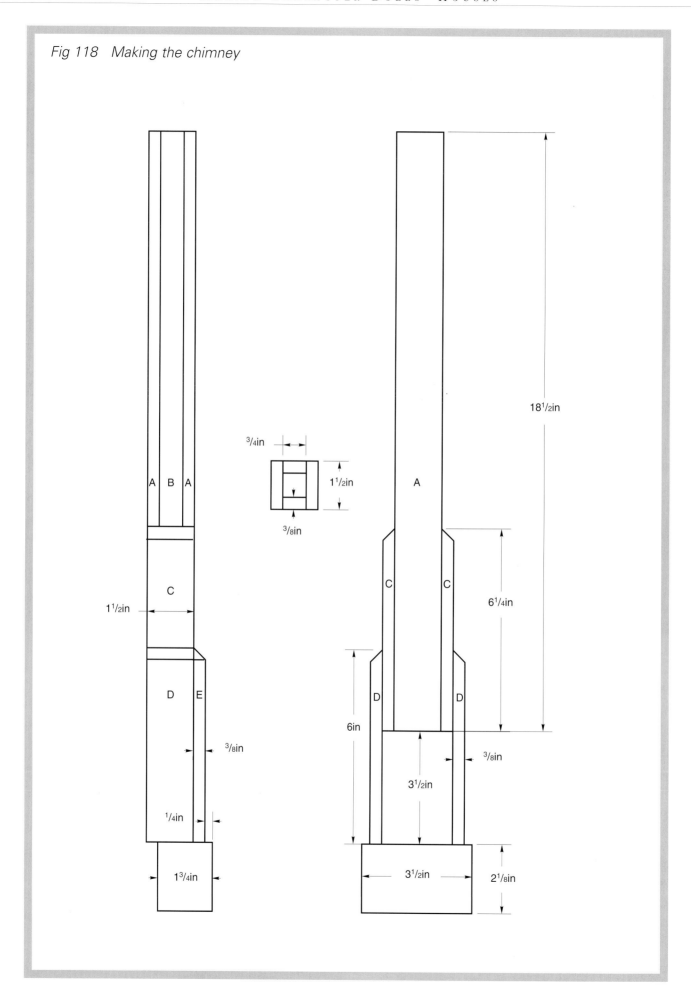

Cottage bedroom

dresser – $3^5/8$in; front bin to millstone hopper – $2^3/4$in. The latter shute has a tube of calico 2in long sewn over its lower end to cover the bottom $1/2$in of the shute.

CHIMNEY
Refer to Fig 118, and start by making the box section ABAB from two strips of $3/8$in plywood B which are $3/4$in wide and $18^1/2$in long, glued and pinned between the two strips A which are again $3/8$in plywood, but this time $1^1/2$in wide and $18^1/2$in long. Add the two thickening pieces C, cut from $3/8$in plywood, which are $1^1/2$in wide and $6^1/4$in long with their tops bevelled to 45°. They are glued and pinned each side of the box ABAB, flush at the bottom and $8^3/4$in below the top. Further thickening pieces D, again from $3/8$in plywood, $1^1/2$in wide and 6in long, are glued and pinned over the lower ends of C, on either side, to project $3^1/2$in below the box. The tops are bevelled to 45° as for C. Now add the outside facing piece E, which is $3/8$in plywood, 3in wide and 6in long. Its top edge is bevelled

and then trimmed back at the corners to match the side bevel on D. Fasten the chimney to the outside of the cottage back wall with glue, and screws from the inside of the wall into D and C. The $2^1/4$in x $3^1/2$in opening in the face of the chimney butting the wall should be aligned with the fireplace opening previously cut in the wall. Note that the base of the chimney overhangs the base frame. A block of mahogany or pine $3^1/2$in long, $2^1/8$in high, and $1^3/4$in deep is glued and screwed to the base frame from inside, so that it fits under the chimney and extends $1/4$in beyond the chimney base at the sides and back.

WIRING
Cir-Kit twin wire, rather than tape, has been used throughout.

Cottage First Floor Drill a $1/8$in diameter hole through the back wall and into the centre of the chimney. This hole should be $1/4$in above first-floor level. Cut a 3ft length of Cir-Kit twin wire and thread this through the hole into the

Cottage interior

chimney and downwards to emerge in the fireplace opening below. Separate the wires at the top, for about 1in, and bare the ends for $^1/_2$in. Using an MH658 plug, press the pins against the wall at the same height as the $^1/_8$in hole, but 1in to the left of it. Now drill a pair of $^1/_{16}$in diameter holes, $^3/_{16}$in deep at these marks, for a pair of CK 1023-2 eyelets. The holes should be spaced at $^1/_4$in centres. Open the holes fractionally with a bradawl. Now wrap a bared end of wire round each eyelet, close under the flange, and hammer them into the holes. Drill a further $^1/_8$in diameter hole through the end wall of the cottage into the motor space, behind the waterwheel. This should be $^1/_4$in above ground-floor level, and $^1/_4$in from the back wall. Lead the wire from the right-hand side of the fireplace, and thread it through this hole.

Cottage Ground Floor A pair of eyelets is fitted 2in to the right of the fireplace, $^1/_4$in above floor level and, from them, a twin wire 18in long is led across the edge of the floor to the right, and through the same hole as the wire from the first floor. Lead both the wires up the wall in the motor space, and across to the connector block.

Allow 2–3in of additional wire at this point, and cut off the surplus. Separate the twin wires at this end and bare them for $^1/_2$in. Now twist together one wire from each source, but do not connect yet. The lights in the cottage are a candlestick in the first-floor bedroom and an oil lamp in the ground-floor room, both from Wood 'n' Wool.

Mill Lamps with conical shades (from Peter Kennedy), are used throughout the mill. These have replaceable bulbs and wire tails long enough to reach the connector block from their positions without the need for plugs and sockets. The mounting hooks will be installed now, and the holes drilled through the mill wall into the motor space, but rather than risking damage by fitting the lights themselves at this stage, temporary wires are led through the holes so that on completion of the building the wire tails from the lights can be drawn through and connected.

Bin Floor Drill a $^1/_8$in hole through the skirting strip into the motor space, 5in from the back wall and $^1/_4$in above the floor. The light will hang from the ridgeboard which is not yet fitted.

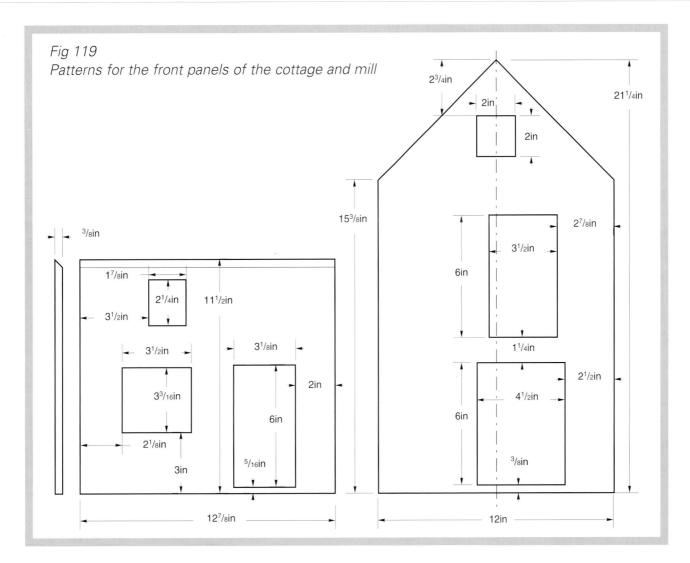

Fig 119
Patterns for the front panels of the cottage and mill

Stone Floor Insert a small hook, bent from brass wire or from a railway track pin, into the underside of the second joist from the back, at a point midway between beam M and the right-hand wall. File a slot $^1/16$in wide and $^1/16$in deep, across the top face of beam M, in line with the light position, and then follow the line through to the left-hand wall, where a $^1/8$in diameter hole is drilled through the floor bearer and the wall to the motor space.

Spout Floor Fit a hook on the third joist from the back, midway between beam K and the right-hand wall. File a slot across the top of K as with beam M, and again follow the line through to the left-hand floor bearer, where a $^1/8$in hole is drilled. Thread the temporary wires at all three points, and tie a bead or washer to each end to stop them unthreading.

INTERNAL PAINTING
First remove all floors, the Hurst frame, and fittings.

Mill This has one coat only of white emulsion on all interior walls. Do not worry about the patchy effect, as the walls need to have a slightly timeworn, grubby appearance. Subsequent handling, while completing the structure, will add to this effect. The floor bearers, floors, ladders, and Hurst Frame are all left natural wood.

Cottage This should have two or three coats of white emulsion, including the floor bearers, joists, and the underside of the first floor. The fireplace lintel, ladder, floors, and handrail are left as natural wood.

FRONT PANELS
The removable front panels for the cottage and mill are now cut from $^3/8$in plywood to the patterns in Fig 119.

Cottage Bevel the top edge of the cottage front to match that on the short section over the water-wheel and the roof slope on the end wall. The front door is identical to that in the Swan

Exterior of the mill and cottage

Inn and should be made and framed following Fig 36 (page 65). The windows have already been made, so the openings can be lined and the windows and sills glued in place. Details of window construction can be found on page 184–5.

Mill Make and frame the two doors following Fig 120. Both have a core of 1.5mm plywood. Note that the upper door opens inwards, and is hung on the right-hand side, with inset hinges as on the Swan Inn. It is planked on both sides, but needs no braces on the inside as this face cannot be seen. The lower door opens outwards, and swings back to lie against the front panel. This is planked on both sides, with braces on the inside face. The door frame is similar to that on the upper door, but reversed.

You will need to make the $2^{1}/_{2}$in x $^{5}/_{32}$in strap hinges from 0.016 x $^{1}/_{4}$in brass strip, (available from Hobby's). Cut two 3in lengths from a strip, and reduce the width to $^{5}/_{32}$in with tin snips. Fold back $^{1}/_{2}$in at one end of each, around a length of $^{1}/_{16}$in diameter rod, and crimp the two faces together with pliers. Bend this end outwards for about $^{1}/_{16}$in, close against the rod. Three holes are now drilled through the hinge, all are $^{1}/_{32}$in diameter and positioned $^{3}/_{16}$in from each end, and in the centre. These will be fastened to the outside face of the door with track pins which are cut off and filed smooth on the inside.

The pivot pins are made from $^{1}/_{16}$in diameter brass rod, bent at right angles and cut to form a vertical locating pin $^{3}/_{16}$in long, with a spigot of the same length for insertion into the door frame.

Houseworks no 1123 handles are fixed to the inside of the upper door, and to both sides of the lower door.

The upper window is made as for the other mill windows which have been fitted already. It has a $^{1}/_{8}$in thick lining at the top and bottom and three mullions, $^{3}/_{16}$in square, set obliquely. The lintels and sills should now be added.

MILL ROOF

Front Truss Cut a triangle of $^{3}/_{8}$in plywood to conform with the profile of the back wall above bin floor level. Trim the bottom corners equally so that, when resting on top of the floor, it fits snugly between the carcase walls at the front of the mill. Its back edge should rest against the front of the $^{3}/_{8}$in skirting strips on either side which stop $^{7}/_{16}$in from the front edge of the

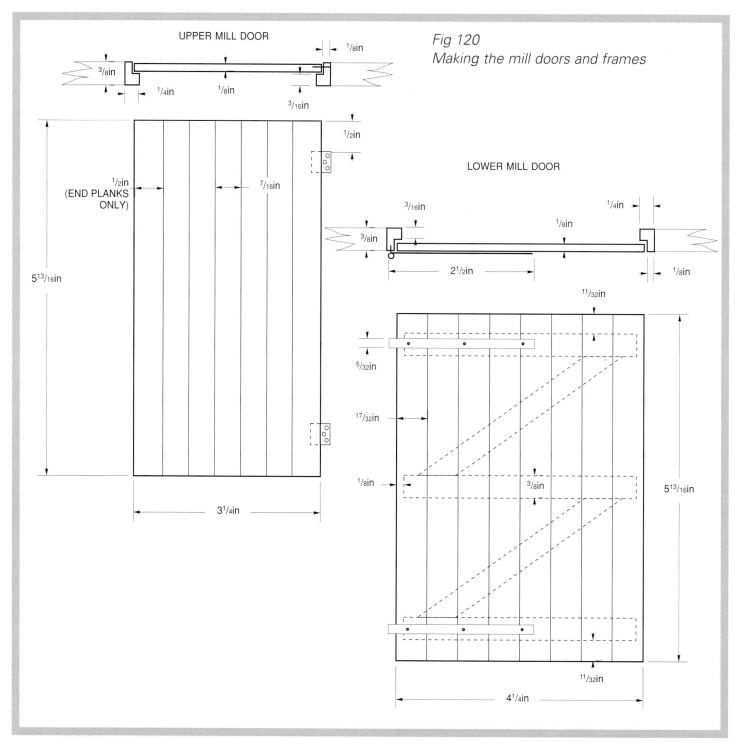

Fig 120
Making the mill doors and frames

walls. Cut away the centre and the bottom edge to leave a truss with roof slopes and short legs, all $1/2$in wide (see illustration on page 158, and Fig 121). Veneer the front face with $1/16$in thick elm to bring the overall thickness to $7/16$in, and therefore flush with the front of the walls and floor. Cut a notch $1/4$in wide and $5/16$in deep centrally in the apex, to receive the ridgeboard. The truss can now be glued and screwed in position from the outside of the walls into the legs. After fixing, remove the floor so that it does not become glued to the undersides of the legs.

Ridgeboard This is made from elm $5/8$in x $1/4$in, $15^3/8$in long (see Fig 122). Both ends are reduced to form tenons $5/16$in deep. At the front end the tenon is $7/16$in long to fit into the slot on the truss, and at the back it is $3/8$in long to fit in the slot on the back gable. Before fixing in place, a hook should be provided for the light on the underside 5in from the back wall. A 1in diameter Meccano pulley should be fitted under the ridge, directly over the central hole in the trapdoor. The mounting bracket for this is formed from a $2^1/2$in long Meccano strip, bent at right

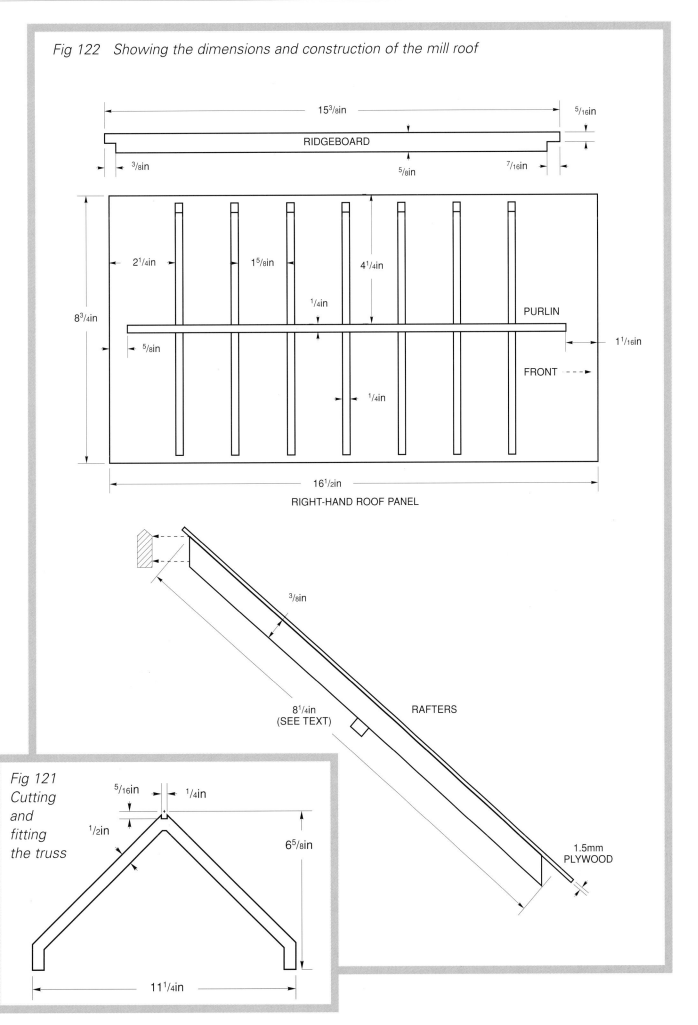

Fig 122 Showing the dimensions and construction of the mill roof

RIGHTBOARD

RIDGEBOARD

15³/₈in

5/₁₆in

3/₈in

5/₈in

7/₁₆in

PURLIN

FRONT

2¹/₄in

1⁵/₈in

4¹/₄in

¹/₄in

8³/₄in

5/₈in

1¹/₁₆in

¹/₄in

16¹/₂in

RIGHT-HAND ROOF PANEL

3/₈in

8¹/₄in
(SEE TEXT)

RAFTERS

1.5mm
PLYWOOD

Fig 121
Cutting
and
fitting
the truss

5/₁₆in

¹/₄in

¹/₂in

6⁵/₈in

11¹/₄in

Fig 123 Constructing the cottage roof

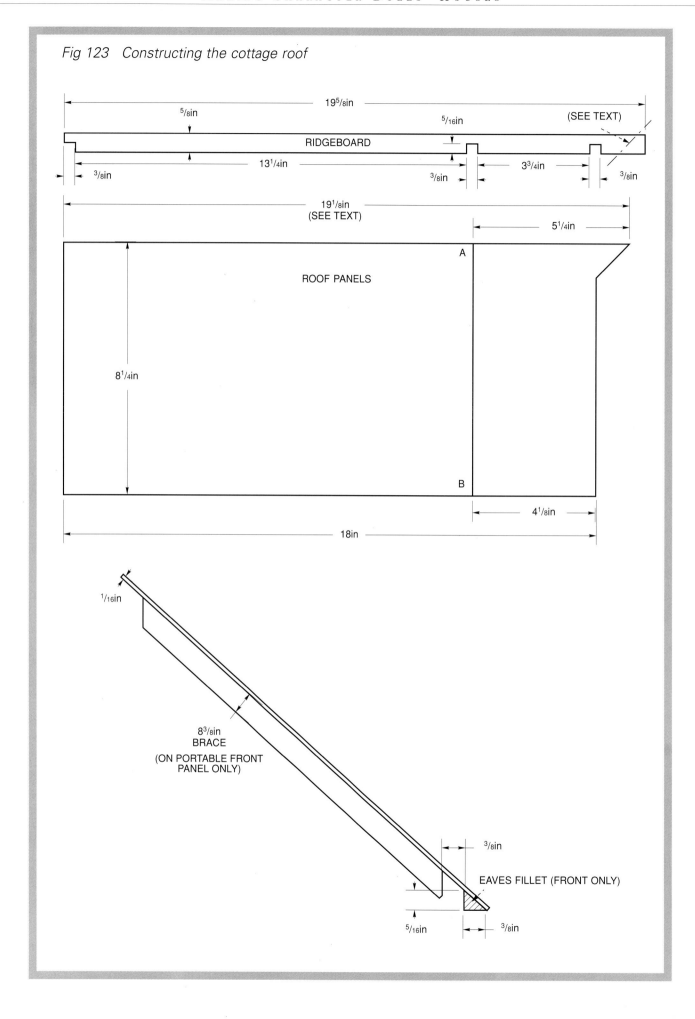

19⁵⁄₈in
⁵⁄₈in
⁵⁄₁₆in
(SEE TEXT)
RIDGEBOARD
13¹⁄₄in
³⁄₈in
³⁄₈in
3³⁄₄in
³⁄₈in

19¹⁄₈in
(SEE TEXT)
5¹⁄₄in

A
ROOF PANELS

8¹⁄₄in

B

4¹⁄₈in

18in

¹⁄₁₆in

8³⁄₈in
BRACE
(ON PORTABLE FRONT
PANEL ONLY)

³⁄₈in

EAVES FILLET (FRONT ONLY)

⁵⁄₁₆in
³⁄₈in

angles, either side of the central hole. It is screwed to the ridge beam through the central hole, with a short length of $^5/_{32}$in diameter Meccano rod used as an axle. Washers will be needed on each side of the pulley, to take up the slack. The ridgeboard can now be glued in place, and its top edge bevelled to the roof slope on each side.

Mill Roof The roof will be tiled, and as no bargeboards are fitted, the roof panels are cut from 1.5mm plywood to avoid unsightly thickness at the ends. Referring again to Fig 122, cut two pieces $8^3/_4$in x $16^1/_2$in. Take one of these, and tack it in position on the right-hand side of the mill roof, ensuring that it overhangs the back wall and the front panel by $^1/_4$in. The top edge should be level and flush along the ridge. Mark the underside with a pencil at the inside of the back wall, inside the truss, and along the top of the skirting strip. Remove the panel, and repeat this operation for the other side of the roof.

You should now cut sufficient $^3/_8$in x $^1/_4$in elm for the seven rafters on each side, which are each approximately $8^1/_4$in long. Note from Fig 122 that the tops are angled to fit against the ridgeboard, and the bottoms angled to fit against the skirting. Their length is best determined by cutting one piece overlength, and trimming one end until a good fit is obtained, taking care that the top edge of the rafter is level with the roof slopes of both the truss and back wall. Use this rafter as a pattern for the others.

Draw parallel lines $^1/_4$in apart on the underside of the right-hand panel where the rafters will be glued. Note that as the rafters are $1^5/_8$in apart, starting from the back, the first pair of lines should be that distance from the line indicating the back wall. The best method of fastening the rafters is with impact adhesive. To ensure correct up and down positioning, after applying the adhesive, the roof panel should be replaced on the building and tacked in position before the rafters are inserted, and pressed into contact with the panel.

Remove the panel and apply further pressure on the rafters to ensure good adhesion. A vice is best here, if you have one large enough. Repeat this operation for the second panel, and then remove it.

Both panels should now have a length of $^1/_4$in x $^3/_{16}$in elm purlin fastened on to the rafters.

Remember that the back end of this purlin should stop $^5/_8$in short of the end of the panel to allow for the wall thickness and overhang. It should also stop $1^1/_{16}$in from the front end, so that it will fit behind the truss. The upper edge of the purlin should be $4^1/_4$in below the top edge of the panel. Secure it to the rafters with a dab of glue and a track pin driven through at each crossing point. These pins are cut off flush on the outside of the panel.

For the tiles to lie flat on each other, a strip of wood, $^1/_8$in square, is glued along the bottom edge of each panel (see Fig 124). Fix these panels in place on the building by gluing and pinning into the roof slopes of the back wall and truss, and into the tops of the mill walls. Glue alone is best along the ridge.

Cottage Roof Start by making and fixing the ridgeboard (Fig 123). It is tenoned at the left-hand end to fit the slot in the end wall of the cottage – the other two slots engage in the top of the right-hand cottage wall and in the pad fixed to the outside of the mill wall. The inner end should be angled to butt against the mill roof.

Both front and back panels are cut $8^1/_4$in deep and $19^1/_8$in long. It is advisable to allow about $^1/_4$in extra length when cutting these panels, and to trim back afterwards. The open ends overhang the end wall of the cottage by $^1/_4$in. The other ends are cut back by approximately $1^1/_8$in to leave a small triangular nib at the top which projects on to the mill roof.

Back Roof After checking that it fits correctly, the back roof panel can be glued and pinned to the three roof slopes, and along the top of the back wall. Glue alone is sufficient along the ridge.

Front Roof Referring again to Fig 123, note that the front roof is cut in two, along the line AB. The smaller right-hand piece is fixed to the building but the left-hand piece will remain portable. Before cutting the panel, check that the cut line will follow the joint between the right-hand cottage wall and the $^1/_4$in thick framing applied to it, thus leaving a $^1/_4$in wide land for the portable section to rest on. Glue and pin the right-hand section in place. Place the cottage front panel in position, and secure it with masking tape.

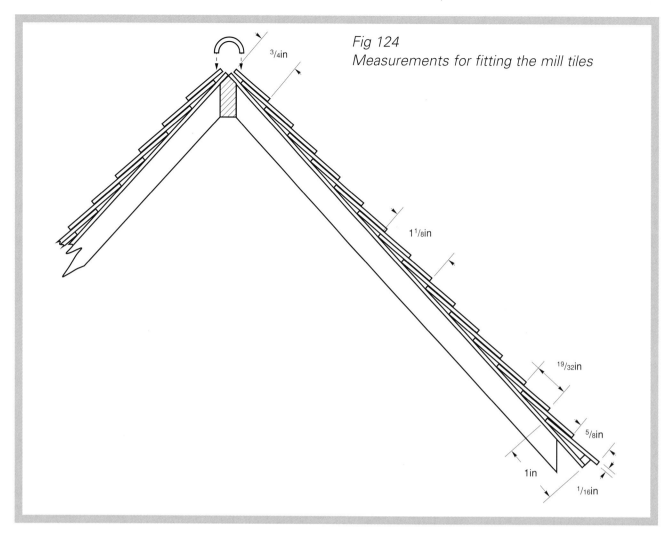

Fig 124
Measurements for fitting the mill tiles

$3/4$in

$1\,1/8$in

$19/32$in

$5/8$in

1in

$1/16$in

Three braces are required under the portable roof. They are cut from $3/8$in plywood, $3/4$in wide, with their ends angled, as for the mill rafters, to be a loose fit in length between the ridgeboard and the inside of the front panel. Glue one of these at the midpoint of the panel, and the other two close inside the walls at either end. Use the same method as for the mill rafters to glue them in place with impact adhesive.

Still referring to Fig 123, glue the triangular fillet under the edge of the front roof outside the portable front wall. Add $1/8$in square strips along the bottom edges of both front and back roof panels, to tilt the lower course of tiles. Cut through the strip at the joint between the two front sections.

Now that the mill roof is fixed, you may need to trim the gable slopes on the portable front panel of the mill so it can be removed easily. Do not trim too much, or it will not stay in place.

TILING

Five bags of fibre tiles are required. These are supplied by Cairn Tiles (see List of Suppliers),

and are of a terracotta-coloured pressed fibre, $1\,3/8$in long, $11/16$in wide and $1/16$in thick. If used straight from the bag, and applied so that half the length of a tile is exposed on each course, they look rather too deep for an older-style roof. To reduce their length to a fair representation of the old hand-made clay tiles is possible, but will necessitate almost twice as many courses, and a lot of extra labour. I have compromised by reducing the length of each tile to $1\,1/8$in, using tin snips or anvil secateurs, thus reducing the exposed depth by $1/8$in, from $11/16$in to $9/16$in. They are fastened to the roof with hot-melt glue from a gun. This is a fairly quick method, as the glue sets in a very short time. Depending on the grade of glue stick used, the setting time ranges from 50 to 90 seconds. Because it is difficult to regulate the thickness of the glue, a rather bumpy texture will be achieved, which is an advantage. Successive courses are staggered by half a tile width.

Mill Roof Following Fig 124, start tiling the right-hand roof panel. First glue a strip of $1/8$in

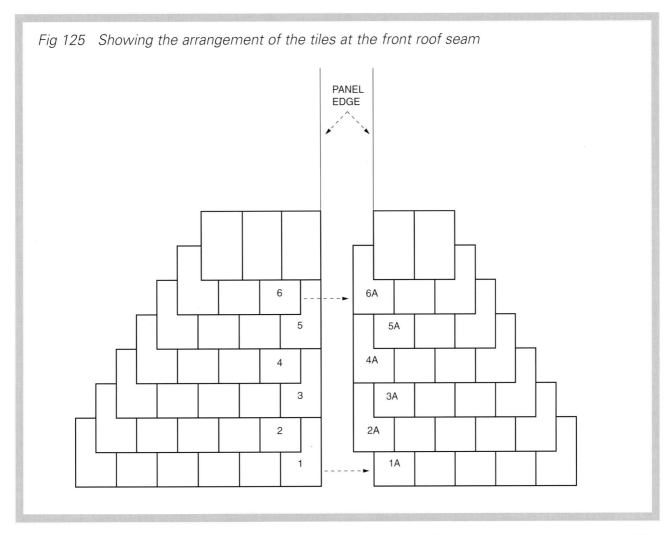

Fig 125   Showing the arrangement of the tiles at the front roof seam

square lime across the bottom edge of the panel to provide a tilt for the first course of tiles, and then draw a line across the roof panel from front to back, 1in above the bottom edge. Starting at the front, lay the first course of tiles with their top edges on this line, the last tile being half width. Now place a further tile on top of the first tile in the course just laid, so that $5/8$in of the lower tile is exposed. Mark the position of the top edge of the upper tile, and draw a line across the roof. Lay the second course to this line, starting at the front with a half-width tile. Sucessive lines are now drawn across the roof at $19/32$in intervals, starting at the top edge of the second course, and continuing to the ridge. Twelve more courses should be laid at this spacing, leaving $19/32$in of tile exposed on each course. The top course is laid with tiles cut to $3/4$in in length which, when partly covered by the ridge tiles, will leave $9/16$in exposed. Repeat this on the other side of the roof. In practice these measurements cannot be strictly adhered to but use them as a target and adjust the spacings so that the $3/4$in top tile (fifteenth course)

finishes flush at the top of the panel. The exposed section of this top tile must not be deeper than those below it.

Cottage Back Roof Lay the bottom course first. Starting at the right-hand end, lay a full tile with its top edge 1in above the bottom of the panel. The tiles are reduced in length when passing behind the chimney, so that their top edges remain in line. Referring to Fig 126, continue to the top and add the last course of tiles, which are now $9/16$in long, so that a clear space between $3/16$ and $1/4$in wide, is left along the ridge at the back, as a land for the ridge tiles on the portable front roof.

Cottage Front Roof The bottom edge of the portable section is $13^{7/8}$in long (Figs 123 and 126). The twenty tiles needed to cover this will take up $13^{3/4}$in if tightly butted. In practice, there will be slight gaps between successive tiles, which will take up the difference. This time the roof is marked for the first course as before, but instead of starting at the end, a full tile is laid on

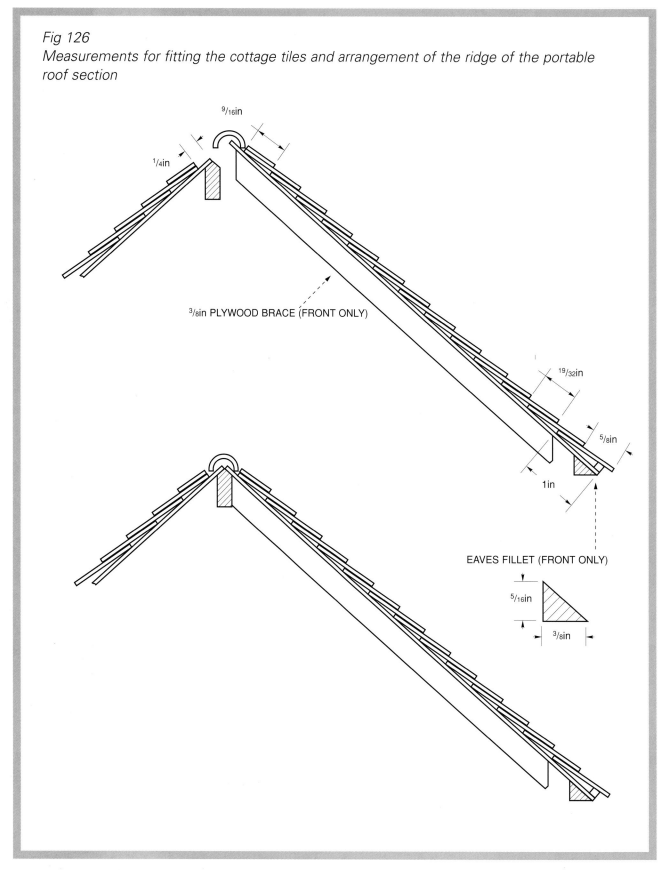

Fig 126
Measurements for fitting the cottage tiles and arrangement of the ridge of the portable roof section

³/₁₆in

¹/₄in

³/₈in PLYWOOD BRACE (FRONT ONLY)

¹⁹/₃₂in

⁵/₈in

1in

EAVES FILLET (FRONT ONLY)

⁵/₁₆in

³/₈in

either side of the joint between the two sections. Continue outwards from here, finishing with a full tile at the left-hand end and a part tile butting the mill wall. To avoid a hard seam line through the courses at the join, the tiles are not cut, but interlaced as shown in Fig 125, and the illustrations on pages 141 and 177. Note that, at the left-hand side of the join, the odd-numbered whole tiles 1, 3, 5, and so on, are glued with their right-hand edges flush with the panel edge.

The half tiles that would have been placed at the ends of the even-numbered courses are omitted and their places taken by the even-numbered whole tiles 2A, 4A, 6A, and so on, which are glued to the right-hand fixed section of roof panel, so that half their width overhangs the edge. When the two roof sections are pushed together, tile no 1 will butt against 1A, with its top section fitting under the lower part of 2A. Similarly tile no 3 butts 3A with its top under the lower part of 4A, and so on to the ridge.

RIDGE TILES

These are available from Cairn Tiles (see List of Suppliers), but since the angle between the upper courses on each side of the roof is rather more than 90°, they do not sit down very well without spreading. You can make your own easily by soaking spare tiles, still at the full length as supplied, in boiling water for a few minutes, and then rolling them lengthways over a length of dowel. These rounded top ridge tiles are quite authentic. After bending to shape, they will spread a little as they dry, leaving a gap of $3/8 - 7/16$in between the sides.

Mill Ridge When thoroughly dry, glue a line of ridge tiles along the mill roof, starting at the front with a tile cut so that its inner end covers only half the width of the second tile on the top course. The others are used full length, with the exception of the last one, which is cut back flush with the roof edge at the back. Hot-melt glue is not very successful for fixing ridge tiles and quick-setting epoxy adhesive is recommended instead.

Cottage Ridge With the portable roof panel in position, glue ridge tiles along its top edge, leaving the back half of each tile unglued and forming a hook which will engage over the clear space left at the top of the back roof. The edges of these tiles will butt against the tops of the $9/16$in tiles laid here, rather than rest on top of them. The remainder of the ridge tiles along the fixed section are glued to both sides of the roof. Take care when gluing either side of the join in the roof, not to stick the two sections together.

Once tiling is completed, the underside of the eaves should be trimmed horizontal with a chisel and a small plane. To achieve a rather more weathered look, chip the bottom corner off one or two tiles with a chisel, and give the roof a

The interlacing of tiles on the portable cottage roof

wash of light and medium oak spirit stain. This should not be applied too evenly as streaks and patches enhance the effect.

Painting The inside of the cottage roof at the back should now be painted to match the rest of the interior. The inside faces of the portable roof and front panels are best varnished, as white paint will soon show fingermarks.

STONEWORK

This can be done with the glue/Polyfilla mix as on the Forge and Cider Barn, or by the alternative method used here, which has the advantage of being less messy, and only one wall need be done at a time. It loses something in surface texture, but the overall effect is quite good.

First paint all outside walls with one coat of textured masonry paint. Any brand of paint should be suitable, but the make used here was Jewsons. Allow the paint to dry thoroughly, then, taking one wall at a time, and not forgetting the garden wall, give each a wash of Liberon light oak spirit stain, applied with a sponge and allowed to flood down the wall. Use a brush to cut in round doors and windows.

While the stain is still wet, apply a further wash over the top, this time of medium oak stain, which should be deliberately patchy, and allowed to streak. Blot the surface with a dry sponge or scrap of foam. The spirit stain has a softening effect on the paint which, after about fifteen minutes, can be scribed with the stonework pattern shown in Fig 5 on page 17. The mortar lines are revealed as white when the stained top surface is cut through. If you find that these lines are again turning brown, it means that the stain is not yet dry enough, so leave it for a little longer. The softening effect would appear to last for about an hour, after which the surface reverts to its original hardness. The stonework effect is now complete, and no further coating or treatment is required.

WIRING

The three lights (Peter Kennedy) should now be installed in the mill. Attach the wire tails to the wires already placed, and draw them through into the motor space. The wires at each light are positioned over the hooks already provided. The wire from the bin floor light passes from the hook down the left-hand roof slope between the roof panel and purlin, before entering the hole in the left-hand wall. The wires from the remaining two lights pass from the hooks across the ceiling, and over beams K and M respectively, lying in the slots provided, and then on through the wall.

All three lights should be connected together in parallel, inside the motor space. Three wires are twisted together, one from each light, followed by the remaining three, to form two tails. These are now secured to one side of the connector block, together with the wires from the cottage. A heavier gauge wire for the feed from the transformer is connected to the other side of the block.

GLAZING

The three cottage windows are now glazed with Glodex or glass, cut as a tight push fit on the inside of the window bars. No glazing is required for the mill.

SACK HOIST

The chain from the winding drum should now be threaded upwards over the pulley on the ridgeboard. A short length of thin wire can be used as a needle to help with the threading. This chain then runs down through both trap-doors to the spout floor.

LANDSCAPING

A bridge formed from two parallel planks of elm, $3/4$in wide, $1/8$in thick, and 8in long, is placed across the millstream, midway between the water-wheel and the front edge of the base frame. The upper contour pad at each side of the stream should be cut away, so that the planks can settle to a level $3/4 - 7/8$in above the bed of the stream. The planks are weathered with vinegar, but not fixed in position until the stream has been finished.

Mill Stream The area under the stream was filled with scrap plywood when the base frame was made. The stream is cast from polyester resin, but before mixing this the bed must be made temporarily leak-proof. This is done by sealing the joints on the underside with masking tape. Note that the stream extends inwards on to the base of the buildings. The banks here will be raised whenever the buildings are separated from the base frame, and must not be coated with resin. To prevent this, they are coated first with Vaseline. The open end of the stream under the water-wheel should have a strip of $3/8$in plywood about $1/2$in wide, cut as a tight push fit across the open end. Seal this with tape at the back.

A 500ml can of resin is needed to fill the river bed to a depth of $3/8$in. Mix this with its hardener as directed on the can, and pour sufficient to cover the bed to a depth of about $1/8$in. Check for leaks, and reseal if necessary. Now fill to the $3/8$in level, adding small stones and pieces of broom bristle at the edges to simulate reeds. Allow to set. At average temperatures, this will take about 45 minutes. The resin heats considerably during the setting process, and the surface will probably distort. This produces a fairly convincing ripple effect on the surface.

As soon as the resin has set, prise up the building base so that the inner banks are clear of the resin, remove the $3/8$in plywood end stop, and allow to cure for 24 hours before handling. The Vaseline residue can then be wiped off the banks, and the building base reset in position. E-Z Water can be used as an alternative to polyester resin (see page 39), after the initial ground work has been prepared, and poured into the stream bed.

Mark out a pathway from the mill, over the bridge, to the cottage door. Glue the bridge planks in position over the stream, and fair the ends into the landscape with Polyfilla. Paint the path, and the yard area in front of the mill, a browny grey. The remainder is grassed over, using railway scenic powders, taking care that the joint between the building base and the base frame is kept clear. If you wish, a cover plate of $^1/_8$in plywood, $6^3/_4$in x $4^1/_2$in, can be screwed to the back wall over the motor space, having first had notches cut in its lower edge for the motor and lighting cables.

WATER MILL – LIST OF SUPPLIERS

And Other Bits: Candlestick.
Sue Austen: Mice and ducks.
Avon Miniatures: Crockery and honey pot.
Bonds: Mill gears, bolts, and rivets.
Bryntor: Sink and dog bowl.
Cassel's: Vegetables and butter dish.
Cairn Tiles: Roofing.
Peter Clark: Heron.
C & D Crafts: Baskets.
Crouzet: Mains motor (Type 82344 FC 10 rpm).
Dijon: Cir-Kit wire and eyelets.
Dolphin Miniatures: Dresser, table, chairs, chest of drawers, sack trolley, and barrel.
Fantasie: Linen basket.
Victoria Fasken: Cockerel plate.
Floriana's Dolls' House Shop: Corn dolly.
Hobby's: Motor, chain, and hinges (the Clearbox is an alternative to the Crouzet motor).
Isobel Hockey: Knitted long johns.
C.A. & B.A. Hooper: Brass tap.
Carol Lodder: Double bed, jug, storage jar, floral plate, and cider flagon.
Mainly Men Minis: Dolls.
Lynne Mitchell: Cut flowers.
M W Models: Supplier of Meccano parts.
Phoenix Model Developments: Kit for range.
Quality Dolls' House Miniatures: Bread bin, trowel, grain, and flour sacks.
Small Sorts: Beehive and Jack Russell terrier.
Sussex Crafts: Bucket and pot of jam.
Thames Valley Crafts: Packet of oats and Virol jar.
John Watkins: Weather vane.
Wood 'n' Wool Miniatures: Cottage lighting, and alternative source of mill lighting

The handcart, watering can, hay rake, and sign, and all the mill lighting (by Peter Kennedy) are from the author's own collection. The knitted bedspread was made by Marie Firkins from a pattern by Isobel Hockey.

IN THE
WORKSHOP

Assuming that you already have a basic wood-working toolkit, this chapter focuses on the more specialised tools and equipment that the DIY woodworker may not have.

SAFETY
The following simple rules should be followed.

■ Never wear loose clothing that can get caught in a revolving machine.
■ Wear safety glasses.
■ Always use properly adjusted machine guards where these are fitted.
■ Keep both hands behind the cutting edge of sharp hand tools.
■ Always unplug power tools before making any adjustments, particularly when changing saw blades or router cutters.
■ Ensure that all plugs are fitted with the correct fuse, and check periodically to ensure that the cable connections are tight. A circuit breaker should be used between the outlet socket and the machine plug.
■ Use push sticks wherever possible, particularly when machining small parts, to keep your fingers out of range of the cutting edge.
■ Do not use power tools in poor light or low temperatures – your concentration should be on the task in hand, *not* distracted by cold fingers or difficulty in following pencilled outlines.
■ Keep the workshop floor clear of obstacles and trailing leads.

POWER TOOLS
A wide variety of small power tools are now produced with the do-it-yourselfer in mind and their cost will be well repaid both in terms of the projects in this book, and for many other jobs around the home. If you do not have the power tools, the projects can still be completed using hand tools alone, but will obviously take considerably more time.

Circular-saw bench
This should have a depth of cut around 2in, and be provided with a rip fence, cross-cutting guide (preferably adjustable for cutting mitres), rise and fall, and tilt adjustment to 45°. The Kity model 511 used in these projects is regrettably no longer available, but the Makita 2708 is a suitable alternative.

A useful addition is the Scheppach model TK, which has a depth of cut a little over $3^{1}/2$in. This saw-bench can be fitted with a folding panel-cutting table, which is useful when handling large sheets of plywood. The extra depth of cut allows conversion of large-dimension timber to your own requirements.

Router
Probably the most suitable router for the projects in this book is the Bosch model POF 500A. Although a little under-powered when cutting through the full depth of $^{3}/8$in plywood, for example when making door and window

Miniature hardware, lighting and roofing materials, gears and alternative motor

openings, satisfactory results can be achieved by taking several shallow cuts and using the template guide provided. When fitted in the drill stand (which is available at extra cost), the Bosch router will cut the carcase joints in the plywood panels with ease, as well as the joints and rebates in small components such as window bars, and door frames. A range of straight cutters will be needed in the following sizes: $^1/16$in, $^1/8$in, $^1/4$in, and $^3/8$in. The latter two sizes are available with tungsten carbide tips. These have a much longer life when used for cutting plywood, where the glue line will soon destroy the edge of a high speed steel cutter. Profile cutters will be required if you make your own mouldings.

Jigsaw

Useful for cutting out door and window openings as an alternative to a router, but not essential if you have a hand fretsaw.

Orbital sander

This is not essential but, when used with a simple jig, makes a better job of cleaning off, and thicknessing window assemblies where a block plane can tear or split small components.

12V Minicraft Drill and Transformer

The Topi is the smallest drill in the Minicraft range, and can be very helpful in tight corners. A wide range of accessories is available, and the Dremel sanding drum can also be used with it. Standard size self-adhesive sanding discs are readily available, but for some applications better results can be achieved when the disc is a little larger than the backing pad, allowing greater flexibility inside curves. The Olfa compass cutter (available from Hobby's) will enable you to cut several small discs of whatever size you choose out of one large disc of 6in to 8in diameter. This method will also provide a much wider range of grit sizes than those supplied as standard.

Soldering Iron

A small soldering iron of about 25 watts will be needed for electrical connections.

Hot-melt Glue Gun

This is the best method of applying the fibre tiles to the roof of the Water Mill, and the yealms of coconut fibre to the roof of the Cider Barn and Forge. Glue sticks are available with differing 'open' times. You should use those of around 60 to 90 seconds so that the tiles or yealms can be positioned before the glue has set.

HAND TOOLS

The following will be needed over the whole range of projects; others with limited application are mentioned in the text where the need arises.

Squares

A 4ft T-square is best for marking out large plywood panels. The 9 inch square used for carcase assembly can be used with a straight edge, but is not as convenient. A very small engineer's square – around $2^{1}/2$in – will be needed for small assemblies such as windows.

Planes

A jack plane around 14in long (Stanley No 5) can be helpful on long straight edges, but with care a normal smoothing plane will suffice.

Apart from its more obvious use, a rabbet plane (Stanley No 78 or similar) will be needed in several situations where the inset blade of a normal plane will not cover the whole surface of the work to be trimmed, as in the angle between a wall and an overhanging roof. A block plane 5in to 6in long is needed for fine cuts on small components, and for end grain.

Fretsaw

Small, shaped components are more easily cut with a fretsaw and it will also cut door and window openings if you do not have a router or jigsaw. It should have a 12in throat.

Cramps

You will need at least two of each of the following sizes of G-Cramp; 2in, 3in, and 4in. Always use a small piece of scrap wood between the cramp and the workpiece, to avoid denting the surface.

Chisels

You should have at least four chisels, preferably of the bevel-edged type: $^{1}/4$in, $^{3}/8$in, $^{1}/2$in, and 3/4in. Additionally, very small chisels, $^{1}/16$in and $^{1}/8$in, can be made from broken needle files.

Scraper

A small Skarsten scraper handle, used with both $1^{1}/2$in and 3in blades, will smooth small parts where a very fine cut is required, and also remove paint splashes or glue – particularly in awkward corners.

Sandplates

Sandvik have a range of self-adhesive hardened-steel sanding plates in a variety of grades. When mounted on a backing of $^{1}/4$in plywood, they are ideal for cleaning up the inside edges of door and window openings. The smaller plates can be used without a backing and, being only a few thousandths of an inch thick, work well in cleaning out the slots in the door jambs.

Pliers

Long-nosed pliers are useful for holding small panel or veneer pins while these are being hammered. This especially applies to work inside a carcase where a hand obscures visibility.

Hammer

A small pin hammer, around 4oz will be needed.

Bevel and Protractor

An adjustable bevel and a protractor are used to mark out and check roof angles, and also to set the mitre guide and tilt on the circular-saw bench, which are normally graduated but often inaccurate.

SMALL TOOLS

The following small tools should also be included. For electrical work, a very small screwdriver and end or side cutters; and for trimming cuts on wood, a razor saw and X-acto knife. A Swann-Morton knife (no 3 handle and no 10A blades), will also be needed, primarily for very light cuts, and for trimming wallpaper. The blades fitted to this knife are not as robust as the X-acto blades, and are not suitable for deep cuts in wood. Where very small holes are to be drilled, a hand-held pin chuck is required. Whilst not essential, a small airbrush or Jennican (both available from Hobby's) will save a lot of time when painting windows – particularly on the Georgian House. The Jennican is a rechargeable aerosol container which is pressurised with a car or bicycle pump. It can also be used empty to blow dust and debris from awkward corners.

MATERIALS

The timber and plywood needed for each project is listed at the beginning of that chapter, classified for ease of reference, in groups with a common thickness. Lengths and areas are approximate and for guidance only. From enquiries received from my first book it appears that many people are having difficulty in getting timber and plywood. With this in mind, for each project a pack containing sufficient plywood, and appropriate hardwoods, cut to convenient sizes, is available from Dolphin Miniatures. Lighting packs are also available. S.A.E. please to the address given on page 188, for details and prices.

Plywood

All the projects are built from birch plywood, mostly $^3/8$in (9mm), $^1/4$in (6mm), and to a lesser degree $^1/8$in (3mm) thick. Doors and some other fittings require a small quantity of 1.5mm ply. Always buy the best quality you can find and make sure that it is flat. Some sheets may have a set in them caused by uneven drying of the various laminates, and although not so important when cut into smaller pieces, this will cause a major problem with large panels.

Mahogany

This is really only required for the stairs in the Georgian House, although it could also be used as an alternative to elm when constructing the bar and shelves in the Swan Inn. Old broken furniture can often provide a supply of the Honduras or Cuban varieties. Some timbers can be stained to resemble mahogany but it is preferable to avoid staining wherever possible as it is never truly convincing and can cause problems, such as inhibiting the drying of some surface coatings.

Elm

This features strongly in all but the Georgian House. Always look for wood with a fine, straight grain and dark brown in colour. Avoid timber with a wild grain pattern, as it will not cut or plane easily and is much more likely to warp.

Oak

English oak is a fair substitute for elm if you can find it with a fine enough grain. Usually it is not dark enough without further treatment.

Lime (basswood)

Very good for small components such as windows, edge veneers and mouldings. It finishes well and is very stable, the only disadvantage being that it is rather soft and marks easily.

Cherry

A nice alternative to lime for flooring, particularly in the Georgian House.

Beech

An alternative to lime but not very good when cut to very small dimensions.

Microwood

A range of plain or self-adhesive veneers is readily available at DIY stores or from Hobby's. Some of the lighter coloured varieties (particularly Anga) are very good for flooring when cut into strips and laid on top of plain plywood.

It is worth repeating here that English hardwoods cannot usually be obtained from DIY stores. You should go to a sawmill or timber merchant.

Glues

Evostik white PVA is best for carcase and window construction. Take care when gluing parts that may later be varnished as it is very difficult to remove all traces from surfaces adjacent to the joint, and these show up as an unsightly milky bloom under the varnish. Wherever possible a sealing coat of varnish should be applied first (not on the surfaces to be glued) to stop glue penetration where it is not wanted.

Evostik contact adhesive is used on some components where an immediate hold is required and pressure can easily be applied (preferably with a vice), and for edge veneering carcases. Do not varnish over contact adhesives for at least twenty-four hours as polyurethanes act as a solvent. Even then, apply the first coat sparingly so that it does not penetrate through to the glued surface.

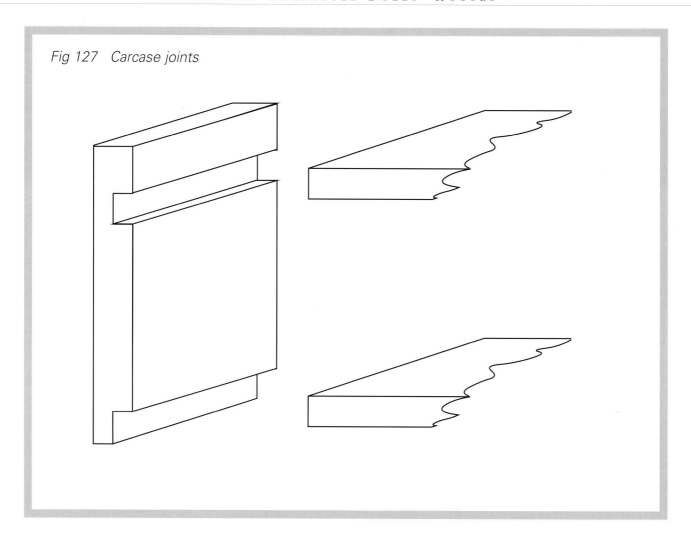

Fig 127   Carcase joints

Quick-setting epoxy resin is used when fitting the door hinges.

Carcases

All the carcases are constructed using lap or housed joints, glued and pinned or screwed (Fig 127). These joints are most easily cut with the router. Intermediate floors on some models are not glued or pinned so that they can be removed for decorating.

Windows

Windows are cross-halved using a router in the following way:

Cut lime a little over $1/8$in thick x 2–3in wide, in lengths according to the height and width of the finished window. (As a general rule a 2in width will produce about ten bars $1/8$in wide, allowing for loss in the saw-cuts.)

Mark these lengths where the joints are to be cut and rout across the full width using a $1/8$in cutter set to a depth of $1/16$in.

Using the circular saw, slice the bars off the block a little over $1/8$in wide (Fig128). *A push*

stick is essential. One or two passes on each cut face with a fine set block plane will prepare the bars for gluing. When you have sufficient vertical and horizontal bars for the window, glue them together and clamp the corners with a spring paperclip. As the basic timber was cut a little over $1/8$in thick you will find after gluing that the outer faces are not level. Prepare a simple jig from $1/8$in hardboard or ply as follows: cut a square approximately 6 x 6in with a cut-out in the middle just larger than the window. Nail this square to a scrap of plywood and clamp it to the benchtop. The window is placed in the centre of the recess and surfaced on one side with the orbital sander, then reversed and sanded down to the $1/8$in thickness of the hardboard or plywood jig.

Lightly plane the edges to fit inside the window linings. A sandplate can be helpful here as there is less risk of splitting out the corners.

Doors

All the doors are made and hung in the same way, although some are panelled and some are

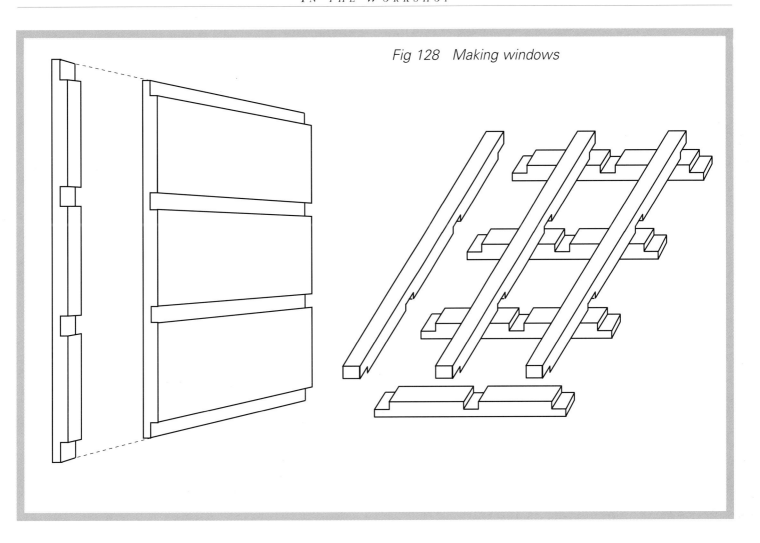

Fig 128 Making windows

planked and braced. Start with a 1.5mm plywood core, cut to the finished dimensions of the door. The brass hinges used are approximately $1/64$in thick and $11/32$in deep, each flap being $5/32$in wide. When fully open the total width is approximately $3/8$in. They are available from most dolls' house shops or from Hobby's. Lay the hinges on the opening side of the door core in the positions shown, $1/2$in from the top and bottom edges of the door, and mark round them with a sharp knife, allowing for half the barrel in addition to the flap. Remove the surface veneer within these marks with a small chisel (Fig 129). The door is then planked or panelled on both sides using wood strip cut to the dimensions specified in each particular project. There is now a pair of slots in the edge of the door a little to one side of centre, on the side which will open outwards. Cut away a little of the surface planking on this side to accept half the hinge barrel. The door jambs are cut and rebated to the measurements given in each project, and slots to accommodate the hinges are cut into the jamb on the hanging side, allowing about $1/32$in

extra in length for vertical adjustment when hanging the door. The door can now be sealed with one coat of matt varnish (or matt white Humbrol paint in the case of the Georgian House), after which the hinges are glued in place with quick-setting epoxy. Take care to remove any surplus, particularly around the barrel, while the adhesive is still slightly rubbery. The door will be fitted, with the other sides of the hinges being glued into the slots in the door jamb, after decorating is completed.

Floors

Apart from the Georgian House the boarded floors in the projects have been scribed directly onto the plywood. Whilst this treatment is quite effective, strips of lime or cherry $1/32$in thick, cut to the appropriate widths, and glued with impact adhesive are a considerable improvement, if you have the time and patience. When selecting Formica for the flagstones try to find offcuts with a differing back colour, this can vary from brown through several shades of grey, and the slight colour variation over a floor adds greatly

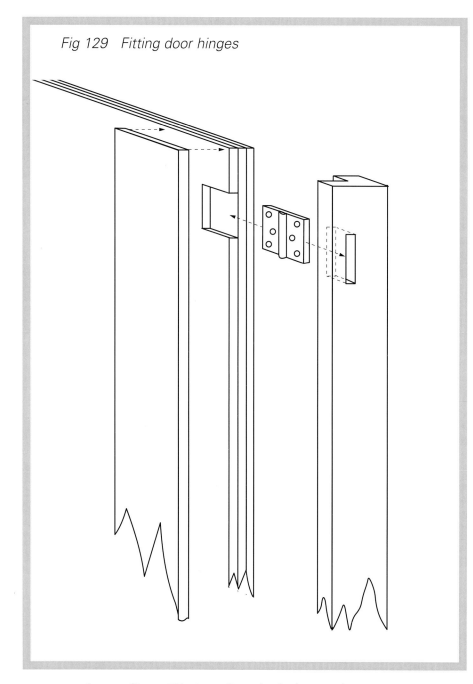

Fig 129 Fitting door hinges

have a full-size application, it is not worth the expense of shaped cutters, as a wide range of mouldings is available from Borcraft.

Wiring and Lighting

Use is made wherever possible of self-adhesive copper tape, which is available in rolls either as a single strip or a twin tape. Cir-Kit Concepts (from the USA, and imported by Dijon) produce a twin tape with surface insulation, which is very convenient, as the two conductor strips are already correctly spaced, and additional insulation on crossovers is not required. Where two lengths are to be joined, a small brass brad must be hammered into the overlap to establish contact between the two layers.

If solder joints are to be made on the surface, a brad should be inserted, and connection made to this. Outlet sockets are available with pins moulded into them, which can be hammered directly into the tape. Alternatively, small brass eyelets can be inserted into pre-drilled holes in each conductor, spaced to accept the plugs.

Lighting is available in two types: fittings with replaceable bulbs; and fittings with grain-of-wheat bulbs where the bulb and wire tails come as one unit, and in the event of failure the whole unit has to be stripped out and replaced. There are obviously some advantages in having replaceable bulbs, particularly if the light is to be sited in an awkward position and there is no provision for a plug-in ceiling rose or backplate. Cir-Kit Concepts have a good range of fittings some with replaceable bulbs, some with grain-of-wheat bulbs. Wood 'n' Wool (UK) have a very attractive range of lighting with a rather more English style – mostly with replaceable bulbs. Both firms supply booklets on using their equipment, and both can supply suitable transformers. But please note that due to differences in mains voltage, US transformers cannot be used in Britain and vice versa. Each project has detailed instructions

to the realism. Having first had their edges sanded to an irregular profile, as shown in Fig 33 (on page 61), the stones are then laid upside down with the back forming the top surface. You should always wear a protective mask when sanding formica.

Mouldings

All the mouldings used in this book (for cornice, window surrounds etc.) can be made on the router table, if you have a fair selection of profile cutters. Most of the cutters available for full-size joinery are too large to be of any use, but in some cases mouldings can be made by using just a part of the cutting edge, or by a combination of two or more cutters. However, unless you regarding installation of tape runs and lighting but remember that wherever there is a join between two tapes a brad must be inserted through each pair of conductors to establish electrical contact. It is worth using a test bulb to check the circuit at each stage of installation to avoid unnecessary problems later on. Good lighting is available from other manufacturers, but fittings from Cir-Kit and Wood 'n' Wool have been used predominantly in this book.

Decorating

The most important part of the finishing process is surface preparation. Unless this is carried out thoroughly, no amount of paint will ever disguise the defects. You must rub down thoroughly between coats with a progressively finer paper, and vacuum away all dust. Three grades of silicone-carbide abrasive paper are recommended: 180, 220, and 400. Stopping or wood filler will also be needed to fill in screw and nail holes.

Where clear varnish is to be applied over light or honey-coloured woods neutral plastic wood produces good results, but for mahogany or elm where a coloured stopping is required, or on wood that is to be painted, Brummer stopping is recommended.

Weathering Before applying the vinegar mixture described in Chapter 1 (Cider Barn) the timber should be textured using the small disc or drum sander to achieve a rough-hewn effect, and the grain accentuated by scratching a broken hacksaw blade along the surface. Remember to test the mix on a scrap of similar wood, and dilute it with more water if it is too dark. The best results are obtained on elm or lime, oak generally turns rather too black.

Chemical blackening Rather than paint some small metal fittings, particularly chain where the small links can get clogged, chemical treatments are available from Liberon Waxes. These products are Haematite for steel, and Tourmaline for brass, bronze, and copper. Full instructions are supplied with the product.

Paints and varnishes Emulsion should be used for plain walls and ceilings, Humbrol matt or satin, either acrylic or oil-based, on doors, windows, and mouldings. Whitewashed exterior walls have a coating of textured masonry paint. Floors are coated with clear matt varnish used both straight from the tin and also mixed with a little walnut varnish stain to produce colour variations on scribed floorboards which would otherwise be a uniform colour.

Wallpapers Normal household wallpaper paste is used but the walls should be sized first to limit absorption, and the paper applied with a generous overlap at openings and front edges. Only when thoroughly dry should these be trimmed using the Swann-Morton knife with a new blade. Always start on the back wall and work outwards. Skirting and dummy doors are best pre-painted and applied over the paper.

Parts of the houses will be very difficult , if not impossible to reach once assembly is finished. Wherever possible you should paint sections before or during assembly, so that the internal paintwork needs no more than a touch-up after construction is completed. Painting special effects, such as stonework, is covered in the relevant chapter.

ACKNOWLEDGEMENTS

FEATURED MAKERS AND RETAILERS

The furniture and accessories featured in this book are from a selection of craftspeople with widely differing marketing policies. Some have small showrooms and can be visited by prior appointment, some sell only at fairs or by mail order, and others are wholesale suppliers whose products are only available from miniatures shops. Most have a catalogue for which a charge is made, but *please remember*, when writing for details, to enclose a stamped, addressed envelope or international reply coupons, otherwise you are unlikely to receive a reply.

As so many telephone numbers are now being changed, following current BT policy, rather than give information which may be wrong at the time of publication they have been omitted.

And Other Bits: 7 Bush Close, Bredgar, Kent ME9 8DR.

Lucy Askew: 5 Sibella Road, London SW4 6JA.

Sue Austen: Folly End Farm, Ashton, Bishop's Waltham, Hants SO3 1FQ.

Avon Miniatures: The Quarterdeck, 20 Brandize Park, Okehampton, Devon EX20 1EQ.

Peggy Birrell: 5 Norwich Road, Exwick, Exeter, Devon EX4 2DN.

Gordon Blacklock: 18 Countisbury Road, Norton, Stockton-on-Tees, Cleveland TS20 1PZ.

Patricia Borwick: Neptune House, Newells Lane, Bosham, W Sussex PO18 8PS.

The Torbay Pottery: 60 Shirburn Road, Torquay, Devon TQ1 4HR

Irene Campbell: Littlefields Studio, Bishopswood, Chard, Somerset TA20 3RS.

Peter Clark: 2 The Ridgeway, Ware, Herts SG12 0RT

C & D Crafts: 133 Lower Hillmorton Road, Rugby, Warks CV21 3TN.

Crafts & Collectables: 1 Oakfield, Newton St. Petrock, Holsworthy, Devon EX22 7LP.

Veronique Cornish: Rose Cottage, The Street, Dilham, North Walsham, Norfolk NR28 9PX.

Terry Curran: 27 Chapel Street, Mosborough, Sheffield, Yorks S19 5BT.

Dolphin Miniatures: The Gallery, The Square, Whimple, Exeter, Devon EX5 2SL

Escutcheon: 28 Queslett Road East, Streetly, Sutton Coldfield, W Midlands B74 2EX.

David Edwards: Available through Royal Mile Miniatures (see shops).

Fantasie: Kestrel, The Lane, Fawley, Southampton, Hants SO4 1EY.

Victoria Fasken: Search Farm House, Stourton, Warminster, Wilts BA12 6QQ.

Isobel Hockey: 25 Branksome Avenue, Upper Shirley, Southampton, Hants SO15 5NX

C.A. & B.A. Hooper: 3 Bunting Close, Ogwell Cross, Newton Abbot, Devon. TQ12 6BU.

Just in Case: 8 Southfields Road, West Kingsdown, Sevenoaks, Kent TN15 6LB.

Carol Lodder: Brooks Cottage, Belchalwell, Blandford Forum, Dorset DT11 OEG.

Lilliput Miniatures: 12 School Close, St Columb Minor, Newquay, Cornwall TR7 3EN.

Mainly Men Minis: 32 Walter Avenue S., Hamilton L8H IA5, Ontario, Canada

Stuart McCabe: 119 Springfield Road, Elburton, Plymouth, Devon.

Miniature Dreams: Millbrook Cottage, Carr Moss Lane, Ormskirk, Lancs L39 8SA.

Lynne Mitchell: Pikes Barn, Uplowman Road, Tiverton, Devon EX16 4LU.

Nursery of Miniatures: Hilltop, Hutgate Road, Honiton, Devon EX14 8SX.

Ottervale China: 8 Coleridge Road, Ottery St. Mary, Devon EX11 1TD.

The Pram Collection: 7 The Vale, S. Ruislip, Middlesex HA4 OSG.

Quaintways Dolls' House Cottage: Lyme Road, Uplyme, Lyme Regis, Dorset DT7 3TQ.

Terence Stringer: Spindles, Lexham Road, Litcham, Norfolk PE32 2QQ.

Bernardo Traettino: 52 Howe Road, East Lichfield, Connecticut 06759, U.S.A

Pat Venning: Pineways, Faircross Avenue, Weymouth, Dorset DT4 0DD.
John & Valerie Watkins: 12 Biddel Springs, Highworth, Swindon, Wilts SN6 7BH.

FEATURED MAIL ORDER SUPPLIERS
Carol Black Miniatures: Sun Hill, Great Strickland, Penrith, Cumbria CA10 3DF.
Blackwells of Hawkwell (*UK distributors for Houseworks and Mini Mundus*):
733/5 London Road, Westcliff-on-Sea, Essex SS0 9ST.
Bonds O' Euston Road Ltd: Arundel House, Rumbolds Hill, Midhurst, Sussex GU29 9NE.
Borcraft Miniatures: 8 Fairfax View, Scotland Lane, Horsforth, Leeds, Yorks LS18 5SZ.
Cairn Tiles: 6 College Green, Bideford, Devon EX39 3JY.
Cassel's: 142 Brockhurst Road, Gosport, Hants PO12 3BA.
Crouzet Motors: Distributed by **Microdrives Ltd**, Aercon House, Alfred Road, Gravesend, Kent DA11 7QF.
W. Hobby Ltd: Knights Hill Square, London SE27 0HH.
M W Models: "Everything Meccano", 4 Greys Road, Henley-on-Thames, Oxon RG9 1RY.
Phoenix Model Developments Ltd: The Square, Earls Barton, Northampton NN6 0NA.
Sussex Crafts : Hassocks House, Comptons Brow Lane, Horsham, W Sussex RH13 6BX.
Thames Valley Crafts: Mere House, Dedmere Road, Marlow, Bucks SL7 1PD.
Wood 'n' Wool Miniatures: Unit 1. Old Co-op Bakery, Kellet Road, Carnforth, Lancs LA5 9LR

FEATURED WHOLESALE SUPPLIERS
Dijon Ltd: The Old Printworks, Streatfield Road, Heathfield, Sussex TN21 8HX.
Liberon Waxes: 6 Park Street, Lydd, Kent
Miniature Model Imports: PO Box 154, Cobham, Surrey KT11 2YE.
Quality Dolls' House Miniatures:
55 Celandine Avenue, Priory Park, Locksheath, Southampton, Hants SO3 6WZ.
Warwick Miniatures Ltd: Bramley Cottage, Weston-under-Wetherley, Leamington Spa, Warks CV33 9BW.

FEATURED SHOPS
Blackwells': 733 London Road, Westcliff-on-Sea, Essex SS0 9ST.
The Dolls' House: Market Place, Northleach, Cheltenham, Glos GL54 3EJ
Dorking Dolls' House Gallery: 23 West Street, Dorking, Surrey RH4 1BY.
Floriana's Dolls' House Shop: 47 Charles Street, Dorchester, Dorset DT1 1EE.
W. Hobby Ltd: Knights Hill Square, London SE27 0HH.
The Mulberry Bush: 9 George Street, Brighton, Sussex BN2 1RH.
The Pram Collection: 7 The Vale, South Ruislip, Middlesex HA4 0SG.
Royal Mile Miniatures: (*Stockists for David Edwards)*: 154 Canongate, Royal Mile, Edinburgh EH8 8DD.
The Singing Tree: 69 New Kings Road, London SW6 4SQ.
Small Sorts: 40 Winchester Street, Salisbury, Wilts SP1 1HG.

MAGAZINES & FURTHER INFORMATION

There are currently four specialist dolls' house and miniatures magazines in the UK. Each has a diary section giving dates of fairs and exhibitions.

Dolls' House and Miniature Scene: By subscription or from W.H. Smith. Bi-monthly.
The Dolls' House Handbook: Annual.
EMF Publishing, 7 Ferringham Lane, Ferring, W Sussex BN12 5ND.

Dolls' House World and The Home Miniaturist: Ashdown Publishing Ltd, Shelley House, 104 High Street, Steyning, W Sussex BN4 3RD. Both are published bi-monthly, subscription only. A free beginner's guide to the dolls' house hobby is available in return for SAE.

International Dolls' House News: PO Box 154, Cobham, Surrey KT11 2YE. Published quarterly, subscription only.

The British Dolls' House Hobby Directory: Published by Nexus Special Interests Ltd, Nexus House, Boundary Way, Hemel Hempstead HP2 7ST. This has a listing of makers and retailers, both alphabetically and geographically, and a product index.

Cir-Kit Electrical Catalogue and Information Sheet : Available from Dijon Ltd, The Old Printworks, Streatfield Road, Heathfield, Sussex TN21 8HX. Enquiries should be accompanied by SAE.

US SUPPLIERS AND MAGAZINES

Due to the enormous following for the hobby in the US, it is impractical to give a full listing. Reference should be made to one or other of the specialist publications. Two suppliers have been listed because their products have been used extensively in this book:

Cir-Kit Concepts Inc: 407, 14th St NW, Rochester MN 55901; suppliers of dolls' house lighting.
Houseworks Ltd: 2388 Pleasantdale Road, Atlanta, GA 30340; suppliers of hardware and building components.

The main publications in the US are *Nutshell News, Miniatures Showcase,* and *The Miniatures Catalog;* these are published by Kalmbach Miniatures Inc, 21027 Crossroads Circle, PO Box 1612, Waukesha, Wisconsin 53187.
Also *The Miniature Collector,* PO Box 631, Boiling Springs, PA 17007.

DOLPHIN MINIATURES GALLERY

The houses featured in this book, and most of those from Brian Nickolls' previous book *Making Dolls' Houses* are exhibited at the following address: Dolphin Miniatures, The Gallery, The Square, Whimple, Exeter, Devon EX5 2SL. A small shop and gallery are open to the public daily except Mondays.

INDEX